THE
BOOK OF
SPICE

ALSO BY JOHN O'CONNELL

I Told You I Was Ill: Adventures in Hypochondria
The Baskerville Legacy
For the Love of Letters
(with Jessica Cargill Thompson) *The Midlife Manual*

THE
BOOK OF
SPICE

FROM ANISE
TO ZEDOARY

JOHN O'CONNELL

PEGASUS BOOKS
NEW YORK LONDON

THE BOOK OF SPICE

Pegasus Books Ltd.
80 Broad Street, 5th Floor
New York, NY 10004

First Pegasus Books hardcover edition July 2016

ISBN: 978-1-68177-152-6

10 9 8 7 6 5 4 3 2 1

Printed in the United States of America
Distributed by W. W. Norton & Company, Inc.

'A chilli,' said Rebecca, gasping. 'Oh yes!' She thought a chilli was something cool, as its name imported, and was served with some. 'How fresh and green they look,' she said, and put one into her mouth. It was hotter than the curry; flesh and blood could bear it no longer. She laid down her fork. 'Water, for Heaven's sake, water!' she cried. Mr Sedley burst out laughing (he was a coarse man, from the Stock Exchange, where they love all sorts of practical jokes). 'They are real Indian, I assure you,' said he. 'Sambo, give Miss Sharp some water.'

William Makepeace Thackeray, *Vanity Fair* (1848)

CONTENTS

INTRODUCTION

I remember vividly the first time I tasted spicy food. I was nine or ten, and we – my mother, sister and I – had come to London to visit Auntie Sheila, a deeply pious Irish Catholic woman who lived in a tiny flat in Marylebone that would now be worth about £16 billion. Auntie Sheila was not actually our aunt but one of our mother's oldest friends, and she fascinated us as children because she claimed an angel had once visited her in the night. (For the record, the angel had 'the most beautiful face you ever saw' and a mass of golden ringlets. It smiled at her, as angels should.)

On this occasion we had a picnic in Hyde Park. Amid the deckchairs and joggers a blanket was spread out and green bags emblazoned with the legend 'St Michael' emptied onto it. There were white fluffy rolls and crisps and bottles of lemonade, tubs of white goo with raw cabbage and tangerine floating in it, Caramel Delight Desserts – liquefied crème caramel topped with star-bursts of cream – and chicken legs coated in something bright red, sticky and oddly yoghurt-smelling.

'Eurgh,' I said, fishing one of these legs out of its plastic tray. 'What the hell's this?'

'It's tandoori chicken,' replied my mother. 'It comes all the way from Tandoor in India.' She leaned forward and whispered sharply: 'Don't say "What the hell" in front of Auntie Sheila.'

I bit into the chicken. It was delicious. One of the most delicious things I'd ever eaten. How clever were the citizens of Tandoor, to have invented such a dish! That creamy sourness. That gentle, peppery heat with a hint of lemon and … hang on, what were those *other* flavours, the ones overtaking on the inside lane as my saliva went to work?

There was only one word for them, a word I had never needed to use before: spicy.

This would have been 1981, possibly 1982 – only a few years after a young woman in the product development department at Marks & Spencer called Cathy Chapman transformed food retail in Britain by introducing a range of high-quality chilled readymeals. The first of these was chicken kiev, a huge hit in 1979. A version of chicken tikka masala, the Nation's Favourite Dish, followed soon afterwards. (Quite possibly, M&S's St Michael-branded tandoori chicken legs were Chapman's idea too. I wouldn't be surprised.)

CTM, as chicken tikka masala is known in the trade, is supposed to be a British invention. The son of chef Ahmed Aslam Ali claims his father invented it in the early 1970s in his Shish Mahal restaurant in Glasgow after a customer complained that his tandoori chicken (and 'tandoori', as we all know now, refers to the clay oven in which the chicken is cooked, not a place) was 'a bit dry'. Ali's solution was to open a can of Campbell's tomato soup, add some garam masala and a dash of cream and pour it over the chicken. 'Pukka', as someone once liked to say.

This is a wonderful story, so wonderful that in 2001 it formed the basis of a famous speech by the then foreign secretary, Robin Cook, to the Social Market Foundation singing the praises of multiculturalism. Cook described CTM as 'a perfect illustration of the way Britain absorbs and adapts external influences': 'Chicken tikka is an Indian dish,' he declared. 'The masala sauce was added to satisfy the desire of British people to have their meat served in gravy.'

Well, yes and no. The current thinking among Indian food historians is that, far from being 'inauthentic' – the meaningless criticism usually flung at CTM – the dish is a bastardised version of murgh makhani, or butter chicken, invented (or at least popularised) by the New Delhi restaurant Moti Mahal shortly after partition in 1947. And if we're going to talk about the appeal of meat in gravy, we can go back, back in time, to ancient Mesopotamia, the land between the Tigris and Euphrates rivers that is now part of Iraq, to prove it's no mere British obsession.

When the French Assyriologist Jean Bottéro deciphered three cracked clay tablets written in around 1700 BC in the Mesopotamian language of Akkadian, he realised not only that they contained the world's oldest extant recipes, but also that these recipes were rich and sophisticated – evidence of a scientifically based cuisine miles from the bland mush of pulses he and his colleagues had expected. Among the recipes curated and glossed by Bottéro in his book *The Oldest Cuisine in the World: Cooking in Mesopotamia* (2004) are proto-curries in which meats such as lamb, goat, pigeon, stag and francolin (a species of wild fowl) are seared until charred before being immersed in a fatty, spiced broth to finish cooking. Using Bottéro as a starting point, author and food blogger Laura Kelley, aka The Silk Road Gourmet, conducted research of her own and concluded that the Sumerians of southern Mesopotamia probably used a wide range of spices, including cinnamon, liquorice, carob, dill seed, juniper, sumac, cumin and asafoetida.

The point I'm trying to make is straightforward, and its implications ripple out across this book: dietary habits change not in a formal, ordered fashion that it is possible or desirable to police, but by accident and, especially, assimilation. My childhood bite of tandoori chicken led me, over the course of the next thirty years, through a network of meandering taste pathways, influencing both the way I cook and the sort of food I want to eat. In short, it made me love spice.

The concept of 'fusion' food that combines elements of different culinary traditions has been with us since the 1970s. But really, is there any other kind?

Consider Mughlai cuisine, which for many people outside India is 'synonymous with Indian food'.[1] In fact, it is a synthesis of the cuisines of northern India, central Asia and Persia – a memento of invasion. Similarly, the roots of that much-maligned curry-house staple vindaloo lie in the Portuguese carne de vinha d'alhos, a dish of pork marinated in wine and garlic which the Portuguese brought to Goa. In Mamak cuisine – the food of Malay Tamil Muslims – the Mughlai dish korma will, unlike elsewhere, contain coconut milk and be seasoned with star anise. When Gujaratis left India's west coast for Kenya and Uganda, they took their cuisine with them, but it melded with indigenous cuisines, yielding results Madhur Jaffrey describes with elegant precision:

> A Kenyan-Indian family might serve the Portuguese-influenced prawn peri-peri, a dish of prawns cooked with bird's-eye chillies (the peri-peri), garlic, cumin and either lemon juice or vinegar one day, followed by green coriander chicken, maize cooked with mustard seeds and a very Muslim pilaf containing rice, meat and cardamom-flavoured stock the next.[2]

Sometimes spice use defines food cultures shared by people who have little else in common. In Jerusalem ownership of local staples such as the spice mix za'atar is fiercely contested by Jews and Arabs. But as Yotam Ottolenghi and Sami Tamimi point out, Israeli and Palestinian food cultures are 'mashed and fused together in a way that is impossible to unravel. They interact all the time and influence each other constantly so nothing is pure any more.'[3]

As with language, so with food: flux is the natural state of things. Any attempt to marshal dishes into rigid canons will fail because of the casual, aleatory way recipes are transmitted in the real world.

Of course, global travel and immigration and the internet have catalysed this process. Last week I had some prunes that needed using up, so I cooked a late-medieval lamb stew from a National Trust cookbook. Reading the recipe, I thought it would be more interesting if, instead of black pepper, I used the Javanese cubeb or the African melegueta pepper (also known as Grains of Paradise), both of which were available in England in the fifteenth century.

Neither was sold in my local Sainsbury's – surprise! – but Brixton Market, in the heart of south London's African-Caribbean community, came up trumps, and even if it hadn't, they would have been simple to source online.

Bottéro observes that all societies develop 'routines and rituals, perhaps even myths, to regulate the use of food, indeed, to confer a value upon food that goes beyond the mere consumption of it'.[4] A glance through Dorothy Hartley's magnificent *Food in England* (1954) makes plain that this country once had plenty of these, from the belief that animals should be slaughtered 'when the moon is on the wane' to the insistence that an egg and lemon jelly will be spoiled if any ends of sponge biscuit are allowed to protrude above the surface. By the 1980s, when I was growing up, such rituals still existed but had ceased to be about cooking. Instead they were about branding, packaging and convenience – the extension of a trend that began in 1953 with the launch by the American firm Swanson of the frozen TV dinner.

On Sundays we ate together as a family. During the week, though, we balanced plates on our knees while watching *Wogan* and *EastEnders*. I agree with the cookery writer Rose Prince that 'the rituals of preparing dinner and laying the table are an enormous part of happiness',[5] but our mother, newly divorced and working full-time, lacked the energy or enthusiasm to cook in the evenings. I recognised her strongly in Nigel Slater's portrait of his mother in his memoir *Toast* (2003) – a 'chops-and-peas sort of a cook' who 'found it all a bit of an ordeal'.[6] We ate a lot of chicken kiev (though not from M&S – too expensive) and microwavable tagliatelle carbonara.

What we didn't eat, the odd leg of tandoori chicken excepted, was spicy food. Opposite our house in Loggerheads – a small village on the border of Shropshire and Staffordshire, 4 miles from Market Drayton, home of Müller Fruit Corners – was a Chinese restaurant called Ambrosia. I couldn't tell you if it was any good because we never went there and never would have done, even if we could have afforded to eat out. If my childhood is anything to go by, the focus of white lower-middle-class culinary aspiration in the mid- to late 1980s was Italy rather than India, China or South-East Asia. (As for Africa, I believed for years, on the basis of Band Aid's assertion that it was a place where 'nothing ever grows', that its cuisine amounted to airdropped bags of rice.)

We dressed salads with olive oil and drank espresso-strength Lavazza coffee by the mugful – even me, as a child, which accounts for a lot. But although we did possess a spice rack, none of the dusty little jars ever saw action. They just sat there, in the glare of the summer sun, gathering dust while their contents grew stale and discoloured.

Not until I left university, moved to London and started working at the listings magazine *Time Out* did I appreciate that there was more to spicy food than supermarket chicken jalfrezi. I remember leafing through the annual *Eating & Drinking Guide* that *Time Out* published – a thick directory of London's best restaurants – and being amazed by the wealth of sub-categories. Contributing to it was obscurely thrilling, as if you were extending some vast codex of urban lore. Who knew that there were so many types of cuisine, and that a single city could accommodate them all?

When Das Sreedharan's Stoke Newington-based Keralan restaurant mini-chain Rasa opened a branch on Charlotte Street, close to our office on Tottenham Court Road, we all trooped along excitedly. (Sadly, Rasa Samudra closed in 2012.) And if the quality of the food in Chinatown wasn't always top-notch, it was still good to have it there, five minutes round the corner, when the desire for dim sum grew overwhelming.

Nowadays my cooking is more international than my Birds Eye Steakhouse grill-munching twelve-year-old self would ever have imagined. I use spices almost every day and try to be as ambitious as I can. But simplicity can be equally effective. One of my favourite recipes, immeasurably useful on those evenings when the kids are late to bed and time is short, is the first 'curry' recipe I ever used – A Quick Lamb Curry, from Nigel Slater's *The 30-Minute Cook* (1994), a book I bought when it came out to commemorate my move to London. I recommend it heartily.

Slater gave me the confidence to experiment. From A Quick Lamb Curry it was but a short step to making spices a part of my daily cooking routine: glazing sweet potatoes with ginger syrup and allspice; stuffing chickens with harissa and dried fruit; baking Cornish saffron buns and hot cross buns and cumin-scented bread. It's hard to think of any food that can't be enlivened by spices. Though my children might tell you that smoked paprika sprinkled on fish fingers is a step too far.

We take them for granted today, now that they are everywhere and, for the most part, dirt cheap, but spices might just be the most important commodities ever – more important even than oil or gold. For most of human history they have been held in sacred regard, despite the fact that in dietary terms they are utterly inessential.

No one ever died for want of spices. And yet thousands died in their name – both the plunderers and the plundered. The desire to control the trade in major spices such as nutmeg, cinnamon, cloves and black pepper led Europe's mercantile powers to commit atrocities on a par with those we're currently witnessing in the more turbulent parts of the Middle East.

Without the wealth generated by the spice trade, however, the Renaissance might never have happened. Alexandre Dumas *père* put it best when he wrote of Venice: 'The intellectual faculties seem to have soared in an enduring exaltation under the influence of spice. Is it to spices that we owe Titian's masterpieces? I am tempted to believe it.'[7] (At the end of the fifteenth century Venice annually imported from Alexandria the equivalent of 500,000 kg of pepper, though over the next hundred years the importance of spice to its success decreased after the Ottoman authorities restricted trade with Syria and Egypt.)

All the major expeditions – the ones that taught us how the world fits together, the ones headed up by legendary, storybook figures like Christopher Columbus (the Italian who, under the auspices of the Spanish monarchy, made four voyages across the Atlantic), Vasco da Gama (the Portuguese explorer who was the first European to establish a sea route to India) and Ferdinand Magellan (also Portuguese; his expedition to the East Indies led to the first circumnavigation of the Earth) – were compelled either wholly or partly by a greedy need to find the places where spices grew, so that the traditional middlemen – the Arab and Phoenician traders who sold spices on to merchants in places such as Venice and Constantinople – might be cut out of the picture.

Before da Gama, spices found their way to Europe along a variety of caravan routes – there was no single 'spice trail' – across the Middle East or along the Red Sea to Egypt. Their ultimate origin was India, Sri Lanka, China and Indonesia. Some spices, like nutmeg and cloves, were indigenous to a cluster of tiny, remote, unmapped islands (the Bandas in the West Pacific for nutmeg; the Moluccas for cloves) and could be obtained only from them. As soon as sea routes were established and blanks in maps filled in, spices came directly within Europe's grasp. Vast corporations like Britain's East India Company and its Dutch equivalent, the Vereenigde Oostindische Compagnie, or VOC, were founded to manage the trade in them and rule the lands where they grew. Once spices began to be cultivated in areas where they weren't indigenous, the monopolies these companies had made it their business to enforce collapsed.

But perhaps, before we go any further, we should define our terms. What exactly is a spice? The word derives from the Latin *specie*, meaning 'sort, kind or type'; the same root as 'special', 'especially' and, obviously, 'species'. The best modern definition for me is the historian Jack Turner's in his *Spice: The History of a Temptation* (2004): 'Broadly, a spice is not a herb, understood to mean the aromatic, herbaceous, green parts of the plant. Herbs are leafy, whereas spices are obtained from other parts of the plant: bark, root, flower bud, gums and resins, seed, fruit, or stigma.'[8] But another authority, the American writer Frederic Rosengarten, who worked for many years in the spice industry, maintains that it is 'extremely difficult to determine where a spice ends and a herb begins, as culinary herbs are in reality one group of spices'.[9]

I don't think this is right, but you can see where Rosengarten is coming from. If you buy his line of thinking, then the aniseed qualities of a herb like tarragon make it more spicy than herby. And it is true that, before spices became cheap enough for ordinary households to afford, what we might call 'spice effects' were produced by using an array of aromatic plants no longer in the repertoire, such as bloodwort, borage, liverwort, tansy and patience.

That said, I'm not sure that chia, the seed of *Salvia hispanica*, a flowering plant in the mint family, deserves to be classed as a spice. Despite meeting Turner's criterion (it's a seed) and being hugely popular as a superfood on account of its high levels of Omega-3 fatty acids, fibre, antioxidants and minerals, chia neither tastes of anything nor has any meaningful culinary application as far as I can tell. I suppose a case could be made on medical grounds for including it here, but I haven't – although it's worth observing, by the by, that spices were the original superfoods.

The story of spice is a global one, which necessarily stops en route at Indonesia, Malaysia, Sri Lanka, India, Egypt, Iran, Iraq, China, Russia and Madagascar, not forgetting the New World of the Americas, Scandinavia, Central and Eastern Europe and Britain. For the formidable food historian Andrew Dalby this also affects the definition: spice is defined by 'distant origin and long-distance trade, as well as unique aroma';[10] spices are 'natural products from a single limited region that are in demand and fetch a high price, far beyond their place of origin, for their flavour and odour'.[11] Much of the time, especially in antiquity, spices were used medicinally rather than to flavour food – also in embalming rituals and as perfumes and cosmetics. But then, as Dalby points out, the line between food and drugs was often rather fuzzy.

The upshot is that in the Middle Ages 'spice' tended to mean anything that was expensive and imported. So as well as cinnamon, nutmeg, black pepper et al. the term encompassed almonds, oranges, ambergris (a waxy substance secreted by the intestines of sperm whales and used in perfumery) and all manner of dyes and unguents and medicinal substances, such as the corpse extract mummia and tutti, scrapings from Alexandrian chimneys that were made into a poultice and applied to weeping sores. Nowadays we think of spices as edible items and shunt the likes of frankincense and spikenard into the siding marked 'aromatics'. But often 'edible' spices were used as incense: the Roman emperor Nero is supposed to have burned the city's entire supply of cinnamon to mark the death of his second wife.

Wolfgang Schivelbusch, in his 'social history of spices, stimulants and intoxicants' (note the way he brackets these together) *Tastes of Paradise* (1979), invents his own category of *Genussmittel* – literally, 'articles of pleasure' – to denote substances eaten, drunk or inhaled to provide sensory gratification, as opposed to substances consumed out of mere necessity. This approach lumps spices in with tea, coffee and sugar as well as alcohol, opium and cocaine. (After much deliberation, and although there is a compelling case to be made for their inclusion – a *much* more compelling one than for chia – I decided not to write about tea, coffee and sugar here. They are such massive subjects that covering them would have created a conceptual imbalance.)

In Europe the use of spices in cooking reached its apogee in the Middle Ages. One canard deserving of swift despatch is the theory, repeated time and again, that spices were used primarily as preservatives and to disguise the taste of rotten food. There were plenty of other methods and substances available for doing this, and they weren't half as expensive. Rather, spices were status symbols. The height of luxury and refinement, they made their consumers feel deeply cultured, as if they were partaking of something so magical and rarefied it could barely be articulated.

On the question of how widespread spice use was there is less agreement than you might expect. Schivelbusch may be overstating things when he claims that in the Middle Ages food was 'little more than a vehicle for condiments which were used in combinations we nowadays would consider quite bizarre',[12] and clearly the lower orders could not have afforded to add spices to their staple diet of foods, such as the cereal pottage frumenty – except perhaps mustard, which was home-grown and therefore cheap. But those nearer the top of the scale certainly would have used spices in their cooking, and from Anglo-Saxon times cinnamon and nutmeg were routinely added to beers and wines.

Ready-made spice mixes were available to buy in the Middle Ages. The most common were 'blanch powder' (pale in colour, made from ginger, cinnamon and sugar), 'powder fort' (hot, dominated by ginger and types of pepper) and 'powder douce' (sweeter, as its name suggests: the author of the fourteenth-century cookery book *Le Menagier de Paris* recommends it contain ginger, cinnamon, nutmeg, galangal, sugar and Grains of Paradise).

We know from the correspondence of members of the upper-class Norfolk family the Pastons, which runs from 1422 to 1509, that Margaret Paston often sent her husband to London to buy items she failed to source locally, among them spices, figs and treacle from Genoa, the last of these newly fashionable as a medicine. In one letter she asks her son, who is in London, to let her know the price of black pepper, Grains of Paradise, cloves, mace, ginger, cinnamon, rice, saffron and galangal, 'and if it be better cheap at London than it is here, I shall send you money to buy with such as I will have'.[13]

The duke of Buckingham used almost 2 lb. of spices per day in the years 1452–3. But this was by no means standard practice. At least one food historian thinks it more likely that large quantities of spices were 'saved up for special meals rather than used every day to provide a light flavouring'.[14]

In medieval Europe, as in ancient Persia, spices were associated with feasting and banquets. Among the treasures of Richard II, recipes from whose court kitchen survive in the book known as *Forme of Cury* (*c*. 1390), were spice-plates for use when spices were served ceremonially at the end of meals with a spiced wine called hippocras. Spices like saffron made possible the 'endoring' of food so that it was brightly coloured and gilded, emphasising the extraordinary transformations a cook had wrought – though the roots of endoring lie in Arab medical lore, where the eating of gold was held to prolong life.

Neat patterns were valued: one capon might be served with a white sauce, the other with a yellow one. Sandalwood extract produced an attractive red; parsley and sorrel green. A popular (camel-)coloured sauce was cameline, a recipe for which can be found in the thirteenth-century French cookbook known as *Le Viandier de Taillevent*:

Cameline: To Make Cameline Sauce. Grind ginger, a great deal of cinnamon, cloves, Grains of Paradise, mace, and if you wish, long pepper; strain bread that has been moistened in vinegar, strain everything together and salt as necessary.[15]

'Deep down,' note the authors of *The Medieval Kitchen* (1998), 'the medieval cook was an alchemist – in a quest for colour rather than for gold',[16] before making the good point that medieval spice mania was not solely a European phenomenon: the dietician to the Mongol court at Beijing in the early fourteenth century used twenty-four different spices in his cooking.

The theory that the huge impact of Arab cuisine on upper-class European cooking in the Middle Ages was a result of the Crusades is treated as a given by most food historians. Frederic Rosengarten maintains that the Crusades stimulated trade, leading to the 'unprecedented availability' of imports from the Holy Land: 'dates, figs, raisins, almonds, lemons, oranges, sugar, rice, and various Oriental spices including pepper, nutmeg, cloves and cardamom'.[17] But there are dissenting voices: Clifford A. Wright believes that 'the Crusaders made no impact on Western European cuisine' because 'the cultural contacts were already occurring by virtue of the dominance of Italian merchants in the East and the presence of Islamic regimes in Spain and Sicily'.[18]

Of course, the story of spices pre-dates the Middle Ages and the Age of Exploration. Or should I say, 'stories', because there are scores of them.

Which one did you hear first? Was it the story of Joseph – of Technicolor Dreamcoat fame – who in Genesis 37: 18–36 is sold by his brothers to a gang of Ishmaelite traders carrying gum, balm and aromatic resin from Gilead down to Egypt? Or the story of the prophet Muhammad, whose first wife, Kadijha, was the widow of a spice merchant and who became a successful merchant himself before he experienced the visions in which the Koran was revealed to him? Or what about Shen Nung, the mythical father of Chinese medicine, who supposedly spoke when he was three days old, walked within a week and ploughed a field at three? His fastidious research into the properties of plants involved testing over 300 spices and herbs on himself, with predictably fatal consequences: the yellow flower of a rogue weed caused his intestines to rupture before he had a chance to drink his antidote.

Perhaps the most entertaining stories are the ones medieval Europe told itself about where spices came from, based on legends circulated by the Arabs and Phoenicians in whose commercial interests it was to keep the true location a secret. The association of spices with distant, magical lands is promoted assiduously in the literature of the period. Consider the idealised garden of the thirteenth-century French courtly poem the 'Roman de la Rose'. In Chaucer's translation

> Ther was eke wexyng many a spice,
> As clowe-gelofre [cloves], and lycorice,
> Gyngevre, and greyn de parys [Grains of Paradise],
> Canell [cinnamon], and setewale [zedoary] of prys,
> And many a spice delitable
> To eten whan men rise fro table.

In the satirical utopia of the anonymous Irish poem 'The Land of Cockayne' (*c.* 1330), where roasted pigs wander about with knives in their backs to facilitate carving, we shouldn't be surprised to find an abundance of spice:

> In the praer [meadow] is a tre,
> Swithe likful forto se,
> The rote is gingeuir and galingale,
> The siouns [shoots] beth al sedwale,
> Trie maces beth the flure [flowers],
> The rind [bark] canel of swet odur,
> The frute gilofre of gode smakke.
> Of cucubes [cubebs] ther nis no lakke.

Spices were, some believed, flotsam carried along by the rivers that ran out of Eden, shown on the Hereford Map of *c.* 1300 as an island in eastern Asia and inhabited, according to the anonymous author of the geographical survey *Expositio totius mundi et gentium*, by a race known as the Camarines, who 'eat wild honey, pepper, and manna which rains from heaven'.[19]

Other quasi-humans believed to inhabit spicy realms were: the Cynophali, who have dogs' heads; the Blemmyae, whose faces are in their chests; and the Sciopods, who hop around on a single huge leg. (Isidore of Seville on Sciapods: 'In summer they lie down on the earth and shade themselves under their great feet.')

Many of these stories found their way into the fantastical *Itinerarium* (Latin for 'road map', meaning 'travelogue') attributed to Sir John Mandeville, allegedly an English knight from St Albans, but thought to have been written by a Belgian monk called Jan de Langhe. Despite being garbled nonsense cobbled together from sources such as the late-medieval Italian explorer Odoric of Pordenone, the *Itinerarium* was used as a reference book by Christopher Columbus on his voyages to the New World. So it led, ironically enough, to the discovery by Europeans of New World spices such as chilli peppers, vanilla and annatto.

As Charles Corn has written, spices conjure up 'a legendary, if not mystical, continuum, a story deeply rooted in antiquity'.[20] Chinese and Arab traders were doing polite business in the Moluccas in the sixth and seventh centuries. Excavations in the Indus Valley show that spices were used there between 3300 and 1300 BC: traces of ginger and turmeric were found inside ceramic vessels and on the teeth of skeletons in burial sites in Farmana in the northern Indian state of Faryana.

The Ebers Papyrus, to which I refer frequently in what follows, is an ancient Egyptian medical directory, believed to date from around 1550 BC and named after Georg Ebers, the German Egyptologist who discovered it in 1874. Full of information about surgical techniques as well as drugs, it makes clear that spices like anise, coriander seed and fenugreek were hugely important in ancient Egyptian medicine. (One cure for stomach complaints listed in Ebers is a mixture of milk, goose fat and cumin. Yum!)

The exotic, flamboyant recipes contained in the Roman cookbook *De re coquinaria* – attributed, probably erroneously, to the gourmet Marcus Gavius Apicius – use spices copiously, especially black and long pepper, which the Romans sourced directly from the Malabar coast. After Rome's annexation of Ptolemaic Egypt in 30 BC it sent ships from the Red Sea to India, taking advantage of the monsoon winds by leaving in July, at the height of the monsoon season, and returning in November.

✲
✲✲

Only a limited *tour d'horizon* is possible here, but the medicinal value of spices as both cures for specific ailments and restorers of equilibrium to unbalanced bodies is worth considering, not least because it enables me to introduce figures such as Pliny, Theophrastus, Dioscorides and Gerard and to explain why they are important – and why they crop up so often in this book.

According to the logic of humoral medicine, health was determined by the balance of the four 'humours', or fluids, believed to control the body: blood, phlegm, choler (or yellow bile) and black bile. Each of these humours could be cold, hot, wet or dry. Linguistic echoes of this system, the dominant one from Hippocrates through to Galen and beyond, are words such as 'phlegmatic', 'bilious', 'choleric' and 'melancholy' to describe character traits. (Ayurvedic medicine, too, is predicated on the idea of balance: of the three elemental *doshas* Vata, Pitta and Kapha.)

Different spices exerted different influences on the humours, whose composition was in any case unique to a person. A hot, dry spice like black pepper counteracted the ill effects of a wet, cold diet. Drugs, many of them spices, were listed and rated in large books called *materia medica*. The most famous of these is probably the five-volume *De materia medica* (*c.* AD 50–70) written by a Greek surgeon to the Roman emperor Nero's army called Pedanius Dioscorides (*c.* 40–90). It lists around six hundred plants (and some animals and minerals too) and about a thousand drugs derived from them. Incredibly, it remained a key pharmacological text well into the nineteenth century, probably on account of its brisk, rational tone.

Before Dioscorides, however, there was Theophrastus (*c.* 371–*c.* 287 BC), born on the island of Lesbos and a pupil of Aristotle, who bequeathed Theophrastus his library and whom Theophrastus replaced as head of the Lyceum in Athens. Regarded as the father of modern botany, Theophrastus wrote two treatises on plants, *On the Causes of Plants* and *Enquiry into Plants*, and was, as the gardening writer Anna Pavord puts it in her wonderful book *The Naming of Names* (2005), 'the first person to gather information about plants, and to ask the big questions: "What have we got?" "How do we differentiate between these things?".'[21]

Theophrastus separated plants into four categories: trees, shrubs, sub-shrubs and herbs. He often comes in for criticism – the redoubtable botanical scholar Agnes Arber, in her *Herbals: Their Origin and Evolution* (1912), felt that 'his descriptions, with few exceptions, are meagre, and the identification of the plants to which they refer is a matter of extreme difficulty'[22] – but Theophrastus is honest about the limits of his knowledge, explaining the paucity of his entries for frankincense and myrrh on the grounds that there simply isn't any more information available to him.

Whatever his shortcomings, Theophrastus was plagiarised by Pliny the Elder (AD 23–79) in the botanical sections of his vast encyclopaedia *Naturalis historia* (*Natural History*) – thirty-seven books organised into ten volumes. In fact, Pliny and/or his copyists introduced numerous errors – he confuses ivy and rockrose because their names are similar in Greek – but it was Pliny whose works continued to be read into the Middle Ages while Theophrastus fell into obscurity, resurfacing only when original Greek manuscripts were found in the Vatican in the early fifteenth century and given to the Greek scholar Teodoro Gaza to translate into Latin – at which point, as we shall see, Theophrastus became important once again.

Fifty years after Pliny's death in the eruption of Mount Vesuvius which destroyed Pompeii and Herculaneum, Claudius Galenus, better known as simply Galen, was born in Pergamon in Asia Minor, the son of a wealthy architect. Galen's interest in spices as drugs was stoked early when he studied as a youth in the trading hub of Alexandria. He gained experience and significant knowledge of anatomy treating the wounds of gladiators and over time produced a huge number of treatises, referred to as the 'Galenic corpus', which laid the foundations for modern medicine.

Galen was an enthusiastic exponent of humoral medicine, and his writings on pharmacology draw on Theophrastus, Dioscorides and Pliny as well as more obscure writer–physicians such as Heras of Cappadocia and Statilius Crito. A drug composed of a single substance was known as a 'simple'. Galen's special skill was compounding drugs from a variety of substances to produce so-called 'galenicals'. His version of theriac, the 'universal antidote' to poisons, contained over a hundred different substances, many of them spices. (Theriac took forty days to prepare and was supposed to be stored for twelve years before use, though Marcus Aurelius drank some only two months after Galen had made it for him and survived ...)

Galen is a colossal, towering figure – truly the bridge between the medicine of antiquity and the scholars of the Renaissance. But he only became this because of the way his ideas were taken up and extended by future compilers of encyclopaedias like Isidore of Seville (c. 560–636) and, in Anglo-Saxon England, medical textbooks such as the ninth-century *Bald's Leechbook* and the *Lacnunga* (c. 1000), a miscellany of prayers, charms and herbal remedies, some of which call for surprisingly exotic spices like ginger, black pepper, cinnamon and zedoary.

The most important developments, however, occurred in the Islamic world, in the intellectual powerhouse that was ninth-century Baghdad. Here, during what is known as the 'age of translation', Muslim scholars translated the ancient Latin and Greek *materia medica* into Arabic. Galen's ideas found particular favour and fed into works like *Paradise of Wisdom* by al-Tabari (838–870) and *The Canon of Medicine* by Ibn Sinna (sometimes called Avicenna), the ingenious polymath who, among much else, invented the distillation process that enabled essential oils to be extracted from herbs and spices and used in perfumes.

The West, mired in the Dark Ages, was centuries behind and didn't catch up until the twelfth century, when the founding of a medical school in the dispensary of an old monastery in Salerno in the south of Italy catalysed Europe's own age of translation, when composites of Greek, Roman and Arab medical books were translated *back* into Latin, creating a whole new European canon.

I quote from a lot of 'herbals' in this book. These plant catalogues have always existed, but the advent of printing in the mid-fifteenth century boosted their popularity: the beautiful woodcut illustrations featured in some herbals meant that they were aesthetically pleasing as well as medically useful. Agnes Arber says the first printed herbal worthy of the term is Richard Bankes's *Herbal* of 1525. The anonymous *Grete Herball*, published in England the following year and derived from a French source, emphasises its Galenic roots in its declared aim to find 'vertues in all maner of herbes to cure and heale all maner of sekenesses or infyrmytes to hym befallyng thrugh the influent course of the foure elementes'. (Bear in mind that at this stage the word 'herbs' means 'plant material' and accommodates what we now regard as spices.)

Two other famous herbals that crop up repeatedly in these pages are those by Nicholas Culpeper (1616–1654) and John Gerard (c. 1545–1612). Culpeper was an apothecary's apprentice who became a doctor to the poor: a political radical who believed medicine should be a public service, not a commercial enterprise. His *Herbal* (1653) was essentially a cheap, vernacular version of the College of Physicians' Latin pharmacopoeia, with a side-order of eccentric-even-for-the-time astronomy. Predictably, it was attacked by the College as a 'drunken labour'.

Gerard was a keen gardener, but his notoriously unreliable *Herball* (1597) is a mash-up of Dioscorides, Theophrastus, Pliny and the Flemish herbalist Rembertus Dodoens. Even the woodcuts in the first edition were recycled from other botanical works. Over time it acquired an authority it doesn't really deserve. But its popularity means it needs to be considered in any study of spice use in Europe.

By the eighteenth century spices had had their moment in the sun: tastes changed, and the European focus shifted to new exotic stimulants like cocoa and coffee. By the nineteenth century England, which had once gorged on spices, regarded them with suspicion bordering on disdain. There was a time and a place for them (the colonies), and the odd bowl of mulligatawny soup probably wouldn't do you any harm. But really, they were best avoided. As Mrs Beeton puts it, quoting a 'Dr Paris in his work on Diet', spices are

> not intended by nature for the inhabitants of temperate climes … The best quality of spices is to stimulate the appetite, and their worst to destroy, by sensible degrees, the tone of the stomach. The intrinsic goodness of meats should always be suspected when they require spicy seasonings to compensate for their natural want of sapidity.[23]

This insular, safety-first attitude would characterise British cuisine for the next hundred years, hardened by wars (where jingoistic self-reliance was the order of the day) and the subsequent bouts of austerity. Foreign muck? Who wanted to eat *that*? My favourite bit in Nigel Slater's memoir of his 1960s childhood *Toast* (2003) is when his family tries to coax his ageing Auntie Fanny into eating spaghetti for the first time: 'Auntie Fanny is looking down at her lap. "Do I have to have some?" I think she is going to cry.'[24]

And now chicken tikka masala is Britain's best-loved dish. The more you think about it, the bigger an achievement it seems.

Actually, the key development in British cooking in the last decade or so – broadly, the years since the start of the war in Iraq – has been the explosion in popularity of Middle Eastern food, a trend kick-started by one of my favourite food writers, Claudia Roden, in the 1960s. A spice that ten years ago would have been available only in specialist stores – sumac – can now be bought in almost every supermarket. And it is common practice for cookbooks to have at least one 'Ottolenghi-style' recipe: for example, the tahini-dressed courgette and green bean salad in *River Cottage Veg Every Day!* (2011) and the cumin-laden shakshouka in 2013's bestselling diet-manual tie-in *The Fast Diet Recipe Book*.

The Oriental influence on fashionable Occidental cuisine seems as great today as it was in the Middle Ages, Holy War stimulating our appetite for foods from across the Levant. The joke powering 2007's satirical *The Axis of Evil Cookbook* was that most Europeans and Americans were completely ignorant about what people ate in countries such as Iraq, Iran and Syria. What a difference a few years make. Head into central London today and you will find, on the sorts of sites where in the mid-1990s there might have been a Café Rouge or Le Piaf, branches of successful Middle Eastern-themed mini-chains such as Comptoir Libanais and Yalla Yalla.

Wondering what might be behind this interest, apart from the obvious tastiness of the food, I remembered the novelist and critic Umberto Eco's theory that every time Europe feels 'a sense of crisis, of uncertainty about its aims and scopes, it goes back to its own roots – and the roots of European society are, without question, in the Middle Ages'.[25]

In a world riven by futile religious wars, gastronomic empathy may be the best route forward, a way of privileging private, domestic narratives – the narratives that bind us, regardless of circumstance – amid the chaos of conflict. As Yotam Ottolenghi and Sami Tamimi put it: 'Food is a basic, hedonistic pleasure, a sensual instinct we all share and revel in. It is a shame to spoil it.'[26]

To call this book a 'narrative encyclopaedia of spices', as I did when I was writing it, suggests a mission to totalise. In fact, my aim has been more basic: to tell a series of entertaining, illuminating stories about the role spices have played in the development of the modern world. To do this I have drawn on a variety of disciplines and the works of hundreds of writers. I hope the result is not too sprawling and eccentric.

There are, quite deliberately, many voices in the book apart from my own. This is my attempt to emulate the food writers I most admire – people such as Jane Grigson, Elizabeth David and Dorothy Hartley, in whose work there is a sense of perpetual dialogue (both with other writers and with the past), of ideas being tested and either waved through or found wanting. The sixteenth-century botanist William Turner attempted something similar in his herbal, published in three parts between 1551 and his death in 1568. His defence of his method makes me smile:

> For some of them will saye, seynge that I graunte that I have gathered this booke of so manye writers, that I offer unto you an heape of other mennis laboures, and nothinge of myne owne … To whom I aunswere, that if the honye that the bees gather out of so manye floure of herbes, shrubbes, and trees, that are growing in other mennis medowes, feldes and closes maye just-elye be called the bees honye, so maye I call it that I have learned and gathered of manye good autoures not without great laboure and payne my booke.

My focus has been broad. I wanted, with each spice, to give a sense of botanical background, historical context and, where appropriate, culinary usage. But *The Book of Spice* is far from the last word and can't possibly be more than an introduction to such a vast and multifarious subject. The magical pull spices once exerted on the imagination may seem quaint, but there is no denying their continuing importance. As Jack Turner puts it, their 'cargo is still with us', the word alone 'a residual verbal piquancy that is itself the echo of a past of astonishing richness and consequence'.[27]

AJOWAN

Trachypermum ammi

Ajowan, sometimes called ajave, carom, Ethopian cumin, omum and bishop's weed, is a member of the parsley family whose stripy red-brown seeds resemble large celery seeds and smell like a coarser, more acrid version of thyme. Ajowan's essential oil, ptycholic, contains around 50 per cent thymol, a pungent phenol that works well as a fungicidal and antiseptic. As a result, much ajowan is grown for export – in India (mostly Rajasthan), Pakistan, Iran and Afghanistan – so that the thymol can be extracted and added to toothpastes and perfumes.

But ajowan is a stomachic too and used in India, especially, as a remedy for diarrhoea, flatulence and other gastric upsets. Sometimes it is chewed whole; more often it is drunk in the form of 'Omum water', a close relative of the gripe water given to babies for colic. Most commercial brands of gripe water use dill or fennel rather than ajowan, and add alcohol.

Ajowan's culinary use is limited, but it crops up in Indian savouries and snacks such as the flatbread paratha and recipes that involve chickpea flour (besan), such as the Diwali snack besan sev – more-ish, mildly spiced sticks of besan. Sometimes, in Indian recipes, it is called lovage. The seeds are sold whole and crushed rather than ground.

The Anglo-Indian manual *The Complete Indian House-Keeper and Cook* (1888) recommends distilling your own Omum water using a pound of ajowan seeds per two quart bottles of water. 'In cholera season check all premonitory diarrhoea with twenty drops of chlorodyne in some ajwain water', the book suggests, though Edmund John Waring's *Pharmacopeia of India* from 1868, while praising ajowan for 'disguising the taste of disagreeable drugs' and relieving 'atonic dyspepsia', considers its powers against cholera to be 'very limited'.

Still, ajowan is supposed to be good for rheumatism, arthritis and (mixed with warm milk, garlic and sesame oil) earache; also asthma, phlegmy coughs and other respiratory disorders, and bad breath. Some pop-Ayurvedic manuals recommend rolling up a quantity of the seeds in cigarette paper and smoking them to relieve migraine. Non-smokers can achieve a similar effect by painting a paste made from crushed seeds onto their foreheads.

Ajowan is often described as being native to India, but Andrew Dalby points out that its Sanskrit name, *yavani*, means 'the Greek spice', suggesting that it arrived on the subcontinent 'by way of one of the Greek kingdoms of the Middle East'.[28] The Romans, who called it ammi, thought it was a variety of cumin, and it is sometimes added to the Ethiopian and Eritrean spice mix berbere (see *A Directory of Spice Mixes*, p. 237) – hence 'Ethiopian cumin'.

SEE ALSO: *Cumin, Dill, Fennel.*

ALLSPICE

Pimenta dioica

The name reflects the flavour, a seeming compound of cloves, cinnamon and nutmeg, although the belief that allspice is the same as mixed spice (see *A Directory of Spice Mixes,* p. 249) persists in some quarters. Also known as pimento (from *pimiento*, Spanish for 'pepper': the substance Columbus initially believed – and desperately wanted – it to be), allspice is the dried, unripe fruit of *Pimenta dioica*, an intensely aromatic evergreen with a smooth, greyish bark and glossy, dark green leaves. Indigenous to the West Indies and Latin America, the trees only start to bear fruit around the age of seven or eight, but hit their stride after their fifteenth year and continue to be active for the next hundred.

In the wilds of Jamaica's limestone hills *P. dioica* grows in clusters, the seeds having been dispersed by birds. But the tree used to be cultivated ornamentally in 'pimento walks' and on commercial plantations. In the nineteenth century most Jamaican plantation pimento was grown alongside other crops – sugar, for example, or tobacco or coffee, introduced to the island in 1728 by its then governor, Sir Nicholas Lawes – compared with which 'the labour demanded by pimento was thought to be minimal'.[29] One English account of Jamaican life from 1807 makes the harvest sound neat and systematic:

> The fruit is gathered by the hand; and one labourer on the tree, employed in gathering the small branches, will give employment to three below (who are generally women and children) in picking the berries; and an industrious picker will fill a bag capable of holding twenty pounds weight in a day.[30]

These 'industrious pickers' were slaves who would also have been charged with chopping down wild pimentos to free up land for other agricultural uses and satisfy the European and American demand for pimento umbrella- and walking-sticks. These were, a source tells us, 'manufactured into almost every variety of fanciful patterns by staining, carving, and other processes', pimentos possessing a rigidity that 'prevents their breaking or becoming crooked'.[31] Export returns for 1881 show that over 4,500 'bundles' of between 500 and 800 pimento sticks were shipped from Jamaica in the first three-quarters of the year. Small wonder legislation was introduced in 1882 to curb a trade widely felt to have spun out of control.

Once picked, allspice berries would be dried in the sun until they turned brown and the seeds inside them rattled. Jamaica's native Arawak and Taino peoples used the berries to flavour and preserve meat, which they smoked over wooden-framed barbecues called *buccans* – the roundabout root (via the French *boucanier*) of the word 'buccaneer'. After Columbus landed on Jamaica on his second voyage to the New World in 1494, the practice was adopted by Spanish settlers and absorbed into their own meat preservation rituals, which resulted in *charqui* – the roundabout root (it is Quechua, i.e., a Peruvian word, rather than Spanish) of the word 'jerky'.

The Spanish brought with them thousands of West Africans to use as slaves. The fortunate ones escaped and either formed their own independent settlements or joined existing Taino ones in Jamaica's mountainous inland regions. They became known as Maroons – from the Spanish for fugitive, *cimarrón* – and aggravated the Spanish occupiers (and, later, the English) by staging regular raids on plantations, for which they were punished by deportation or worse.

Jerk-spiced meat is really Maroon food – an adapted amalgam of three different cooking traditions: Spanish, Taino and West African (specifically Ghanaian). But while its preparation drew on ancestral African methods such as wrapping the meat in leaves or burying it in a pit filled with hot stones so that it could steam in its own juices,[32] its four most important ingredients were local: thyme, which grows plentifully in Jamaica; the scotch bonnet pepper, which gives jerk seasoning its fiery kick; ginger, introduced to Jamaica in the early sixteenth century; and allspice, whose wood is burned in the smoking process and whose crushed or ground berries are added to the jerk marinade or dry-rub.

Whether you favour the 'wet' or 'dry' approach to preparing jerk is down to personal taste, and possibly your willingness to regard one approach as more authentic than the other. Helen Willinsky in her *Jerk: Barbecue from Jamaica* (1990) favours dry, but the wet seems now to be more popular, possibly because of the tenderising effect of the vinegar or soy sauce or citrus juice – whichever you prefer – on indifferent supermarket meat.

The strong sense of local pride that jerk engenders isn't surprising: its popularity represents the triumph of the militant tendency over an oppressive ruling class. As Winston Currie, owner of the Best Jerk Center in St Ann, Jamaica, told the *New York Times*: '[Jerk] is a dish that is ours, not coming from England like the patty, or from India like the roti.'[33]

Given how popular allspice was to become in England, it is curious how long it took to make an impact outside Jamaica and Mexico (where it was used in spice mixes for moles). It was certainly known in England in the early seventeenth century, as the word 'allspice' dates from 1621. An abundant supply was guaranteed after the British succeeded the Spanish as Jamaica's rulers in 1655, but at first low prices made it 'hardly worth the while of the proprietor of the fragrant trees to gather the berries'.[34] On 8 April 1694 Margaret Banks of Kingston Lacy, a country house in Dorset, spent 2 shillings on 4 oz. of nutmegs and 3 shillings on 4 oz. of cloves and mace. Yet a single shilling bought her half a pound – i.e., 8 oz. – of allspice.[35]

Between 1793 and 1807 the average quantity of allspice exported from Jamaica was a mere 1,767,500 lb. This rose to 5,347,900 lb. for the period between 1835 and 1838, and by 1858 had exceeded 9 million lb. Slavery having been abolished in 1835, an 1878 history of the island recommends that 'what was neglected by the slave-holding proprietor or his attorney [i.e., harvesting pimento] is well worth the attention of the free negro'.[36]

In England, allspice found favour in custards, pies and puddings. Its affinity with sweet, exotic fruits such as the pineapple – first cultivated in Europe in the early seventeenth century, then by the Victorians in glass-covered trenches called 'pineapple pits' – was recognised and admired. In Yorkshire, Jane Grigson tells us, allspice was known as 'clove-pepper' and used in curd tarts; also in Cumberland currant cake (aka 'squashed fly cake'), which Grigson remembers eating as a child while visiting relatives in the north-east of England.[37] A speciality of the North Yorkshire moors was pepper cake, enriched with treacle and brandy, which 'probably gained its name from the use of Jamaica pepper or allspice',[38] though some recipes use nutmeg, caraway and ginger instead or as well.

Almost all European pickling marinades feature allspice as their principal spice. Oily fish such as herrings and mackerel turn rancid so fast that before the age of refrigeration they needed to be eaten or salted within a day of being caught. The pickling of these fish (and sprats, oysters, cockles and mussels) by marinating them in spiced vinegar was called 'caveaching' and was practised across Europe with only slight regional variations – for example, sometimes the fish were fried first in lard, or the raw fillets wrapped around onions, as in Danish rollmops. 'Sousing' involves poaching the fish in spiced vinegar before pickling.

Not so long ago, the trade in pickled herrings underpinned entire economies, turning small Scottish fishing communities like Peterhead into boomtowns. But rampant over-fishing between the early 1950s and the mid-1960s caused North Sea stocks to drop by over 50 per cent.[39] While in Britain the taste for pickled herrings has become a minority one in the last twenty years as the generations reared on them have died out, they remain popular in Scandinavia. In Sweden, matjessil is traditionally served on Midsummer's Eve, accompanied by sour cream, chives and dill-flavoured boiled potatoes.

Elizabeth David tells us that spiced, salted beef, another recipe where allspice is mandatory, is an English Christmas country-house dish. So it is – chef Rowley Leigh has called it 'plum pudding, a richly cloved ham and mulled wine rolled into one'[40] – but almost every country has a variant with its own unique qualities: biltong in South Africa, Turkish pastirma, Italian bresaola etc. Irish dry-cured beef, 'meticulously boned', had a reputation for never spoiling,[41] and for this reason was bought in huge quantities by the French, who shipped it out to the Caribbean to feed the slaves on their sugar plantations – until they realised New England salt cod was cheaper. Salted beef and cabbage remains a popular Irish festive dish, albeit one more often served in Irish bars in America than in Ireland itself, where, according to *Irish Traditional Cooking* (2012) author Darina Allen, it is now 'almost a forgotten flavour'.[42]

In Britain and Ireland this salted beef was sometimes called 'corned beef', a term first used by Robert Burton in his *Anatomy of Melancholy* (1621). Note that 'corn' here refers to coarse grains of salt rather than anything to do with maize. From the Middle Ages onwards, saltpetre (potassium nitrate) was often used too to maintain colour. Tinned corned beef, the 'bully beef' of the First World War, is a whole other product and a whole other story: it was invented by the German chemist Justus von Liebig when he was looking for a cheap way to use up meat from Uruguayan cattle which had been slaughtered for their hides.

In *Pickled, Potted and Canned* (2000) Sue Shephard cites a delicious-sounding 1864 recipe for 'Melton Hunt Beef' in which a huge joint of ox is air-dried before being rubbed every day with a mix of ground allspice, bruised juniper berries, coarse brown sugar, coarse salt, black pepper, minced shallots and dried bay leaves. But this is not the end of it. Saltpetre, garlic and rock salt are added, and after ten days the joint is shaped and skewered, the final touch being a week of smoking over beech and oak chips and turfs of fern or grass.[43]

Wet-brined beef brisket is one of the archetypal Jewish foods – *pickelfleisch* in Yiddish. Hannah Glasse in 1747 refers to 'the Jews' way to pickle beef, which will go good to the West Indies, and keep a year good in the pickle, and with care, will go to the East Indies'. But *pickelfleisch* too was called corned or 'corn' beef. The craze for over-stuffed salt-beef sandwiches spread in the 1930s and '40s from New York to other American cities with significant Jewish populations: 'A strip of East Lombard Street in downtown Baltimore, once the centre of the city's Jewish life and dotted with delis, was nicknamed "Corn Beef Row".'[44] By the 1960s it had become a mainstream American food. *Pickelfleisch* is different from pastrami, which was introduced to New York by Romanian Jews in the 1870s. In pastrami the beef is cured slightly before being smoked and coated with spices, garlic and red pepper.

Elizabeth David notes that 'there are those who use lavish quantities of [allspice] in Christmas puddings',[45] somehow making it clear that she would rather die than be counted among them. (David famously disliked Christmas, which she called the 'Great Too Much'.) As far as I can gather, the earliest written recipes for plum pudding, among them those of Eliza Acton and Hannah Glasse, privilege nutmeg and ginger over other spices, though in the Scottish journalist Christian Isobel Johnstone's *Cook and Housewife's Manual* (1862), published under the *nom de plume* Margaret Dod, 'a little allspice' is called for in her 'common small plum-pudding' – even if her more lavish Trinity pudding, garlanded with holly to deter witches, requires cloves, cinnamon and nutmeg.

SEE ALSO: *Cinnamon, Cloves, Nutmeg.*

AMCHUR (MANGO)
Mangifera indica

Different regions in India favour different souring agents. Cambodge (the pumpkin-like *Garcinia gummigutta*) is specific to Keralan fish cuisine, while kokum (*G. indica*) is mostly used in the Konkan region to flavour dhal and make digestive sherbets. In both cases the spice constitutes sun-dried strips of the de-pulped fruit's skin. These are stored in airtight jars away from sunlight and with a layer of salt over them as a preservative.

Better known in the West, probably because it is easier to find, amchur is the same sort of thing, but in powdered form and derived from mangoes. Amchur is specific to northern India, though intact (i.e., not dried and ground) unripe mangoes are also used as souring agents in southern Indian cooking in dishes such as the Keralan manga chertha mathi kari (sardine curry with unripe mango) that is one of the highlights of Vijayan Kannampilly's *The Essential Kerala Cookbook* (2003).

Mangoes are so common in India, where they have been cultivated for over four thousand years, that it's hardly surprising they have been put to so many uses, or that they should play such a significant role in Hindu mythology and ritual – such as the mango leaves that are placed inside the metal Kalasha pot, their tips just touching water, in honour of Kāmadeva, the god of love. The flat, oblong seed in the centre of each mango can be ground into a flour high in potassium, magnesium and calcium – a so-called 'famine food' capable of delivering a basic level of nutrition in hard times. Even when preserved, mango is an important source of vitamins C, E and A. Preserved mango was traditionally used as an anti-scorbutic (in other words, to prevent scurvy) on sea voyages and when fresh mangoes were not available.

Once commonly made at home, amchur is now usually bought ready-ground. It is beige in colour, with a distinctive dusty-tropical-warehouse smell and a coarse texture. Sometimes it contains added turmeric. It has a bittersweet, slightly resinous taste and is used, like tamarind, in curries, soups and chutneys as well as some blends of char masala (see *A Directory of Spice Mixes*, p. 238). Amchur's affinity with vegetarian dishes doesn't stop it being an effective tenderiser of fish and meat when it is added to marinades. In the spice mix for the Rajasthani baked-fish dish machchi ke sooley it complements another tenderising spice, kachri, made from the ground, sun-dried skin of *Cucumis pubescens*, a species of wild cucumber indigenous to Rajasthan.

Amchur's main advantages over tamarind are that it keeps

better in high temperatures and requires no preparation. But if you use too much, the flavour can be overpowering.

SEE ALSO: *Sumac, Tamarind.*

ANGELICA
Angelica archangelica

The candied, lysergic-green stems of this plant, a tallish (up to 7 feet) member of the parsley family with a thick stem and white flowers, used to be mandatory in the sort of fruit cakes your grand-mother made. They are now surprisingly hard to get hold of. If you can find fresh angelica – good luck with that – it's easy to boil the stems yourself in sugar syrup. Adding sodium bicarbonate during this process 'fixes' the bright green colour.

Angelica is, of course, a herb, its holy name a nod to its alleged potency as a charm against witchcraft. But you can eat any part of it, and both the seeds (used to flavour gin and absinthe) and the fragrant, spongy root (which trails long, twisted rootlets and looks like some sort of wood-carved squid) qualify as spices. Angelica root has been used medicinally for thousands of years, mostly to treat lung disorders and typhoid, though John Gerard recom-mends a decoction of it in wine to cure the cold shivering of agues. It reduces swelling, he says: 'One dram of the root in pouder given certaine daies together, is a remedy for them that have the dropsie, and also for those that are troubled with convulsions, cramps, and the falling sickenesse … It cureth also the Haemorrhoids, if the fundament be bathed with the decoction of the leaves and roots, and the soft and tender sodden herbes laid thereon very hot.'[46]

Mrs M. Grieve recommends ingesting the spice as an infusion:

Pour a quart of boiling water upon 6 oz. of Angelica root cut up in thin slices, 4 oz. of honey, the juice of 2 lemons and 1/2 gill of brandy. Infuse for half an hour.[47]

Angelica was introduced to Britain in the sixteenth century, probably from Syria, but was embraced most readily in Scandinavia, where the root was sometimes made into bread. A Victorian guide to Iceland, Greenland and the Faroe Islands advises:

The A. archangelica is accounted a great delicacy by the natives of this and the neighbouring countries, who use both the stalk and the root. It is found of the greatest size and perfection on those mountains near the coast where the sea-fowl build their nests. In Greenland it is called quannek ... and it is considered better flavoured in those northern regions than in warmer countries.[48]

SEE ALSO: *Orris.*

ANISE

Pimpinella anisum

Most Mediterranean countries have at least one anise-flavoured tipple – France has its pastis, Greece its ouzo, the Middle East arak. Looking further afield, the Colombian version of aguardiente contains anise – though that flavour, of the fragrant compound anethole, may be derived from fennel or star anise rather than anise. The ribbed, grey-green seeds of *Pimpinella anisum*, a dill-like annual with yellowish-white flowers, resemble tiny mandolins and are used in cooking much as fennel seed is. Indigenous to Egypt and Greece, anise was one of the aromatics used to flavour the ancient spiced wine conditum and the Byzantine medical wine anisaton, a precursor of ouzo, which was traditionally drunk in April.

SEE ALSO: *Fennel, Liquorice, Star anise.*

ANNATTO

Bixa orellana

In 1866 Emperor Napoleon III began to worry about the dietary habits of France's urban poor. (This is one theory. More likely is the alternative explanation that he was worried about the ballooning costs of feeding France's army.) So he initiated a quest for a cheap but nutritious spread that convincingly mimicked butter. Any chemist who could create such a product was promised a generous financial reward.

Step forward, three years later, Hippolyte Mège-Mouriès, who mixed beef tallow with skimmed milk and churned it into what he called 'oleomargarine' after the saturated fatty acid margaric acid, a trace component of the milk fat of ruminants.

Margarine, as it became known, was an immediate hit, and not just in France. The only problem was that in its natural state margarine is an unattractive, lardy white. When manufacturers added yellow colouring, America's dairy lobby lost its sense of humour. Its determined anti-marge crusade resulted in the margarine industry being heavily penalised. Even after US law was amended in 1902, Congress levied a tax of 10 cents per pound on any margarine that used yellow dye, never mind the fact that butter is routinely colour-enhanced when grass quality affects its natural hue.

Margarine manufacturers circumvented the law by leaving it to purchasers to add the colour themselves at home. Little packets of yellow dye were supplied with margarine, which had to be mixed in with a spoon. In the early 1950s packaging technology improved so that kneading the margarine packet ruptured a tiny dye-containing capsule, resulting in a more even colour distribution. Not until the mid-1950s was this anti-colouring legislation repealed, and not until 1968 was it legal to sell margarine in Wisconsin, America's dairy heartland. (It is still illegal in Wisconsin to serve margarine instead of butter in restaurants.)

The man who, more than anyone else, understood how important it was for margarine to be yellow was Louis Cheskin, one of the last century's great marketing gurus and the creator of the Marlboro Man. Cheskin's theory of 'sensation transference' held that people transfer their impressions of a product's packaging onto the product itself. Call a margarine 'Imperial', wrap it in foil, put an image of a crown on it – and really, who will care that it hasn't come from a cow? Nobody, as long as the margarine is the correct shade of yellow.

In his *Color Guide for Marketing Media* (1954) Cheskin explained that 'in Western civilisation we are conditioned to associate red with festivity, blue with distinction, purple with dignity, green with nature, yellow with sunshine, and so on.'[49] So it was in the pursuit of sunshine that margarines were coloured yellow with, in the beginning, coal-tar dyes such as dimethylaminoazobenzene. By the late 1930s, however, worries that this entire class of dyes was carcinogenic triggered an industry-wide shift to the natural dyes carotene and annatto – E160b, as it is known in Europe.

Also deployed as a spice, annatto comes from the triangular seeds and seed pulp of *Bixa orellana*, a small tree which has glossy, ovate leaves with reddish veins and pink or white flowers and is indigenous to tropical South America and the Caribbean. Its spiny red fruits each contain around fifty seeds covered with a waxy red pulp. Achiote (ah-cho-tay), as annatto is sometimes called, especially in a culinary context, is a Nahuatl word. Another name, Lipstick Tree, is helpfully explicit about the cosmetic use to which the pigment within the seed husk has traditionally been put.

The Aztecs added annatto to their hot chocolate because they liked the way it coloured their mouths red. This was a reminder, says Andrew Dalby, that 'drinking cacao was, in Aztec thought, parallel with drinking blood'.[50] Mayan Indians used it in their war paint, as did Caribs: the French clergyman and botanist Jean-Baptiste Labat (1663–1738) observed women in Dominica painting their husbands' bodies with what they called *uruni* – annatto dissolved in oil – before they set off on raids into other villages: 'This cosmetic shields their skin, so that it will not crack or burn in the sun and wind, and it protects them from the bites of mosquitoes.'[51] The Ecuadorian Tsáchila tribe still use it to dye their hair red.

In his *General History of the Dichleamydeous Plants* (1831) the Scottish botanist George Don explains how the spice was extracted from the seeds:

> The contents of the fruit are taken out and thrown into a wooden vessel, where as much hot water is poured upon them as is necessary to suspend the red powder or pulp, and by diligently stirring

and pounding the pulp is separated from the seeds, or gradually washed off with the assistance of a spatula or spoon. When the seeds appear quite naked they are taken out, and the wash is left to settle; after which the water is gently poured away, and the sediment put into shallow vessels, to be dried by degrees in the shade. After acquiring a due consistence it is made into balls or cakes, and set to dry in an airy place until it is perfectly firm … Arnotta [*sic*] of a good quality is of the colour of fire, bright within, soft to the touch, and dissolves entirely in water.[52]

Don considered annatto 'cooling and cordial' – 'a good antidote to dysentery and disorders of the kidneys'. A tea made from the seeds and the plant's leaves is supposed to have aphrodisiac qualities.

Annatto is still used on an industrial scale to colour popcorn, ice cream, fish fingers, instant mashed potato, crisps, custard, coleslaw, chorizo, cheese (for example, Red Leicester) – anything yellowy-orange. It is sometimes called 'poor man's saffron', but the chef Rick Bayless thinks this is unfair: 'If it's not fresh or if it's used in tiny pinches, the orangey colour is all you notice. More than a pinch of fresh achiote gives any dish an exotic, earthy perfume that to me is as captivating as good, musky saffron; it's certainly less expensive.'[53] In the Yucatán peninsula the ground seeds are mixed with garlic, salt, oregano and other spices – normally cumin, cloves, cinnamon and allspice – to create the marinade recado rojo or achiote paste. Annatto is considered essential in the spicy pulled pork dish cochinita pibil.

SEE ALSO: *Saffron, Vanilla.*

ASAFOETIDA

Ferula assa-foetida

The clue is in the name: *assa* ('resin' in Persian) and *foetida* ('foul-smelling' in Latin). This spice smells rank, like pickled eggs covered in manure. So rank that in France it is known as *merde du Diable* ('devil's dung'). So rank that you have to be careful how you store it – in an airtight container – or it will contaminate the other spices in your rack. That said, some animals seem to love it: it is used as a bait for wolves, fish and moths, among others.

Asafoetida was known to the Romans as Syrian or Iranian silphium, an inferior version of the Cyrenaic silphium they valued so highly (see *Silphium*). A perennial with yellow flowers which grows between 6 and 12 feet high, it derives from several species of giant fennels and is indigenous to Afghanistan and Iran, where it grows in dense forests, though one type, the shorter *Ferula narthex*, grows in northern Kashmir. Plants are 'tapped' in the spring and must be at least four years old before they are ready to yield.

Asafoetida is supposed to have been discovered by Alexander the Great and his army as they passed through north-eastern Afghanistan. At first they thought that what they had found was silphium, but quickly realised their error. Still, it became a popular substitute for Cyrenaic silphium after that was farmed into extinction. Dioscorides points out the main difference between the varieties:

> The Cyrenaic kind, even if one just tastes it, at once arouses a humour throughout the body and has a very healthy aroma, so that it is not noticed on the breath, or only a little; but the Median (Iranian) is weaker in power and has a nastier smell.[54]

The milky resin is extracted from the thick stems and carrot-shaped fleshy root, which is covered in bristles. It is pearly when fresh but darkens over time. The bad smell, caused by disulphides, disappears when the spice is tempered, to be replaced by the more appetising scent of onions fried in garlic. More cautious cooks prefer to use powdered asafoetida, where the hard resin has been ground and mixed with flour.

Although it was little-used in the West until the 1970s, asafoetida (or hing, as it is called in India) is a common spice in Indian cookery, especially Tamil, Gujarati and Keralan vegetarian cuisine, where it lends a leeky-garlic base flavouring to beans and pulses and has the convenient bonus effect of countering flatulence.

In certain devout Hindu castes in which onions and garlic are deemed impure and so not eaten, asafoetida makes an effective substitute. Garcia da Orta, one-time physician to the Portuguese governor of Goa, noted its popularity with Hindus in his *Colloquies on the Simples and Drugs of India* (1563):

> You must know that the thing most used throughout India, and in all parts of it, is that Assafetida, as well for medicine as in cookery. A great quantity is used, for every Gentio [Hindu] who is able to get the means of buying it will buy it to flavour his food ... These [people] flavour the vegetables they eat with it, first rubbing the pan with it, and then using it as seasoning with everything they eat.[55]

For da Orta it may have been 'the nastiest smell in the world',[56] but Tom Stobart, ever measured, calls it 'part of the special magic which has enabled Indians to solve the problems involved in trying to create tasty vegetarian dishes'.[57] You would struggle to make a decent Indian pickle without it, and its horrible smell doesn't seem to rob the process of romance, judging by the novelist Anuradha Roy's nostalgic account of watching her aunt make pickle from wild plums – 'a gooey mixture of mustard oil, molasses, a five-spice mixture, asafoetida and chilli. It would mature gently taking in the lemony colour and warmth of the winter sun until it was just right.'[58]

The Mughals brought asafoetida into India when they invaded the north in the sixteenth century. We know from *Ain-i-Akbari*, an account of life at the court of the sixteenth-century Mughal emperor Akbar written by a high-ranking minister, that it was used in his kitchens. The *Baghdad Cookery Book* (1226) shows that all parts of the asafoetida plant were used in Abbasid (the third Islamic caliphate after Muhammad) cuisine, with the leaves considered a particular delicacy.

Medicinally, asafoetida is something of a cure-all, praised as both a sedative and a stimulant, though in the former capacity it was often mixed with opium, so it is hard to tell what was doing the sedating. In traditional Indian medicine it was, like silphium, prescribed as an abortifacient. In Thailand it is the active ingredient in a topically applied gripe water called *mahahing*, which is smeared on the abdomen.

Asafoetida in tincture form was used in Western medicine in Victorian times. When treating Alexis St Martin, the Canadian fur-trader who in 1822 ended up with a permanent gastric fistula after he was shot at close range with a musket, American army surgeon William Beaumont 'administered wine, with diluted muriatic acid, and thirty or forty drops of the tincture of asafoetida, three times a day; which appeared to produce the desired effect, and very much improved the condition of the wound'.[59]

A related species, *F. galbaniflua*, produces a more aromatic gum resin called galbanum, which is used in incense and in commercial perfumes such as Vol de Nuit, by Guerlain, and Chanel No. 19.

SEE ALSO: *Silphium*.

AVENS

Geum urbanum

An excellent example of a herb that produces a 'spice effect' (see *Introduction*, p. 9), avens, sometimes called colewort or St Benedict's herb, was popular in Tudor kitchen gardens because its roots smell strongly of cloves.

Avens is a perennial in the Rosaceae family, which likes woods and damp hedgerows and grows to around 12 feet high. While its leaves were used in salads – John Evelyn recommends a 'goodly sallet' with lettuce, leeks, mint, rocket and 'colewort-tops', dressed with oil and egg[60] – avens root was added to beer, soups and stews, as cloves would have been, and folded among linen to keep it smelling fresh and to ward off moths. A decoction of the root can be gargled as a cure for halitosis.

Note that the word 'colewort' today is sometimes used generally to describe plants in the Brassica family.

SEE ALSO: *Cloves.*

BLACK PEPPER

Piper nigrum

On 26 May 735 the Venerable Bede, author of the *Ecclesiastical History of the English People*, died at the monastery in Jarrow where he had lived for over fifty years. Despite the 'frequent attacks of breathlessness' which his disciple Cuthbert says overcame Bede in his last days, the Father of English History had enough strength to ask for a box containing his 'few treasures' to be brought to him so that they could be divided among the community.

These treasures turned out to be: two handkerchiefs, some incense and a stash of peppercorns.

We know from a riddle devised by Aldhelm, bishop of Sherborne, that pepper was at this time a rare, expensive foodstuff which '[seasoned] delicacies, the banquets of kings, and the luxuries of the table'. That a monk should have possessed enough of it to be worth distributing after his death may strike us as odd. But there is a duality at work: while Anglo-Saxon monks were, in most respects, austere and self-denying, the monasteries where they lived were major landowners with easy access to all the meat, wheat and vegetables they wanted. The result was, well, intemperance. Bede himself blamed Coldingham Abbey's holy inmates for the building's destruction by fire in 683. They paid the price, he wrote, for 'gluttony and drunkenness and idle gossip and other unlawful transgressions'.[61] (Coldingham was open to both monks *and* nuns, so arguably was asking for trouble.)

Besides which, Anglo-Saxon monks were often what Aelfric in his *Lives of the Saints* calls 'nobly born men who had been used to eating delicacies'. Even though feasting was technically forbidden, a much-abused dispensation in the *Regularis concordia* – a sort of monastic rulebook – permitted it in cases of 'unexpected hospitality when travelling', and generally it proved hard for monks to remain aloof from conspicuous consumption in a society where, as Ann Hagen points out, 'kings, nobles and landowners rewarded their retainers and servants and demonstrated their status by holding feasts'.[62]

Bede's pepper would have had a long journey to Jarrow. Robert Lacey and Danny Danziger speculate that it was probably picked up by English merchants in the northern Italian town of Pavia, the ancient capital of Lombardy. Pavia was 'the great centre of commercial exchange between north-western Europe and the East, and accounts of the time describe merchants' tents being pitched in the field beside the River Ticino on the outskirts of the city'.[63] It would have been brought to Pavia from Basra by Muslim traders, who collected in turn what they needed from Europe – grain, timber, textiles, iron.

The pepper's ultimate source, however, was India's south-west seaboard, where the perennial climbing vine *Piper nigrum* grew wild in the forests of Malabar and Travancore. 'It grows well in the lowlands, but with far more luxuriance in the elevated tracts and along the hills and mountains', observed the VOC (Dutch East India Company) pastor Jacobus Canter Visscher, writing in the early eighteenth century. 'It is not planted in open fields, but in the close neighbourhood of trees, around which the branches climb, as the plant requires support.'[64] It also needs shade: pepper vines exposed to direct sunlight for too long will yield few berries. Pepper grew elsewhere in India too. In 1637 the East India Company merchant Peter Mundy found a 'pepper garden' in Surat in Gujarat. He recorded the experience in his journal:

> Att the Foote of these trees they sett the pepper plant, which groweth uppe about the said tree to the height of 10 or 12 Foote, Clasping, twyning and fastning it selff theron round about as the Ivy Doth the oake or other trees with us [i.e., the English]. They continue 10 to 12 yeare yielding good pepper; then they sett new plants, soe I was told. This yeares Croppe was newly gathered, some of it then lying a Drying in the sunne; yet were there a few clusters, both greene and ripe, left among the leaves on the plant. The berry when it is Ripe beecommeth ruby red and transparent cleare ... as bigge as small pease, sweet and hott in tast.[65]

Visscher calls pepper 'the cheapest but by no means the least useful' of spices, which is broadly how it is regarded today. Pepper is so commonplace, so widely and indiscriminately used, that few people regard it as a spice, let alone as anything special. 'It would be otiose to list the uses of pepper as it occurs in practically all main courses, soups, savoury sauces, salads and entrées', declare Carolyn Heal and Michael Allsop in *Cooking with Spices* (1983), and they have a point.[66]

To add insult to injury, the vagaries of nomenclature mean that pepper shares its name with a host of other substances to which it is mostly unrelated botanically, even if they possess similar properties (heat, intensity): chilli pepper, melegueta pepper (Grains of Paradise), Szechuan pepper, cayenne pepper ... Like 'spicy', 'peppery' is used to describe anything hot.

Black pepper is the second most widely traded spice after chilli peppers. Like sumac, it is exceptionally versatile – equally effective as a condiment and as a cooking ingredient; as richly, earthily pungent on strawberries as it is on steak – and versatility breeds a shrugging complacency.

As Elizabeth David once observed, it is often overused: 'French restaurant cooks tend to overdo the pepper on steak au poivre to the point where their victims choke on the very first mouthful.'[67] And yet the suggestion that there is a standard, classic way of cooking this dish – the dish that springs instantly to the minds of many Europeans and Americans when they hear the word 'pepper' – ignores its rather dubious provenance.

Far from being a traditional French recipe passed down through the generations, steak au poivre was probably invented – there are rival claims: see *Larousse Gastronomique* – in the early 1930s by Émile Lerch, a chef at Paris's Restaurant Albert, who realised that adding a peppery crust was an effective way to enliven the shipments of bland, frozen beef he was receiving from America.

The tendrils of *P. nigrum* bear elongated clusters of peppercorns on thin spikes. The plant starts fruiting after three to five years and continues to do so every third year for up to forty years. To harvest pepper, pickers move from vine to vine on small ladders, handpicking spikes on which some of the berries are red – a sign of maturity – but most are still green. After sorting, the green berries are dried on mats in the sun until they turn black and wrinkled. To make white peppercorns, which have a cleaner, drier heat when ground, red and orange berries are packed in sacks and soaked for a week under running water. This rots the outer husk so that it can be removed by hand. Green peppercorns are sometimes sold fresh on the stem but are more usually pickled. They are used in Thai cooking (the stir-fry pad cha, for instance) and in French cuisine – terrines, pâtés, creamy sauces.

Although the finest varieties of pepper still come from Kerala – Tellicherry and Wynad, for example – others, such as Sarawak (from Malaysian Borneo), Kampot (from Cambodia), Penja (from Cameroon) and Muntok (from Indonesia), are also highly regarded. After a shaky start when much of its pepper was deemed only FAQ ('fair average quality' in the grading parlance), Vietnam is now a leading producer, accounting for around 30 per cent of global production – 150,000 tonnes a year compared with India's 45,000.[68] Vietnamese pepper typically has a high piperine content and aromatic top notes.

Pepper should always be bought whole, as ground pepper loses its aroma very quickly, and should be added towards the end of the cooking process. Mignonette pepper is a mixture of black and white peppercorns; in parts of Canada these are augmented with coriander seed to create 'shot pepper'. The belief that white pepper is preferable in white sauces because specks of ground black pepper are unsightly is still widely held. Odd, as you would think the fact that its slow-glowing heat complements creamy textures so well was more significant.

For some reason black pepper has never, for all its importance, been included in what the spice historian Charles Corn calls the 'holy trinity' of spices that set Europe up for the Renaissance and the ensuing age of barbaric mercantilism – cloves, nutmeg and mace. In the early Middle Ages rents, taxes and dowries were often paid in pepper; hence the term 'peppercorn rent', which now, revealingly, means a nominal sum. It was a different story in the

1430s, when, according to the household accounts of the earl of Oxford, a pound of pepper cost as much as an entire pig.[69]

When a guild was established in London in 1180 to represent spice merchants and ensure their goods were 'garbled' (cleansed) to a reasonable standard, it was called the Guild of Pepperers. Among the recipes from Richard II's kitchen collected as *Forme of Cury* (1390) is a pepper sauce for veal and venison, what we would now call sauce poivrade: 'Take brede and fry it in grece. Draw it up with broth and vynegar. Take thereto powdor of peper and salt and sette it on the fyre. Boile it and messe it forth.'

By the early sixteenth century, however, the spice had lost its cachet. No longer associated with royalty, it became symbolic of crude, rustic cooking – a result, perhaps, of the European oversupply that followed Vincent da Gama's arrival in Malabar on 20 May 1498 and Portugal's subsequent wresting of control of the spice trade from Venice. Pepper plantations were also spreading beyond India into Sumatra and western Java. The money generated funded the rise of the sultanate of Aceh in the sixteenth century.

A similar narrative had played out in ancient Rome. In 13 BC we find Horace discussing pepper as a rare delight, 'wrapped insecurely in scraps of paper'. But as the Roman empire expanded it began to be regarded as a necessity rather than a luxury. For this reason it was excluded from the so-called Alexandrian Tariff issued by the emperor Marcus Aurelius between 176 and 180, which listed fifty-four commodities subject to import duties at Alexandria on their way to Rome.[70]

So much pepper was needed that in AD 92 the emperor Domitian built dedicated pepper warehouses in Rome's spice quarter, north of the Sacra Via. And in 408, 3,000 pounds of it was part of the ransom demanded (and obtained) by Alaric the Visigoth before he would agree to lift his blockade on Rome.

Apicius uses pepper in almost every recipe in *De re coquinaria*; it is often the first ingredient he lists – although John Edwards claims that the word 'was used in an extended sense to include cinnamon, cardamom and nutmeg'.[71] What we can be sure of is that as a condiment it was served in pots called *piperatoria*, which were elaborate and often made of silver. The Romans brought pepper – and therefore *piperatoria* – to every territory they conquered, which explains why so many of them have been found scattered around Europe.

The British Museum's Hoxne pepper pot, stumbled upon by a Suffolk farmer in 1992 while he was looking for a missing hammer with a metal-detector, resembles a statue of a Roman matron wearing dangly earrings and with her hair in plaits. ('She is obviously a seriously *grande dame* and very fashionable', observes Neil MacGregor in *A History of the World in 100 Objects*.) The pot would have cost a small fortune to fill, yet was one of three owned by the household – 'dizzying extravagance'.[72]

Pepper was often given at the Roman festival of Saturnalia, where gifts signified a bond: they had to be of equal value, or a relationship might be thought to be unbalanced. Martial describes a wealthy Roman receiving a present of pepper alongside such exotic goods as frankincense, Lucanian sausages and Syrian grape syrup. But if pepper was omnipresent in ancient Rome, it wasn't to everyone's taste. Pliny, for one, couldn't understand what all the fuss was about:

It is remarkable that the use of pepper has come so much into favour, as in the case of some commodities their sweet taste has been an attraction, and in others their appearance, but pepper has nothing to recommend it in either fruit or berry. To think that its only pleasing quality is pungency and that we go all the way to India to get this![73]

Pepper was the basis of Roman trade with India. The relationship would not have been possible but for the work of Hippalus, a Greek sailor (though a Roman *subject*, based in Egypt) who in around AD 45 worked out that the wind over the Arabian Sea, the monsoon, changed direction seasonally, blowing south-westward between May and October and north-eastward between November and March. Hippalus' story cropped up in the first-century *Periplus of the Erythrean Sea*, a kind of proto-*Lonely Planet* for would-be merchants, packed with seafaring tips and advice about which ports were best for which goods.

Romans collected their pepper from the port city of Muziris, near what is now Cochin in Kerala, which according to the *Periplus* 'abounds in ships sent there with cargoes from Arabia, and by the Greeks [... Kings] send large ships to these market towns on account of the great quantity and bulk of pepper.' According to the Muziris Papyrus, a Greek contract between an Alexandrian merchant and a financier dating from the second century AD, a single shipload of pepper was worth 7 million sestertia.

Sailors knew they were approaching Muziris when they saw vast shoals of sinister red-eyed sea-snakes writhing in the water. The French navy officer and slave-trader Louis de Grandpré wrote in the 1790s that between the Maldives and the Malabar coast he saw 'on the surface of the water a great number of living serpents ... They begin to appear as soon as we get within the Maldives; but they are not very numerous till we arrive at about eight or ten leagues from the coast, and their numbers increase as we approach.' Those off the Malabar coast were black and short, with dragon-shaped heads and, yes, 'blood-red eyes'.[74]

After the collapse of Rome, the Arab world dominated the trade in spices, and the Indian Ocean became, in Jack Turner's words, 'a Muslim lake, home to the seaborne civilisation that gave rise to the tales of Sinbad and his voyages to the magical realms of spice, giant birds and monsters, genii and gold'. The true source of pepper was effaced, or at least mystified. Isidore of Seville knew that pepper grew in India, where there were forests of pepper trees. But he also believed these trees to be guarded by poisonous snakes – an interesting echo of the 'sea-snakes' story. To harvest the pepper, he thought, natives had to set fire to the trees to scare off the snakes, scorching the white peppercorns until they were black and wrinkled:

> It is the flame that blackens the pepper, for pepper is naturally white although its fruit varies. Unripe pepper is called 'long pepper'; that which has not been through the fire is called 'white pepper' [...] If pepper is light, it is old; the heavy kind is fresh. One should watch out for fraudulent merchants who sprinkle very old pepper with silver foam or lead to make it weigh more.[75]

Actually, long pepper (*P. longum*) is completely different (see *Long pepper*).

Dioscorides believed that 'all pepper in general is warming, urinary, digesting, attracting and dissolving, and cleans away things that darken the pupils'.[76] He recommended drinking pepper-water as a cure for the shivering that accompanies fever. (This is an Ayurvedic remedy too.) The Ayurvedic supplement *trikatu*, usually taken to improve gastric function, is a mixture of black pepper, long pepper and ginger. Meanwhile, a paste of ground white pepper and butter, licked at intervals, is supposed to do wonders for a sore throat. Hippocrates recommended pepper mixed with honey and vinegar for menstrual irregularities, while Pierre Pomet, Louis XIV's pharmacist, wrote that 'a few drops of the oil [of pepper], in any proper liniment, rub'd upon the perinaeum three or four times will restore a lost erection'.[77]

Several studies since the 1980s have suggested that piperine's main health benefit may be the way it increases 'bioavailability', helping nutrients and drugs work more effectively by stopping metabolic enzymes from compromising their absorption by the body.

One of the most popular Anglo-Indian dishes, mulligatawny, has its roots in colonial Madras, where native chefs baffled by British requests for soup repurposed sour, hot rasams or 'pepper-waters' (*milagu thanni* in Tamil), adding rice, vegetables and meat to a basic stock thickened slightly with split peas and spiced with lightly roasted black peppercorns, cumin seeds and coriander seeds. The dish 'quickly spread to the other British settlements dotted around the subcontinent and "very hot mulligatani soup" was invariably served at every Anglo-Indian dinner party and ball'.[78]

Mulligatawny became a Sunday-lunch staple of the mixed-race Anglo-Indian community – the descendants of the British men who had come to India in the seventeenth and eighteenth centuries and taken Indian wives. Colonel Arthur Kenney-Herbert, author of *Culinary Jottings from Madras*, considered it a comfort food, best eaten with rice and nothing else: 'There are so many condiments, spices and highly flavoured elements in its composition – not to mention the concomitant ladleful of rice which custom decrees – that he who partakes of it finds the delicate power of his palate vitiated.'[79] Recipes abound, most of them stipulating curry powder or cayenne pepper over *P. nigrum*. Neither Mrs Beeton nor Eliza Acton (whose recipe in *Modern Cookery for Private Families*, from 1864, is reckoned to be the first in an English cookery book) mentions black pepper specifically. Daniel Santiagoe's recipe in his *The Curry Cook's Assistant* (1887) suggests 'a pinch'; but then he, a Ceylonese cook brought back to London by John London Shand, makes clear that his milky brew of saffron, ginger, cumin and coriander is a concoction devised for Europeans.

SEE ALSO: *Grains of Paradise, Grains of Selim, Long pepper, Pink peppercorns, Szechuan pepper.*

BLUE FENUGREEK

Trigonella caerulea

In her book *The Georgian Feast* (1999) Darra Goldstein expounds a gorgeous Georgian creation myth: when He was making the world, God took a break for supper. But He became so involved in his meal that he tripped over the peaks of the Caucasus mountain range and spilled a little of everything from his plate onto the land below: 'So it was that Georgia came to be blessed with such riches, table scraps from Heaven.'[80]

Georgia's finest herbs and spices grow in Svaneti, in the mountainous north-west – an isolated, magical realm dotted with medieval villages and the stone towers that were built to defend them. One such plant is *utskho suneli*, which translates as 'strange and fragrant smell from far away': probably it was introduced into Georgia from India. More commonly called blue fenugreek (*Trigonella caerulea*), it is milder than ordinary fenugreek (*T. foenumgraecum*), smells like hay and has three main uses: in the Georgian spice mix khmeli suneli; in the Swiss cheese Schabziger; and in certain types of Tyrolean rye bread, such as schüttelbrot.

As with garam masala in India (see *A Directory of Spice Mixes*, p. 248), there is no set recipe for khmeli suneli. Generally, its components are blue fenugreek (the ground seeds and pods), coriander seed, garlic, dried marigold flowers (known locally as 'Imeretian saffron'), chilli and pepper, but the proportions change according to the dish being cooked. The recipe in Paula Wolfert's *The Cooking of the Eastern Mediterranean* (1994) also includes cloves, dried mint and basil.

Khmeli suneli can be used as a rub for meat or in stews. Specific uses mentioned by Goldstein are: in spicy meatballs (abkhazura, served with tkemali or plum sauce) from Abkhazia on the Black Sea coast – the meatballs are wrapped in caul fat (the lacy membrane encasing an animal's internal organs), as with the Cypriot sausage sheftalia; in cabbage with walnuts (kombostos ruleti nigvzit); and in the aubergine salad badridzhani mtsvanilit.

The hard, green, strongly flavoured cow's-milk cheese Schabziger (Sap Sago in the US) is made exclusively in the Swiss canton of Glarus, where monks invented it in the eighth century and manufactured it using blue fenugreek grown in their monastery's garden. At an open-air parliament on 24 April 1463 local citizens passed a law obliging Schabziger to carry a stamp of origin, making it one of the earliest branded products. Pre-moulded into a conical shape, Schabziger is usually eaten grated – sprinkled over pasta, for example – or mixed with butter to make a sharp, pungent spread. This use of blue fenugreek is technically beyond the compass of this book as it involves the dried, ground stems and leaves rather than the seeds and pods – blue fenugreek as a herb, not a spice – but is too interesting not to include.

Blue fenugreek seeds are used in Chinese medicine to relieve 'painful swollen testes'.[81]

SEE ALSO: *Fenugreek*.

CALAMUS

Acorus calamus

The roots of this marsh plant, indigenous to North America but first cultivated in Poland in the thirteenth century, were once candied and eaten as a sweetmeat, especially on the east coast of England, where they were believed to ward off 'Fen fever', a type of malaria endemic in East Anglia.

The best root is reddish or greeny-white and has a sweet smell, a pungent, acrid taste and a firm texture. Mrs M. Grieve's *A Modern Herbal* (1931) recommends calamus root as a substitute for cinnamon, nutmeg and ginger in cookery. She continues:

> The rhizome is largely used in native Oriental medicines for dyspepsia and bronchitis and chewed as a cough lozenge, and from the earliest times has been one of the most popular remedies of the native practitioners of India. The candied root is sold as a favourite medicine in every Indian bazaar.[82]

Snuff was commonly adulterated with ground calamus, and it was an ingredient in a once popular tonic drink called Stockton Bitters.

Dioscorides calls the plant acoron, after *coreon*, the Greek word for the pupil of the eye, diseases of which calamus was reputed to cure.

SEE ALSO: *Orris*.

CARAWAY

Carum carvi

In Agatha Christie's penultimate Miss Marple novel, *At Bertram's Hotel* (1965) – I'm discounting 1976's *Sleeping Murder*, which, while the last to be published, was written in 1940 – the fusty London establishment of the title, a hang-out for the decrepit remnants of old county families, represents a way of life for which the ageing Christie had grown nostalgic: 'Inside, if this was the first time you had visited Bertram's, you felt, almost with alarm, that you had re-entered a vanished world. Time had gone back. You were in Edwardian England once more.'[83]

When Lady Selina Hazy and Colonel Luscombe take tea there, their solicitous waiter is quick to recommend the hotel's 'very good seed cake'. 'Seed cake?' responds Lady Selina. 'I haven't eaten seed cake for years. Is it *real* seed cake?' The waiter insists that it is: 'The cook has had the receipt for years. You'll enjoy it, I'm sure.'[84]

The waiter's certainty here is touching. Whatever its symbolic value, few cakes divide people like caraway seed cake, which originated in East Anglia and was traditionally made in the spring to celebrate the end of wheat-sowing, when it was distributed among farm workers. Most of the best-known early cookbooks contain a seed cake recipe – some more than one, so that the best-quality cake might be matched to the smartest occasion. Eliza Smith's *The Compleat Housewife* (1727) boasts three, versions of which filtered through into Hannah Glasse's *The Art of Cookery* (1747) and Mrs Beeton's *Book of Household Management* (1861).

Essentially a highly flavoured version of pound cake, seed cake is, admits Arabella Boxer in her *Book of English Food* (1991), 'enormously popular with some, but anathema to others'.[85] Elisabeth Ayrton goes one step further: '[Seed cake] is almost universally disliked', she writes in *The Cookery of England* (1974), as 'very few people can stand the taste of caraway seeds'.[86] Boxer quotes with sympathy the author and cook George Lasalle's comment that, as a boy, he was 'once frightened by a seed cake in a cricket pavilion', but declares that she finds it delicious 'in a somewhat austere way'.

And yet seed cake need not be austere, as some of the older recipes for it demonstrate. It was supposed to be a rich and dense cake, kept moist with Madeira wine, brandy, rosewater or milk. Like Christmas cake, it was a 'keeping cake', designed to last for several weeks. But it was also rustic and unsophisticated; hence the ripple of awkwardness when, in Elizabeth Gaskell's *Cranford* (1853), the retired milliner Miss Barker serves it to snooty Mrs Jamieson, a widow with aristocratic connections:

> I saw Mrs Jamieson eating seed-cake ... and I was rather surprised, for I knew that she had told us, on the occasion of her last party, that she never had it in her house, it reminded her so much of scented soap. She always gave us Savoy biscuits. However, Mrs Jamieson was kindly indulgent to Miss Barker's want of knowledge of the customs of high life; and, to spare her feelings, ate three large pieces of seed-cake, with a placid, ruminating expression of countenance, not unlike a cow's.[87]

That Christie's Lady Selina should be so enamoured of such a cake is odd. But what seems to have happened is that, between the 1850s and the early years of the twentieth century, seed cake ascended into respectability, possibly via the nurseries of the late-Victorian upper and upper-middle classes, whose children learned to look back on it as adults with pernickety nostalgia: 'Is it *real* seed cake?'

It was, at any rate, good enough for Bloomsbury – that crucial social acid test. According to *The Bloomsbury Cookbook* (2014), seed cake was in the repertoire of the artist Vanessa Bell's long-serving cook Grace Higgens, who developed from the 'quite incompetent' sixteen-year-old she was when Bell first employed her into the 'treasure' of Charleston. Higgens was even the recipient of requests from Bell's sister Virginia Woolf for her recipes 'as I can't get any cakes made except yours that I like to eat'.[88]

Whatever the truth of the matter, here is the 'best' recipe from *The Compleat Housewife*:

> Take five pounds of fine flour well dried, and four pounds of single refined sugar beaten and sifted; mix the sugar and flour together, and sift them through a hair sieve; then wash four pounds of butter in rose or orange-flower water; you must work the butter with your hand till it is like cream, beat twenty eggs, half the whites, and put to them six spoonfuls of sack [sweet sherry]: then put in your flour, a little at a time; you must not begin mixing it till the oven is almost hot; you must let it lie a little while before you put the cake into the hoop [circular tin]; when you are ready to put it into the oven, put into it eight ounces of candied orange peel sliced, as much citron, and a pound and a half of carraway comfits; mix all well together, and put it into the hoop, which must be papered at the bottom, and butter'd; the oven must be quick; it will take two or three hours baking; you may ice it if you please.[89]

The combination of alcohol and candied peel here and in recipes by Hannah Glasse, Elizabeth Moxon and Mrs Beeton (who adds brandy and lots of nutmeg and mace) would have made these cakes very different from the dry — and, yes, austere — between-the-wars cake that Arabella Boxer has in mind: the recipe *she* cites, from Catherine Ives's *When the Cook Is Away* (1928), relies on orange peel alone to dial down the acrid pungency of the caraway. Smith's genius stroke, though, is the addition not of rough caraway seeds, as used in the more basic recipes, but potentially tooth-shattering (one would think) caraway comfits, otherwise known as sugar-plums.

In Clement Clark Moore's *A Visit From St Nicholas* (1823),

visions of sugar-plums dance in the heads of children. But these are not what most of us imagine: sugar-plums have nothing to do with plums. Comfits are sweets consisting of multiple layers of sugar built up around a central seed or kernel – usually caraway or cardamom seeds, or almonds – using a labour-intensive process called 'panning'. 'Plum' in the name was a nod to the sweet's ovoid shape.

Carum carvi, the plant whose detested seeds kept Tom Stobart up half the night picking them out of his bread – an 'impossible task' which nevertheless became 'a prelude to almost every ascent I made in the Austrian Alps during my apprenticeship as a mountaineer'[90] – is a biennial in the family Umbelliferae with tufty, frilly leaves and umbels of creamy-white flowers. Its roots and leaves are edible, but it has always been grown commercially for its seeds – dark brown, with lighter ridges.

Caraway seeds' bitter liquorice taste was popular with the Romans, who knew them as *karo* or *careum* (from Caria, according to Pliny: the region in western Anatolia where the plant was supposed to hail from; 'caraway' is from the ancient Arabic *karawya*). Apicius uses them in numerous sauces, such as ius in elixam allecatum (fish-pickle sauce for boiled meats), though in negligible quantities – a 'pinch' is usually stipulated. They are a staple of German, Austrian and East European cooking, turning up in sauerkraut and goulash and a Czech rub for chicken, much loved by my children, which teams them with paprika, sage and black pepper.

Their affinity with game has been exploited since at least the fourteenth century; also their ability to counteract the fattiness of pork and goose: *Forme of Cury* (1390) contains a delicious recipe for cormarye – pork braised in garlic and red wine with caraway and coriander. And, of course, caraway is one of the most popular flavourings of Scandinavian and East European rye breads, where it complements the sour, bitter taste imparted by the sourdough culture.

Caraway flavours the Scandinavian liqueur akvavit and the German kümmel – its name in German (and also the German word for cumin: in several European languages the spices share a name; in France caraway is called *cumin des prés*) – and cheeses such as the Swedish Bondost and the Danish Havarti. The Alsace cheese Munster Gérome is usually served with a small dish of caraway seeds on the side.

The seeds' use outside Europe is limited to some formulations of the North African chilli paste harissa (see *A Directory of Spice Mixes*, p. 246) and Middle Eastern puddings like moghli (or meghlie), traditionally prepared to celebrate the birth of a son: 'It is said that a family will serve it on the birth of a daughter only if they are truly pleased to have one after a succession of four sons.'[91]

The habit of sprinkling caraway seeds on cabbage-based dishes suggests they are good at preventing indigestion and flatulence. (Incidentally, the recipe for cabbage leaves with caraway cheese stuffing in Jane Grigson's *Vegetable Book* (1978) is much less disgusting than it sounds.) They were held to be especially effective in this regard when eaten with apples, as Shallow invites Falstaff to do in Shakespeare's *Henry IV, Part 2*:

Nay, you shall see my orchard, where, in an arbour, we will eat
a last year's pippin of my own grafting, with a dish of caraways,
and so forth.

Caraway's other health benefits are more questionable. Dioscorides recommends caraway oil as a tonic for pale-faced girls. Culpeper believes that caraway 'helps to sharpen the eye-sight' and that 'the powder of the seed put into a poultice, takes away black and blue spots of blows and bruises'.[92]

SEE ALSO: *Celery seed, Dill, Fennel, Fenugreek, Nigella, Sesame.*

CARDAMOM

Elettaria cardamomum

My favourite story about cardamom is told by Tom Stobart in his *Herbs, Spices and Flavourings* (1970). The mountaineer, zoologist and film-maker was in Bombay, as was, when an Indian friend found what he thought was a cockroach in his curry:

> He fished it out and called the waiter. The waiter called the manager who, in turn, called the cook. At this point, according to the classic Italian story, the cook should have eaten the cockroach, smacking his lips and exclaiming, 'You do not like zis wonderful little fish?' But the Indian cook respectfully pointed out that the cockroach was, in fact, a large hairy 'cardamom' seed.[93]

Cardamom is a perennial in the ginger family which grows wild in southern India and Sri Lanka, but is now cultivated in other tropical countries such as Guatemala, the main producer, and Tanzania. The stalks or racemes bearing the seed pods – small, ovoid pellets containing between fifteen and twenty seeds in three double rows – grow out from the base of the plant and trail on the ground. After harvesting, the pods are washed, then dried in the sun or in ovens. Cardamom is best bought in pod form, as the seeds lose their eucalyptus flavour quickly once decorticated, and even more quickly after they are ground.

In ancient Greece the inferior grades ('false cardamom') were called *amomum* and the superior ones ('true cardamom') *kardamomom*. Several varieties of 'true' cardamom exist, and the difference between 'true' and 'false' cardamom is, on balance, greater than that between, say, cinnamon and 'false cinnamon', or cassia. Uncertainty remains over what *exactly* the Greeks' amomum was, but their grading carries through into the Linnaean formulation:

false cardamoms carry the species name *Amomum* – e.g., *A. subu-latum* or 'black cardamom' – which may have been the identity of Stobart's friend's cockroach.

The numerous varieties of Chinese cardamom are used in tra-ditional Chinese medicine rather than cooking (though cardamom does feature in some Szechuanese red-cooked dishes). *A. globosum* and *A. villosum* are used to treat stomach pain and nausea, while Li Shih-chen's sixteenth-century *Herbal Pen Ts'ao* considers 'bastard cardamom' or *A. xanthoides* – at one time commonly substituted for true cardamom by wily traders – to have 'tonic, stomachic, stringent, carminative, sedative, and tussic properties':

> [Its seeds] are used as a preserve or condiment, in flavouring spirit, and are said to hasten the solution of copper or iron cash, fish bones, or any other metallic or foreign substance acciden-tally swallowed.[94]

The habit of grading spices as 'true' and 'false' is connected to market value, and cardamom is costly: the third most expensive spice after saffron and vanilla. Besides, some types of false carda-mom are entirely acceptable, even preferred. In Ethiopian and Eritrean cuisine *Aframomum corrorima*, or korarima, is used in spice mixes like berbere and the spicy mitmita (see *A Directory of Spice Mixes*, pp. 237, 249), and black cardamom's devotees insist its smoky, camphorous kick enlivens potentially bland rice and lentil dishes. (Cardamom has long been an important ingredient in pilaf.)

Still, the best varieties of cardamom are held to be the green *Elettaria cardamomum* sub-types Malabar and Mysore, the latter containing the largest amount of the fragrant compounds cineol and limonene. The smaller and paler green the pods, the better the flavour. White pods are ordinary green pods which have been chemically treated with peroxide – allegedly to improve their appearance in milky sauces or rice puddings such as payasam, where the greenness might jar, though really, it's hard to imagine anyone would care. Another theory is that, when cardamom pods were being shipped from India to Scandinavia, they were bleached by the sun during the long journey.[95] Scandinavians had been introduced to the spice by the Vikings, who acquired it in the course of their raids on Constantinople and grew accustomed to the milder-tasting bleached pods which they used to pickle herring and in pies and breads such as the Finnish pulla. Presumably, as shipping speeds increased, the need arose to bleach the pods at source rather than leave it to the vagaries of nature.

(Frederic Rosengarten cites another reason for cardamom's Scandinavian popularity: 'In Sweden a man who has been drinking liquor will frequently chew cardamom seeds so that on returning home his wife will not smell alcohol on his breath.'[96] If this sounds unlikely, consider the fact that Wrigley use cardamom as an ingredient in chewing gum.)

Sixty per cent of the cardamom produced in the world goes to Arab countries, where it is a major component (40 per cent or greater) of Bedouin coffee or gahwa. Gahwa's serving is highly ritualised: the spiced beans – saffron, cloves and cinnamon are added too – are roasted at home, ground and brewed while guests wait, then served in tiny portions from a special pot called a dallah. 'The long, beak-like spouts of their brass coffee pots are usually stuffed with a few opened cardamom pods', says Stobart, with the authority of one who has seen them (and drunk the coffee) for himself.[97] 'Nothing is more characteristic of the infuriating frontier posts and police stations of the Near East than the taste of cardamom-scented coffee.' Rosengarten adds that it is 'good form to accept up to three cups and make an audible slurping noise'.[98]

Sometimes a host's approach to preparation can be more *ad hoc*. 'The Arabs, indeed, appear fond of cardamoms, and generally use this spice with their coffee', says James Baillie Fraser in his *Travels in Koordistan, Mesopotamia, &c.* (1840), explaining:

When you enter the tent of a petty Sheikh, or head of a family, and coffee is got ready before you, you may generally observe your host, just before the pot boils for the last time, or about that stage of the process, take from his own private purse or pocket, a few grains of something which he hands to the cahwachee to be infused in the beverage; they are grains of cardamom and it is held, I believe, as an indispensable compliment to a guest whom they desire to honour.[99]

The resulting brew is 'as strong as brandy, and as bitter as gall, but fine, warm, refreshing stuff. When we had sipped one or two of their thimble-full cups of it we rose and withdrew.'[100] On the question of slurping, Fraser is disappointingly silent.

SEE ALSO: *Ginger, Grains of Selim.*

CAROB

Ceratonia siliqua

We know from Matthew 3:4 that John the Baptist 'was clothed with camel's hair, and with a girdle of a skin about his loins; and he did eat locusts and wild honey'. Does this mean he *actually ate locusts* – as in the swarming, short-horned grasshoppers? No, because we are told elsewhere that his diet was 'purely vegetable'. 'Locust' here means 'locust bean', or the seeds of the flowering shrub in the legume family we call carob, from the Middle French for locust bean pod, *carobe*.

Carob pods are between 6 and 12 inches long, flattened, shiny, wrinkled and browny-black, like scorched runner beans. The seeds, arranged along a wide but shallow central groove, are ruddy-coloured, ovoid and very hard. When the seeds' skins have been removed in acid and the endosperm milled, the result is the yellow-white powder locust bean gum – the thickening agent used in a range of edible and inedible products from yoghurts to shoe polish, insecticides and cosmetics. As a foodstuff, carob has always been low-rent – a famine food (carobs are resistant to drought), usually given to livestock, as in the parable of the prodigal son (Luke 15:16):

> So he went and hired himself out to one of the citizens of that country, and he sent him into his fields to feed swine. And he would have gladly filled his stomach with the carob pods that the swine were eating, and no one was giving anything to him.

Carob seeds have a reliably consistent mass of 0.21 g. For this reason they were used as a scale-weight by Arab jewellers: hence the word 'carat', from the Greek word for the tree, *kerátion*. The gold Roman coin called the solidus, introduced by Constantine I in 312, weighed 24 carob seeds. This, pub-quiz fans, is why '24-carat gold' means pure gold.

Another type of powder is made from the ground, de-seeded pods themselves. Carob powder has a warm, chocolatey aroma and is frequently used as a chocolate substitute. The idea that it is healthier than chocolate is, however, false. While carob has only half the fat of cocoa and does not contain caffeine or theobromine, the main allergen in cocoa, it is naturally high in sugar. Carob molasses is popular in Middle Eastern cookery: in stews and mezze dishes like nazuktan, the Turkish dish of aubergine purée and crushed almonds, and added to tahina with mint to make a dip. Carob juice is traditionally drunk in Egypt during Ramadan – the best is supposed to come from Alexandria – while in Malta a syrup made from carob is used as a cough medicine.

Carob trees are indigenous to Mediterranean and the Levant but now grow anywhere that citrus fruit will grow. The Egyptian name for carob fruit is written on pottery vessels found in a First Dynasty tomb at Saqqara, though Theophrastus, who called carob pods 'Egyptian figs', wrote that the plant 'does not occur at all in Egypt, but in Syria and Ionia and also in Cnidos and Rhodes'. The Greek island of Crete has one of the largest natural carob groves at Tris Ekklisies.

SEE ALSO: *Vanilla.*

CASSIA

Cinnamomum cassia

A lesser variety of cinnamon popular in China.

SEE *CINNAMON.*

CELERY SEED

Apium graveolens

The celery we know today, the self-blanching *Apium graveolens dulce*, was developed in the seventeenth century by Italian gardeners from a foul-smelling wild celery called smallage which grows in salt marshes: the horses of the Myrmidons graze on it in Homer's *Iliad*. Today, celery is a big deal in Italy – usually braised

and gratinéed to within an inch of its life – and grows most notably
in Puglia, Calabria and Campania. Sicily produces its own small-
stemmed variety, which is used in the vegetable stew caponata.

By the time John Evelyn was writing his *Acetaria: A Discourse of Sallets* in 1699, newfangled Italian celery was positively
fashionable:

> Sellery, apium Italicum, (and of the Petroseline Family) was for-
> merly a stranger with us (nor very long since in Italy) is an hot
> and more generous sort of Macedonian Persley or Smallage ...
> and for its high and grateful Taste is ever plac'd in the middle of
> the Grand Sallet, at our Great Men's tables, and Practors feasts,
> as the Grace of the whole Board.[101]

A. graveolens is a herbaceous biennial in the parsley family which
yields a mass of tiny, ridged, grey-brown fruits every second year.
It grows best in cool to moderate climates and needs a lot of mois-
ture as its roots are shallow. Strictly speaking, celery 'seeds' (actually fruit) are usually smallage seeds. You harvest them by cutting
the stalk and hanging it upside down to dry with the seed head
covered.

Celery seeds should be bought whole, crushed at home just
before they are needed, and used sparingly as they have a strong,
bitter flavour, 'like a very pronounced version of the cooked
stalks'.[102] They work well with egg dishes, fish, salad dressings
and sprinkled over cucumbers and tomatoes (and tomato juice),
in breads and, especially, biscuits or savoury pastries intended to
be eaten with cheese. The condiment 'celery salt' is a combination of ground celery seeds and salt and is a common seasoning
for American hot dogs, quails' eggs and, of course, Bloody Marys.
Note that celery salt is missing – along with Tabasco (see *Chilli
pepper*) – from the earliest versions of the restorative cocktail.
Its first appearance is in one of the three Bloody Mary recipes in
former Waldorf PR Ted Saucier's book *Bottoms Up* in 1951, shortly

before the first-ever sighting of a celery-stick garnish – in Byfield's Pump Room, the Chicago restaurant that inspired the title of Phil Collins's 1985 album *No Jacket Required* when it turned the singing drummer/drumming singer away for failing to meet its dress code.

In ancient Greece smallage was grown for its medicinal qualities – as a carminative and diuretic – and in ancient Rome as a pain-killer, according to Celsus' *De medicina* (*c.* AD 40). The Greeks associated smallage with death and wove funeral garlands from its leaves. Apiol, the chemical compound it contains, is an aborti-facient. Oil distilled from celery and parsley, which also contains apiol, was used in medieval times to induce abortions and treat menstrual disorders. Consumed in large quantities, it can cause liver and kidney failure.

Fresh smallage leaves can be used in salads and sauces. The stalks, which have a harsh, bitter taste, are sometimes used in French cuisine but usually blanched first to draw away the bit-terness and make them sweeter. Turnip-rooted celery, or celeriac, bred from the same source as *A. graveolens*, is *sedano rapa*.

CHILLI PEPPER

Capsicum annuum, C. frutescens et al.

In 1987 a Portuguese-born audio engineer called Fernando Duarte took his friend Robbie Brozin to a Portuguese restaurant called Chickenland in Rosettenville, a suburb of Johannesburg. They liked the place so much they bought it – Brozin was an entrepre-neur, he could do that sort of thing – and renamed it Nando's in Duarte's honour.

What made Chickenland so appealing? It served flame-grilled

chicken which had been marinaded in peri-peri sauce. Peri-peri, or pili-pili, is the Swahili name for the chiltepín, or bird's-eye chilli pepper, a variety of the most common chilli pepper species, *Capsicum frutescens* – native to the Americas but disseminated across Europe, Asia and Africa by the Spanish and the Portuguese, who were helped by the fact that the seeds remain viable for two or three years.[103] Nando's sauce, made with bird's-eye chillies grown in Mozambique, is a version of the marinade that Portuguese settlers brought with them to South Africa: crushed chillies mixed with citrus peel, garlic, onion, salt, pepper, bay leaves, lemon juice, paprika (of which more later), pimiento (ditto), tarragon, basil and oregano.

No wonder it tastes good. And where Nando's is concerned, goodness means hotness. Musing on the way the restaurant chain has managed to combine massive global popularity with not being awful, the novelist John Lanchester revealed: 'My standard Nando's order is a chicken breast burger served "medium", which is still fairly spicy. But on my Ofsted-style inspection visit [to a local branch], I ordered it "hot". After my first mouthful, I burst into tears and went crimson. Lord only knows what "extra hot" is like.'[104]

The modern use of the word 'spicy' as a synonym for 'hot' is almost entirely the fault of chilli, the Aztec (Nahuatl) name for the fruit of the numerous varieties of *Capsicum* plant. (The pods are technically berries, but horticulturalists call them fruits.) In their excellent *Complete Chile Pepper Book* (2009) – 'chilli' can be spelled several ways – Paul W. Bosland and Dave DeWitt clarify chilli's status, not the first occasion on which they are obliged to disperse the fog enshrouding this most complex and multifarious of plants: 'When harvested at the green stage, the pods are considered a vegetable; when harvested in the dried mature colours [e.g., red or orange], they become a spice.'[105]

For many people chilli *is* spice, its heat connoting danger and sexuality. It even has its own dedicated unit of measurement for heat, the Scoville Heat Unit (SHU), devised in 1912 by the American pharmacist Wilbur Scoville. Not all chillies are hot and pungent, but when they are, it is because they contain large quantities of the volatile compound capsaicin. Capsaicinoids bind with receptors in our mouths and throats to create a burning sensation which raises our heart rate, makes us perspire and goads our central nervous systems into producing endorphins, the opiate-like neuropeptides that induce feelings of contentment and euphoria. It is possible to become addicted to eating chilli, just as people become addicted to exercise.

Scoville's interest in chillies was medical rather than culinary. He wondered whether chilli compounds might, when applied to the skin, be effective counterirritants – that is to say, create pain or inflammation in one area with the goal of lessening it in another. The way to find out, he thought, was to find the number of dilutions necessary for sensations to disappear, then use this 'bite threshold' as an estimate of potency.

Despite numerous modifications over the years to the system for compiling them, Scoville ratings, while they have captured the public's imagination, will always be slightly dubious: capsaicin desensitises testers, sometimes within a single testing session. And besides, the use of threshold measures is controversial in sensory evaluation: thresholds are 'only one point on an intensity function, and thus they don't tell us anything about above-threshold responding';[106] also, they 'may depend so much on the conditions of measurement that they do not exist as a fixed point with any physiological meaning'.[107]

As a broad indicator, though, Scoville is acceptable. A chilli pepper with a high Scoville rating is going to be very hot, and that's as much as most of us need to know.

Our obsession with foods that hurt us perplexes psychologists. Many people who dislike chillies at first later come to love them. The mechanics of this learned preference are intriguing, not least because they cross the species barrier. Rats won't eat chilli pepper but 'can learn to prefer it if they're exposed to other rats that have eaten it', according to Alexandra W. Logue in *The Psychology of Eating and Drinking* (2004).[108] Similarly, chimpanzees will not seek it out but can acquire a preference for it through contact with people.[109]

Humans are the only omnivores that regularly eat chilli. A 1980 study found that Mexicans typically eat chillies several times a day. One British book from the mid-1980s observes, memorably, that 'chillies are widely consumed in India, South America and Africa in quantities that would be dangerous for the delicate Western palate'[110] – echoing, over a century on, Mrs Beeton's worries about spices in general (see *Introduction*, p. 20).

Spice expert Gernot Katzer thinks they 'make everything better', that people who do not agree on this point 'simply suffer lack of experience and training'.[111] This rather overlooks the fact that people taste things differently. One person's 'scorching hot' is another's 'mild'. So-called 'supertasters' with a higher than normal number of fungiform papillae on their tongues and thus an enhanced ability to taste phenylthiocarbamide (PTC) and 6-*n*-propylthiouracil (PROP) will feel a greater burn from chilli than others and may be more inclined to dislike it.

The evolutionary psychologist Jason Goldman explains love for spicy foods in terms of a mechanism he calls 'hedonic reversal' or 'benign masochism': 'Something happens, in millions of humans each year, which changes a negative evaluation into a positive evaluation, like flipping a light switch.'[112] Logue speculates that we enjoy chilli because 'the pain that accompanies eating [it …] seems dangerous but is actually safe – a manifestation of the sensation-seeking trait'.[113]

How safe, though, is safe? Capsaicin can burn literally as well as figuratively. You should always wear gloves when handling chillies, and if you forget and burn yourself, remember that splashing cold water on the burn will have no effect. Capsaicin is soluble in alcohol and oils, so you should either coat your hands in vegetable oil, then wash them with soap and water, or rub the area with iso-propyl alcohol. If you burn your mouth, eat thick cream or Greek yoghurt: casein, found in dairy products, strips the capsaicin molecules from the receptors.

It would be a mistake, though, to define chillies solely in terms of their heat. The popularity of the bland bell pepper and English iterations of chilli con carne which reduce it to an infinitesimally spiced, nursery-food bolognese-with-beans shows that people like the flavour of chilli without the burn. In Szechuan cuisine chillies are browned in hot fat to lessen the impact of the capsaicin in dishes such as kung pao chicken, where they are used in tandem with Szechuan pepper. And while heat is extremely important in south-east Asian cooking, it is designed to be experienced in the context of more subtle taste atmospheres in which herbs such as lemongrass and spices like galangal also play a crucial role. Think of the way a Thai green curry benefits from these ingredients, not to mention kaffir lime leaves, garlic, shrimp paste etc.

Like aubergines and tomatoes, capsicum species are members of the family Solanaceae. Native to tropical regions in North and South America, they are perennials in their native habitats but grown as annuals in more temperate zones. The main global producer is now India, especially the state of Andhra Pradesh, but chillies are easy to grow, which is why, as Jack Turner remarks, the chilli 'was never the major money-spinner that the true Eastern spices had been for thousands of years'.[114]

Chilli plants are often grown domestically, and the internet teems with chillihead blogs and forums debating the hottest cultivars and how best to grow them. (Be warned: the chilli world attracts fanatics and obsessives, and there is an unpleasantly macho, hyper-competitive tang to some chillihead discourse.) Many of these grower-bloggers are American, as you would expect, but there is a solid community of UK home-growers (see a site like thechileman.org); small-scale professional growers, too, like Bedfordshire's Edible Ornamentals, whose hydroponic chillies are sold in Waitrose and Fortnum & Mason. Chillies must be the only spice to have their own dedicated research centre: the Chile Pepper Institute at New Mexico State University, founded in 1992 and still 'the only international, non-profit organisation devoted to education and research related to Capsicum or chile peppers'.

'Peppers', of course, is Columbus's misnomer, an echo heard down the centuries of the confusion he felt when he first tasted the spice in Hispaniola in 1492. 'There is also plenty of *aji*,' he wrote, 'which is their pepper, which is more valuable than [black] pepper, and all the people eat nothing else, it being very wholesome.' Shocked by its heat, and believing it to be a species of *Piper nigrum*, he shipped fifty caravels of it back to Spain. From there chillies found their way to Portugal and thence to India and Africa and, courtesy of invading Turks, to Central and Eastern Europe, where paprika was taken up enthusiastically in rustic meat stews like the Hungarian goulash (from the Hungarian *gulyás,* meaning 'herdsman'), pörkölt and paprikash, and their numerous local equivalents. Northern Europe only took an interest later, in the nineteenth century, when, as Lizzie Collingham explains, chilli peppers 'entered the cookery books in Indian curry recipes, further conflating them in the British mind with the Indian subcontinent rather than with the Americas'.[115]

Paprika is generally very mild, so much so that Katzer considers it separately from 'proper' chillies on his website, feeling that it 'does not make much sense to discuss mild and hot species together, as their applications are wildly distinct'. This may be true, but in the interests of efficiency, and because most non-specialists would expect to find paprika discussed alongside other types of chilli, I am mentioning it here – though you can also find it on p. 177.

At first chilli was known in India as 'Pernambucco pepper', suggesting it came from Brazil via Lisbon. But in Bombay it was called Goan pepper, as Goa was its point of entry. Indians took to chilli because it looked and tasted similar to long pepper, which they used copiously, but kept longer and was easier to grow. South Indian cooking makes particular use of chilli. Collingham mentions a Keralan recipe that 'uses green chillies and chicken in proportions of a hundred grams of chillies to seven hundred grams of chicken, plus generous helpings of ground red chilli powder'.[116]

In India chillies were used by Ayurvedic practitioners to treat cholera. Frederic Rosengarten mentions a West Indian stomachic called mandram, which is prepared by adding cucumbers, shallots, lime juice and Madeira wine to mashed-up pods of bird's-eye peppers.[117]

Classification is a big problem with chillies. Because of the ease with which they cross-pollinate, there are hundreds of different types and sub-types, and some of these not only have several names but share the same names – 'a minefield', says one book;[118] 'the number and range of [varieties] is astonishing and defies any exhaustive description', says another;[119] Delia Smith entreats us: 'Forgive the pun, but the whole subject of chillies is a hotbed of confusion: there are so many varieties, and availability fluctuates from one variety to another.'[120] Even Katzer, who is rarely fazed, admits that there are 'almost innumerable names ... for different cultivars in Latin America, especially Mexico'. As long ago as 1529 the Franciscan friar Bernardino de Sahagun was writing in his Aztec encyclopaedia that 'the good chilli seller sells mild red chillies, broad chillies, hot green chillies, yellow chillies, cuitlachilli, tenpilchilli, chichioachilli':

> He sells water chillies, conchilli; he sells smoked chillies, small chillies, tree chillies, thin chillies, beetle-like chillies. He sells hot chillies, early-season chillies, hollow-based chillies. He sells green chillies, pointed red chillies, late-season chillies, chillies from Atzitziuacan, Tochmilco, Huaxtepec, Michoacan, Anauac, the Huaxteca, the Chichimeca ...[121]

And so on. Chillies are highly nutritious – rich in vitamins A and C – and as cultivation in New Mexico continued and the size of the pods grew, their value as a vegetable (rather than just a spice) increased. The problem was their irregular size and shape, which 'made it very difficult for farmers to determine which chilli they were growing from year to year'.[122] In 1888 a horticulturalist called Fabian Garcia attempted to standardise varieties, breeding chillies to create pods of a uniform size and heat – the sort of peppers shops would want to sell and consumers would want to buy. In 1921 the fruit of his labour was released: New Mexico No. 9, a hybrid of three types of *C. annuum* from the famous chilli-growing terroir of Hatch Valley. Descendants of New Mexico No.9 are used widely in North America: for example, the Californian Anaheim pepper.

New Mexico is still the largest producer of chilli peppers in the US, with around 35,000 acres devoted to them. Chillies are central to life in the region, commercially, culinarily and symbolically:

> All the primary dishes in New Mexican cuisine contain chilli peppers: sauces, stews, carne adovada, enchiladas, tamales, and many vegetable dishes. The intense use of chillies as a food rather than just as a spice or condiment is what differentiates New Mexican cuisine from that of Texas or Arizona ... [In New Mexico] houses are adorned with strings of dried red chillies, called rustras. Images of the pods are emblazoned on signs, T-shirts, coffee mugs, hats and even underwear. In the late summer and early fall, the rich aroma of roasting chillies fills the air all over the state.[123]

At the last count there were believed to be thirty-two species of chilli, of which *C. annuum* is the most common. *C. annuum* mostly gives us mild chillies like bell peppers, sweet peppers, pimientos (the very mild chillies used to stuff olives: they have nothing to do with pimento, also known as allspice) and paprika, though also jalapeños (usually eaten green) and cayennes. Chipotles are smoked, ripe jalapeños, often canned in adobo sauce but used fresh in salsas. Cayenne pepper – long, wrinkled and sometimes oddly shaped, hence another common name for it, 'cow-horn pepper'

– has nothing to do with Cayenne in French Guiana, the region after which it is named, and is mostly grown in India and East Africa. Note that commercial cayenne pepper, generally a finely ground powder, is often a blend of different chilli types and may also include varieties of the lesser-regarded species *C. baccatum*.

There are four other main species. *C. frutescens* we have encountered already. It includes two famous sub-types: bird's-eye chilli, and tabasco chilli, the main ingredient in Tabasco sauce, made in southern Louisiana since 1848 and named after the Mexican state from which the chillies were originally imported. (Katzer is sceptical about Tabasco – he is unimpressed by *C. frutescens* generally – and reckons that 'the unique aroma of Tabasco sauce mainly stems from the long ripening period in wooden barrels, not from the underlying chilli material'.[124]) There are plenty of other types, though, including the Filipino siling labuyo or tagalog, whose leaves are used in the soup-like tinola.

C. chinense was discovered in 1776 by a Dutch botanist, Nikolaus Joseph von Jacquin, who thought it originated in China. (It didn't.) It boasts some of the hottest varieties: for example, datil, grown mostly in Florida, which has a spiciness level of between 100,000 and 300,000 SHUs; habanero, a staple of Yucatecan food (100,000–350,000 SHUs); and the scotch bonnet, so called because it resembles a Tam o' Shanter, used in Caribbean cuisine in jerk spice mixes alongside allspice, and possibly the true identity of the *aji* encountered by Columbus, though that may have been *C. baccatum*. It's impossible to say for sure.

For a while, a few years ago, the world's hottest chilli was the Trinidad Moruga Scorpion, a variety of *C. chinense* with a heat rating of more than 2,000,000 SHUs. Paul W. Bosland, co-author of the *Complete Chile Book* and director of the Chile Pepper Institute, which identified it, describes the sensation of eating it: 'You take a bite. It doesn't seem so bad, and then it builds and it builds and it builds. So it is quite nasty.'[125] The Institute's senior research specialist, Danise Coon, says that she and the two students responsible for harvesting the peppers went through four pairs of latex gloves while they were picking them: 'The capsaicin kept penetrating the latex and soaking into the skin on our hands. That has never happened to me before.'[126] New claimants are constantly emerging, and at the time of writing the world's hottest chilli is widely held to be the Carolina Reaper (2,200,000 SHUs), a cross between a red habanero and a Bhut Jolokia, or 'ghost pepper'.

The last of the main chilli species is *C. pubescens* ('hairy', because of its leaves), which gives us the popular and hot rocoto pepper – called caballo ('horse') in Guatemala, because it kicks like one, and levanta muertos ('raising the dead') in Mexico, though at 30,000 SHUs its heat rating is puny compared to the big beasts of *C. frutescens*. Rocotos are often mistaken for bell peppers, which they resemble. This can be unfortunate. Rocotos are popular in Peru, where they are stuffed with minced beef or hard boiled egg, topped with cheese, then baked.

The serrano pepper, a type of *C. annuum*, is the dominant chilli in the Maghrebian spice paste harissa (see *A Directory of Spices Mixes*, p. 246). Chilli peppers may have been introduced to the region when the Spanish occupied part of Tunisia between 1535 and 1574.[127]

SEE ALSO: *Black pepper, Paprika.*

CINNAMON

Cinnamomum zeylanicum and C. cassia

No spice's origin has been more persistently mystified or misconstrued than that of *Cinnamomum zeylanicum*. Columbus thought he had found it in America – or, as he believed, the Indies – in

1493. But the promising-looking bits of bark he brought home inspired only confusion: 'A witness reported that the twigs did look a little bit like cinnamon but tasted more pungent than pepper and smelled like cloves – or was it ginger?'[128] To be fair, Columbus's 'cinnamon' was probably the bark of *Canella winterana*, a tree known as 'wild cinnamon' and used widely in pot pourri and perfumes, so he wasn't as wide of the mark as all that.

The ancient Egyptians procured cinnamon (and frankincense, and myrrh) from somewhere they called Punt. Conceived by them as a distant, fantastical realm, it was probably present-day Eritrea, Ethiopia or Somalia. According to a relief on the walls of the Pharaonic cemeteries at Thebes, Queen Hatchepsut despatched five Punt-bound galleys out into the Red Sea in around 1500 BC. While routine in one sense, such expeditions were still a major undertaking. As Joyce Tyldesley explains in her biography of Hatchepsut, the Egyptians were 'not particularly well versed in the hazards of sea travel': the voyage to Punt would have seemed 'something akin to a journey to the moon' for present-day explorers.[129] But the substantial rewards outweighed the risks. The Thebes murals show men carrying sacks and trees across gangplanks and on to vessels for the return journey. Below these images are hieroglyphic inscriptions which translate as:

> The loading of the ships very heavily with marvels of the country of Punt; all goodly fragrant woods of The Divine Land, heaps of myrrh-resin, with fresh myrrh trees, with ebony and pure ivory, with green gold of Emu, with cinnamon wood, khesyt wood, with ihmut-incense, sonter-incense, eye-cosmetic, with apes, monkeys, dogs, and with skins of the southern panther, with natives and their children. Never was brought the like of this for any king who has been since the beginning.[130]

Once the laden ships had returned to Egypt, Hatchepsut offered up their cargo to the god Amon:

Her majesty herself is acting with her two hands, the best of myrrh is upon all her limbs, her fragrance is divine dew, her odour is mingled with Punt, her skin is gilded with electrum [a pale yellow alloy of gold and silver], shining as do the stars in the midst of the festival-hall, before the whole land.[131]

So all is well: ecstatic, even – except that cinnamon would not have grown in the Horn of Africa, which has the wrong climate, so must have been brought there and sold on to Hatchepsut's hardy crew. But how? And from where? And by whom?

Questions about cinnamon's origins sorely taxed the usual authorities. 'In what country it grows is quite unknown', observes Herodotus, who then repeats a bizarre, obfuscatory story spread by Arab merchants:

The Arabians say that the dry sticks, which we call kinamomon, are brought to Arabia by large birds, which carry them to their nests, made of mud, on mountain precipices which no man can climb. The method invented to get the cinnamon sticks is this. People cut up the bodies of dead oxen into very large joints, and leave them on the ground near the nests. They then scatter, and the birds fly down and carry off the meat to their nests, which are too weak to bear the weight and fall to the ground. The men come and pick up the cinnamon. Acquired in this way, it is exported to other countries.[132]

Theophrastus gets it right when he declares that 'it is the bark and not the wood which is serviceable', and is careful to emphasise that the following story is 'sheer fable':

They say that [cinnamon] grows in deep glens, and that in these there are numerous snakes which have a deadly bite; against these they protect their hands and feet before they go down into the glens, and then, when they have brought up the cinnamon, they divide it in three parts and draw lots for it with the sun; and whatever portion falls to the lot of the sun they leave behind; and they say that, as soon as they leave the spot, they see this take fire.[133]

Pliny, writing some four hundred years later, is dismissive of these 'old tales'. He has heard, or somehow intuited, that cinnamon comes from Ethiopia; or at least, it is traded by Ethiopians who obtain it from 'cave dwellers' (inhabitants of Eritrea and Somalia) with whom they are 'linked by intermarriage'. Spice historian Andrew Dalby believes Pliny's use of the term 'Ethiopians' encompasses inhabitants of the far eastern shore of the Indian Ocean. This is significant: it means Pliny 'knew that cinnamon came from south-eastern Asia and crossed the whole breadth of the Indian Ocean on its way to the West'. How else to explain Pliny's comment that the journey took the traders 'almost five years there and back' and carried a high risk of death?

Centuries passed. The mystification continued. In the 1340s the Moroccan explorer Ibn Battuta came to the island of Sri Lanka, as it has been called since 1972, and found the town of Puttlaman in the north-west 'covered with the trunks of cinnamon trees brought down by the rivers'. One wonders if he was surprised or whether, as a Muslim who had spent time in the trade hub of Alexandria, he had been tipped off by merchant friends. A few Europeans, such as the Italian Catholic missionary John of Montecorvino, had joined the dots, but in the main it was still a Muslim secret that Sri Lanka was the source of what we regard as 'true' cinnamon: Sri Lanka, formerly Ceylon, formerly Sarandib, from which word (via Horace Walpole's reading of the Persian fairy-tale 'The Three Princes of Serendip') we end up with the concept of 'serendipity' or 'fortuitous happenstance' ... The titular princes were, explained Walpole in a letter to a friend in 1754, 'always making discoveries, by accidents and sagacity, of things which they were not in quest of'.

Probably there was more sagacity than accident behind Portugal's discovery that cinnamon came not from birds' nests or snake-filled glens but from wild trees growing on Sri Lanka's west coast in a 200-mile-long strip.

C. zeylanicum is a bushy evergreen in the laurel family with dark green, veined leaves, strong-smelling greenish flowers and purplish-black berries. It grows best at low altitudes and likes shelter and moderate rainfall. Each tree has eight to ten lateral branches. After three years the bushes are mature enough to be harvested – in the rainy season, when the humidity makes their bark easier to peel. The 'quills' of bark which mostly constitute the spice (though the leaves and buds are valuable too) are rolled by hand, then graded according to appearance, thickness and aroma. The terminology is cutely expressive: broken quills are 'quillings'; the inner bark of twigs 'featherings'; coarse bark remnants 'chips'.

Traditionally, harvesting was the job of the island's Sinhalese Salagama caste, who handed over the finished quills to the state as a form of taxation. When the Portuguese arrived in Sri Lanka in the early sixteenth century and seized control of the cinnamon trade, they allowed this practice to continue but otherwise exhibited the brutality they employed so successfully at Malacca, where Albuquerque ordered all the Muslim inhabitants to be massacred or sold into slavery. In 1518 the Portuguese viceroy Lopo Soares de Albergaria built a fort-cum-factory and forced the king of the lowland kingdom of Kotte to declare himself a vassal of King Manuel I: 'The agreement, which was engraved on sheets of beaten gold, made provision for an annual tribute of 300 *bahars* of cinnamon, 12 ruby rings and six elephants.'[134]

By 1658 the Portuguese had been ousted by the Dutch. They absorbed Sri Lanka into their Dutch East India Company (VOC), which by 1669 had become a country in its own right with over 50,000 employees, a 10,000-strong private army and the authority to mint money, fight wars and sign treaties. Visit Galle Fort on Sri Lanka's south-west coast today and you will see, on the main gate, the Dutch coat of arms with 'VOC' inscribed in the centre – a relic of the Netherlands' imperial apogee.

The vacuum left by the eventual collapse of the VOC was filled by Britain, who first occupied the island's coastal regions in 1796 during the Napoleonic Wars but did not achieve full sovereignty until 1815 – by which time the cinnamon trade was in decline as tastes changed and tea, coffee, sugar and exotic fruits like oranges replaced spices as the world's most desirable commodities. (See *Introduction*, p. 20.)

Our dominant sense now is of cinnamon as a flavouring for food. But before the Middle Ages it was prized more highly as a perfume – soaked in fat or oil, then gently heated to release the scent. (Perfume comes from the Latin *per fumum*, 'through the smoke'.) Sappho tells us that the smell of cinnamon permeated the wedding of Hector and Andromache, while in Lucan's epic poem *Pharsalia* Caesar is entranced by Cleopatra and her entourage at a lavish banquet thrown in his honour: seduced by smell as much as taste, for 'in their locks was cinnamon infused/Not yet in air its fragrance perished'.

In ancient Egypt, Greece and Rome cinnamon was associated with funeral rites and embalming. After the Roman emperor Nero murdered his pregnant second wife, Poppaea, in a fit of rage – Suetonius tells us that he kicked her in the stomach during a row when he came home late from the races; Tacitus paints it as a casual outburst of domestic violence – he was so filled with remorse that he ordered a year's supply of cinnamon to be burned at her funeral.

The point of using cinnamon in embalming was not preservation, as with some other spices, or even deodorisation, but the conferral of sanctity, of blessing a soul's passage from one world to the next: celebrating its rebirth, not lamenting its extinction. The interesting thing about *this* association is that it ties in with the legend of the phoenix, returning us to Herodotus' mountain birds *and* Theophrastus' solar sacrifice and showing them to be cut from the same mythopoetic cloth.

In some versions of the phoenix myth cinnamon is a component of its nest and pyre, and so essential for its resurrection. (It is cinnamon that the poet Robert Herrick has in mind when he writes: 'If I kisse Anthea's brest,/There I smell the Phenix nest ...'. Which leads him, incidentally, to conclude: 'For my Embalming, sweetest, there will be/No spices wanting, when I'm laid by thee.') If the phoenix loses its cinnamon, it cannot be reborn and will die for the final time.

Like Herodotus' birds, the phoenix is responsible for bringing cinnamon from distant realms to the world of man. And like the cinnamon in Theophrastus' tale, the phoenix is consecrated to the sun and will spontaneously combust once it has offered the sun its age-ravaged body. As Roelof van den Broek makes clear in *The Myth of the Phoenix* (1972), the collecting of cinnamon by an old phoenix should be seen in the context of ancient burial practices: 'It was customary to place many kinds of scented materials on the deathbed, the bier, and beside and in the grave, as well as to combine them with the pyre and mix them with the ashes in the urn.'[135] When the phoenix covers itself with cinnamon – 'an act that in the world of man fell to the relatives of the deceased' – it is preparing to die at its own funeral.

In Chinese mythology, too, cinnamon represents the sun and eternal life. Cinnamon is the Tree of Life which grows in the Garden of Paradise at the headwaters of the Yellow River and cannot be cut down – its flesh repels the woodcutter's axe. Any pilgrim who enters the Garden and eats the Tree's fruit will win immortality.

This cinnamon, however, would be not *C. zeylanicum* but *C. cassia*, known as 'Chinese cinnamon' or *gui* or just plain cassia, which also grows in the eastern Himalayas and has for many years formed the bulk of what Westerners believe to be cinnamon.

(Another type, *C. loueirii* or 'Saigon cinnamon', grows in Vietnam.) In the US, the Food, Drug and Cosmetic Act of 1938 allows this potent but cruder varietal to be sold as cinnamon. Not so in Britain, where if you look on the side of your Schwartz jar of ground cinnamon you will see the grudging admission: 'Ingredients: cinnamon (cassia).'

Cinnamon and cassia are often written about as though they are interchangeable, but even in the fifteenth century John Russell was adamant in his *Boke of Nurture* (*c.* 1460) that cassia was inferior – not as 'fresche, hoot, and swete' in your mouth as 'true' cinnamon, whose sticks are 'thynn, bretille, and fayre in colewre'. What the Romans called malobathrum and the Indians tejpat is *C. tamala* – or at least its leaves, which were used in cookery (it features in Apicius) and processed into oil for use in medicine and as a perfume. Whether the 'sweet cinnamon' in God's holy anointing oil is *C. zeylanicum* or some other varietal we will never know for certain.

In terms of its everyday culinary application, cinnamon has fared better than others in its cohort of one-time world-conquerors. Like nutmeg, it is used in milk and rice puddings, in that British Sunday-lunch staple apple crumble and in apple-based cakes. Like cloves, it turns up in mulled wine and stews and lends a sleek, caramel smoothness to poached fruit. If these spices feel complementary, part of the same family, that may be because they all contain the chemical compound eugenol, although cinnamon's distinctive flavour is down to cinnamaldehyde.

Cinnamon has a strong affinity with sugar, which explains the popularity of cinnamon toast and its ungodly breakfast-cereal spin-offs Cinnamon Toast Crunch, Curiously Cinnamon etc. Jane Grigson traced cinnamon toast back to 1666 and Robert May's *The Accomplisht Cook*: 'The rather brief instructions tell you to toast the bread and top it with cinnamon mixed with sugar and claret.'[136] *Claret*? It adds 'an extra goodness', she says.

Actually, it is more accurate to say cinnamon has an affinity with breakfast, from the Aleppan semolina pudding ma'mouna to those chewy Starbucks cinnamon rolls with the cream cheese icing. The maize-based porridge atol has been a breakfast staple in the Americas for millennia. In the sixth century BC the Zapotecs of Mexico's Oaxaca Valley began adding cacao seeds and allspice to their atol to make champurrado, but 'once Spaniards brought exotic spices to the New World in the sixteenth century, cinnamon became another integral ingredient'.[137] The Turkish hot chocolate salep, thickened with a flour made from orchid tubers, is sipped through a thick crust of powdered cinnamon.

Dorothy Hartley's *Food in England* (1954) has a recipe for cinnamon sticks dating from 1600. They were 'considered good for colds, or children in church'. To make them, you melt a lump of gum arabic in hot rosewater, then fill the liquid with sugar and an ounce of powdered cinnamon. 'Work it and beat it out flat on a slab and cut it into thin strips as it stiffens, and "roule" them into the "forme" of a cinnamon stick.'[138] Rosemary Hemphill in the *Penguin Book of Herbs and Spices* (1966) recommends cinnamon sprinkled over treacle tart, but admits this is not traditional.

For Gervase Markham (*The English Huswife*, 1615) the savoury pie was a jewel of the English kitchen which contained 'all the art of seasonings'. His chicken pie, which Elisabeth Ayrton in *The Cookery of England* (1974) declares 'rather too rich', is heavy on the cinnamon. Ditto his herring pie, which, perhaps put off by its candied crust, Ayrton admits she has 'never dared to try'.

Cinnamon features in almost all manufactured spice mixes for Sri Lankan curries, whose notorious heat is usually offset with coconut milk. In Sri Lanka every family will have its own spice mix; regional variations, too, can be marked. In Kerala it is used in the likes of irachi varutharachathu (meat cooked with ground coconut) and panniyirachi vindaloo (pork vindaloo), a dish that originated in Kerala's Latin Christian community – Malayalis who converted to Christianity after the arrival of the Portuguese, hence the similarity to Goan cuisine. (Cinnamon is important in vindaloo because its sweetness takes the edge off the vinegar's sourness and the chillies' ferocious heat, especially if those chillies are the local *kanthari* bird's-eye chillies, which have a capsaicin value of 0.504 per cent.)

In Greece cinnamon is used in the Béchamel sauce for moussaka. Elizabeth David mentions a Cypriot restaurant where a bowl of powdered cinnamon was offered with the hot egg and lemon soup avgolémono – 'a beautiful idea' – and sprinkled on courgettes.[139] Its use in pastries extends to the Cretan cheese pies kallitsounia and the syrup for the custard-filled filo tarts galaktoboureko.

The best cinnamon still comes from Sri Lanka and grows in the 'silver sands' coastal belt of the Negombo district, just north of Colombo.

CLOVES

Eugenia aromatica

In around 1720 BC, in the Syrian town of Terqa, not far from the Iraqi border, the house of a man called Puzurum burned down. The simple dwelling, a perfect example of its type, was just up the road from a temple devoted to Ninkarrak, the Babylonian goddess of healing, and consisted of three rooms arranged around a courtyard. This courtyard would have been the main living and cooking area.

Between 1976 and 1986 a team of archaeologists led by Giorgio Buccellati, an emeritus professor in the Department of Near Eastern Languages and Cultures at UCLA, dug through the charred ruins and found a collection of pillow-shaped clay tablets. After so many years they ought to have crumbled to dust. But because they had been fired hard by the blaze they were perfectly preserved and the inscriptions on them still legible.

The cuneiform markings revealed Puzurum to have been a moderately successful estate agent. Not an astonishing fact in itself, perhaps. But in the light of what the team found next – a small ceramic pot containing a handful of cloves – it had far-reaching implications.

In 1720 BC the only places in the world where the clove tree *Eugenia aromatica* grew were the neighbouring volcanic islands of the Moluccas (now Maluku) – over six thousand miles away from Syria.

That the islanders, had, for centuries, harvested the dry, unopened flower buds of this evergreen – a member of the myrtle family – and sold them on to passing Arab, Malay and Chinese traders was well known. What *wasn't* known until the Terqa dig was the breadth of the spice's dissemination. 'Before our excavations,' writes Buccellati, 'there was no evidence for this spice having been used in the west before Roman times ... That a middle-class private individual like Puzurum not only possessed this spice but used it (for cooking or medicinal purposes) indicates a high degree of trans-cultural absorption.'[140]

As Buccellati suggests, the Romans knew the buds and used them. Pliny, in his *Natural History*, mentions 'a grain resembling that of pepper, but larger and more brittle, called *caryophyllon*, which is reported to grow on the Indian lotus tree: it is imported here for the sake of its scent'. But Pliny's entry is based on hearsay. Probably he never saw a clove, and certainly he never saw the tree. No European did until 1500. (Marco Polo claimed to have seen clove trees growing in south-western China, but he was mistaken.)

The Arab writer Ibrahim ibn Wasif-Shah heard that cloves grew on an island somewhere near India, where, it was said, there was a Valley of Cloves: 'No merchants or sailors have ever been to the valley or have ever seen the kind of tree that produces cloves: its fruit, they say, is sold by genies.'[141]

Their resemblance to nails supplies their name in English and other languages: 'clove' is from the French *clou de girofle*. Young trees are conical but become cylindrical over time. They have glossy green leaves and clusters of crimson flowers and can be productive for up to 150 years.

As with nutmeg, the one-time value of cloves is hard to credit at this distance. Elizabeth David's majestic put-down of the spice may date from 1970, but it still holds for many people: 'A small amount of cloves goes a long way, at least to my taste. I do not buy whole cloves, beautiful though they are, since for me they spoil the taste of apple pie, which is their main destination in the English kitchen.'[142] She concedes that they are 'indispensable for Christmas puddings, mincemeat and hot cross buns'. But that's about it. The stubby little buds are nothing to write home about; nothing worth crossing the world for.

And yet cloves more than any other spice set in motion the Age of Discovery, bequeathing us some of the most incredible and unlikely seafaring yarns. Of these, none is more incredible or unlikely than the story of Magellan's circumnavigation of the world.

To understand the extent to which the Portuguese were prime movers in destroying Venice's virtual monopoly of the European spice trade, we need to know first about Vasco da Gama.

Da Gama was ordered by Portugal's King Manuel I to seek a sea route to India, and on 8 July 1497 four ships duly set off from Lisbon. They rounded the Cape of Good Hope, sailed up to Mozambique and Malindi, then on 24 April 1498 plotted an east-north-east course across the Arabian Sea. Aided by the monsoon winds, they arrived at Calicut on India's west coast on 20 May with a jubilant cry of 'Christos e espiciarias!' – for Christ and spices!

The friendly welcome da Gama received must have been a relief. A logbook kept by one of his crew records the message allegedly sent from the zamorin of Calicut to King Manuel. Written on a palm leaf using an iron pen, it declared: 'Vasco da Gama, a gentleman of your household, came to my country, whereat I was much pleased. My country is rich in cinnamon, cloves, ginger, pepper, and precious stones. That which I ask of you in exchange is gold, silver, corals, and scarlet cloth.'

The guilelessness of this is heartbreaking. The zamorin wasn't to know that the cargo da Gama finally brought back to Portugal was worth sixty times the cost of the expedition.

King Manuel wanted spices to be cheaper still, and in 1512 Portuguese forces took the entrepôt of Malacca on the south of the Malay Peninsula – what Jack Turner has called 'the choke point through which all Eastern spices headed west'.[143]

But when Ferdinand Magellan – a nobleman who as a teen had been a page in Portugal's royal household – suggested it might be possible to sail westwards to the Spice Islands, avoiding the need to sail around the tip of Africa, he was rebuffed. King Manuel, with whom Magellan had fallen out over his refusal to grant Magellan a pension, withdrew his hand when Magellan stooped to kiss it: the ultimate insult.

Stung, Magellan offered his services to Spain instead. He arrived in Seville for his audience with Charles I on 20 October 1517. The theory with which Magellan intended to woo the eighteen-year-old king was that, far from being a legitimate province of Portugal, the Moluccas were really Spain's for the taking. A decree by Pope Alexander VI had granted Portugal all non-Christian lands east of an imaginary north–south line approximately 300 miles west of the Cape Verde islands. Spain, on the other hand, was allowed all the land to the *west* of this line. (The Vatican had overlooked the fact that the world is round.)

Magellan and his co-conspirator, the nautical scholar Rodriguo Faleira, met with Charles, whose grandparents Ferdinand

and Isabella had sponsored Columbus, and Magellan read out letters from his old friend and brother-in-arms Francisco Serrão, who was sitting pretty on Ternate, having made it there in 1512 on a stolen junk, formed an alliance with the island's sultan and married a local woman: 'I have', he wrote to Magellan, 'found a New World, richer, greater and more beautiful than that of Vasco de Gama ...'

Next, Magellan brought out his maps and laid them before the king. Most maps at the time were nonsense scribbles. But Magellan's were high-end, designed by the cartographer Jorge Reinel, whose father Pedro had been the first mapmaker to draw a latitude scale on the prime meridian. Despite being the best available, though, they still grossly underestimated the breadth of the Pacific and the earth's circumference. The comfort Magellan drew from the consensus at the time – that the Spice Islands lay less than a week's sailing west of the coast of Mexico – was, in hindsight, unfortunate.

The Spanish crown agreed to fund Magellan's expedition. Five ships, provisioned for two years and manned by 234 officers, left the port of Sanlúcar de Barrameda on 20 September 1519. Magellan understood that under no circumstances was he to violate Portuguese territory. Other than that, he had no real idea where he was going.

Magellan sailed south-west across the Atlantic and down the coast of South America. But the longed-for passage from the Atlantic to the Pacific proved elusive. Almost by accident, the fleet entered the narrow, winding, 350 mile-long strait that would later be named after Magellan on 1 November 1520. They emerged thirty-eight days later into waters so calm that Magellan named them the Pacific, but were sorely tested by the next challenge: three months and twenty days of sailing without any fresh water or provisions. Magellan's Boswell, a young Italian crew-member called Antonio Pigafetta, is graphic about what this entailed:

The biscuits we were eating no longer deserved the name of bread; it was nothing but dust, and worms which consumed the substance; and what is more, it smelt intolerably, being impregnated with the urine of mice. The water which we were obliged to drink was equally putrid and offensive. We were even so far reduced, that we might die of hunger, to eat pieces of leather with which the main-yard was covered to prevent it from wearing the rope. Sawdust was also eaten as well as mice which, when caught, could be sold for half a ducat apiece.[144]

It was another two years and three months before the remnants of Magellan's fleet, the *Trinidad* and the *Victoria*, entered Moluccan waters. Of the other ships, one had been wrecked, another scuttled and another seized by mutineers in Patagonia and sailed back to Spain.

Eight months earlier, Magellan had been killed in a dispute with natives on the island of Mactan, next to Cebu, where he had stopped to recuperate and take on provisions. The irony of his having survived the journey (Magellan avoided scurvy by eating preserved quince) only to fall so close to the goal, hacked to death by bamboo spears, was almost too much for Pigafetta to bear: 'Thus they killed our mirror, our light, our comfort and our true guide. When they wounded him, he turned back many times to see whether we were all in the boats.'[145]

Soon after the attack force returned to Cebu, the island's formerly friendly sultan turned against them, forcing the fleet to drift for months across the China Sea. They found the Moluccas almost by accident after they shanghaied a ship and took a prisoner who claimed to have been a guest in the house of Francisco Serrão on Ternate:

The pilot who remained with us told us that they were the Moluccas, for which we thanked God, and to comfort us we discharged all our artillery. Nor ought it to cause astonishment that we were so rejoiced, since we had passed 27 months, less

two days, always in search of these Moluccas, wandering hither
and thither for that purpose among innumerable islands.[146]

The *Trinidad* and the *Victoria* spent six weeks in the islands. Magellan had refused to allow the men to bring women on board, but
now they took full advantage of the old tyrant's absence. They bar-
tered for cloves using goods they had plundered from other ships
en route. In the end the *Trinidad*'s hold burst apart. The ship had to
be careened – unloaded, turned on its side, repaired, reloaded. The
process took three months, so long that the man who had assumed
the position of captain-general after Magellan's death died himself
before it was completed.

Ever dutiful, Pigafetta used the time to investigate how and
where cloves grew:

> The tree from which they are gathered is high, and its trunk is
> as thick as a man's body, more or less, according to the age of
> the plant. Its branches spread out somewhat in the middle of the
> tree, but near the top they form a pyramid. The bark is of an
> olive colour, and the leaves very like those of laurel. The cloves
> grow at the end of little branches in bunches of ten or twenty
> ... are white when they first sprout, they get red as they ripen,
> and blacken when dry ... The leaf, the bark, and the wood, as
> long as they are green, have the strength and fragrance of the
> fruit itself ...[147]

Of the five ships in Magellan's original fleet, only the *Victoria*
completed the circumnavigation. The *Trinidad*, laden with 50 tons
of cloves, had to turn back to Tidore, where she was captured and
plundered by the Portuguese, while the *Victoria* limped back to
Spain with twenty-one survivors and a cargo of spices, mostly
cloves, worth ten thousand times their original price.

*
**

For the next two centuries the Portuguese and then the Dutch controlled the spice trade. In their desperation to maintain the upper hand, no practice was too sharp or brutal. The Dutch, who had 'more ships, more men, better guns, and a much harsher colonisation policy',[148] thought nothing of destroying an entire clove crop to create an artificial scarcity across Europe and drive the price higher. As Jack Turner observes, rebellious natives were not tolerated by the VOC (the Dutch East India Company): 'In 1750, the Dutch governor, despite being bedridden, insisted on personally knocking out the teeth of a Ternatean rebel commander, smashing the roof of his mouth, cutting out his tongue, and slitting his throat.'[149]

In the end the Dutch monopoly was broken by one Pierre Poivre, who in 1770 smuggled seedlings from what is believed to be the oldest clove tree on Ternate to Mauritius, where the trees flourished. (Poivre's antics are believed to be the basis for the children's rhyme 'Peter Piper picked a peck of pickled pepper'.) In 1799 the VOC went bankrupt. Nowadays the world's largest producer of cloves is Zanzibar.

Cloves were used as breath-fresheners by dignitaries at the Chinese imperial court during the Han dynasty (200 BC). Eugenol, the chemical compound found in many parts of the clove tree – not just the buds – is still used in toothpastes and gargles. Trusted by generations as a bulwark against toothache, clove oil is used in local anaesthetics and to treat ulceration and inflammation.

Use of cloves with roasted meat is widespread in sixteenth- and seventeenth-century recipes, including Gervase Markham's for Roasted Venison with Cloves in his housewives' handbook *The Well-Kept Kitchen* (1615), where the haunch is studded with them 'like a ham', Andrew Boorde's Summer Soup with Meatballs (1542) and as part of the spice mix in Hannah Wolley's Barthelmas Beef. Every other recipe in Eliza Smith's *The Compleat Housewife* (1758) uses them: White Mead involves twenty cloves.

Their use in the fourteenth and fifteenth centuries would have been primarily in royal or aristocratic households. *Forme of Cury* (1390) has a recipe for Spiced Fish:

> Tak Lucys or Tenches and hack them small in gobbets and fry them in oil de olive and seeth nym vinegar and the third part of sugar and minced onions small and boil altogether and cast therein cloves, maces & quibibs [cubebs] and serve it forth.

The Cold Spiced Chicken dish served at the coronation feast of Henry IV on 13 October 1399 anticipates Rosemary Hume's Coronation Chicken, invented for the banquet which followed Queen Elizabeth II's coronation in 1953, but uses cloves as the main spice. A 1381 recipe for meatloaf with almonds, 'bruet of Sarcynesse', shows the influence of Arab cookery in medieval England (though doubt has been expressed about the illicit use of wine):

> Take the flesh of the fresh beef and cut it all in pieces and bread and fry it in fresh grease take it up and dry it and do it in a vessel with wine and sugar and powder of cloves, boil it together till the flesh have drunk the liquor and take the almond milk and quibibs maces and cloves and boyl them together, take the flesh and do thereto and mix it forth.

Cloves fell out of fashion in the English kitchen after the eighteenth century except in puddings. But they are a component of Chinese five-spice powder and East European pickling spice mixes, and are used extensively in African and Middle Eastern cuisines as an ingredient in baharat and in traditional dishes such as kawareh bi hummus (calf's feet with chickpeas). The dominance of cloves (and, for that matter, nutmeg and cinnamon) in Keralan Christian and Muslim cooking reflects Kerala's historical trade contact with the Portuguese and the Dutch. Although grown now across Kerala and Tamil Nadu, clove trees have only existed in India since 1800, when they were introduced by the East India Company.

The bulk of the world's cloves are used not in cooking or medicine but in Indonesian *kretek* cigarettes, most of which are manufactured in Kudus in Central Java. In 2004 Indonesians smoked 36,000 tons of cloves a day.

Whole cloves have a long shelf life but deteriorate rapidly once ground. When making your own powder, you need only grind the bud at the top of the 'nail'.

SEE ALSO: *Allspice, Cinnamon, Nutmeg.*

CORIANDER

Coriandrum sativum

One clue that you are suffering an infestation of bedbugs (*Cimex lectularius*) is the smell. When a group of the parasites is disturbed, they exude 'alarm pheromones' to alert each other and trigger dispersal. The result is a horrible burning-rubber aroma which reminded Pliny of a certain plant with a bright green slender stem and umbels of small pink, blue or white flowers. Pliny knew it as a remedy for cancer and malaria; also as an antidote to the bite of a mythological ant-eating serpent with chicken-like feet and two heads – 'as though it were not enough for poison to be poured out of one mouth' – called the amphisbaena. The unpleasant smell was a sign that the plant's fruits were immature: once they had ripened and dried, it went away.

Pliny named the plant *coriandrum*, from the Latin for bug, *coris*. But it has other names – cilantro (in the United States and Latin America), dhana (in India), Chinese parsley (in China, presumably). It is an annual in the parsley family, at any rate;

indigenous to southern Europe and the Mediterranean but adept enough at tolerating heat and drought to have been cultivated successfully across the world, especially in Russia, India, Morocco and Australia.

This is no recent occurrence. Coriander seeds are mentioned in the Book of Exodus and in the Minoan Linear B tablets from Knossos, and were found in Tutankhamun's tomb. Despite the fact that they would have been imported and therefore expensive, they were used extensively in Egyptian medicine. The Ebers Papyrus recommends coriander seed as an all-purpose analgesic – though it also prescribes beer froth and half an onion as a 'delightful remedy against death', so who can say?

Coriander 'now seems a typical Indian spice and a typical southeast Asian herb',[150] says Andrew Dalby, but this is a false impression: it was only introduced into India on a significant scale in the third century BC; imported from Persia, probably, by the Buddhist emperor Aśoka, who was 'proud of his activity in transplanting aromatic and medicinal plants'.[151] The roots can be eaten as well as the leaves (frilly, parsleyish) and seeds (yellowish-brown, ribbed, separated into two mericarps), but this only seems to happen in Thailand. The leaves are sharp and citrusy, the seeds warm and sweet, with undertones of burnt orange. Coriander seed should be used immediately after it has been ground, as it loses its flavour very quickly.

Coriander seeds are especially popular in Cyprus and Greece, where they spice sausages and lend a nutty clarity to green olives when added to lemon-based marinades. The Cypriot pork-belly-in-wine dish afelia relies heavily on coriander seed; likewise the Greek cabbage salad lahanosalata. Boiling gammon in water charged with coriander seeds, cloves, cinnamon and bay leaves evokes, for me at least, something very close to the essence of Christmas.

Like caraway seeds, coriander seeds are added to rye bread. Dan Lepard's *The Handmade Loaf* (2004) contains an excellent recipe for coriander-flavoured rye bread similar to that served in traditional cafeterias in Russia and the Ukraine. The coriander seed gives the crumb 'a slight bitterness, like the white pith of an orange', though Lepard admits that this is an 'acquired taste'.[152]

Coriander was introduced to Britain by the Romans, who used the seed to flavour barley porridge and boiled greens and, at the other end of the social spectrum, oysters. Anglo-Saxon ethnobotany recommended that a bracelet of twelve coriander seeds be worn by a woman high on her left thigh, 'close to the "kindling limb" [vulva]', to determine the gender of an unborn child.[153] It enjoyed widespread popularity as a pickling spice and in recipes for black pudding and game until the eighteenth century, when it fell out of fashion except as a flavouring for gin and in beer-brewing.

That said, Elizabeth David cites a lovely-sounding recipe for ham cooked in milk with coriander seed from William Verral's 1749 book *The Cook's Paradise*. Verral owned a pub near Lewes called The White Hart and probably bought his coriander locally as it was cultivated in Sussex at the time, although more was grown in Essex and Suffolk, especially Ipswich.

The seed is still used in brewing, mostly in top-fermented Belgian-style white beers such as Hoegaarden: 'Typically, coriander is added at a dose of 2.11–8.3 ounces per barrel during the last five to 20 minutes of boiling in the brewkettle.'[154] The short boiling time is to ensure that aromatic compounds are not volatilised away. Often coriander seed is used in conjunction with orange peel.

Like fenugreek and turmeric, coriander seed has long been a cheap staple of Indian curry powders. But it is milder and more versatile, self-effacing even – its most notable quality may be its ability to synthesise disparate flavours. It probably found its way into early Anglo-Indian versions of curry powder by way of the south Indian spice-and-split-peas mix sambar, in which coriander is the dominant spice. But it is also important in the Lebanese spice mix taklia, usually added at the end of cooking, and the pan-Middle Eastern baharat (see *A Directory of Spice Mixes*, p. 236).

SEE ALSO: *Fenugreek, Turmeric.*

CUBEB
Piper cubeba

This berry, similar in appearance to black pepper but with a distinctive tail attached, tastes like a cross between black pepper and allspice, though with a bitter overtone. Grown in Java and Sumatra, it was popular in medieval European cookery but is now mostly used to flavour gin. In West Africa the word cubeb is sometimes used for the similar but milder *P. guineense*.

See *Grains of Paradise* for discussion of the complex variety of African peppers.

CUMIN
Cumimum cyminum

In terms of impact and ubiquity, the dried fruit of *Cumimum cyminum*, a small annual herb in the parsley family, is one of the most important spices of all. With a strong, persistent odour that suggests lemons and brown sugar, cumin is the dominant flavour in many commercial and home-made curry powders and in spice mixes such as advieh (Persia), char masala (Afghanistan), baharat (Middle East), garam masala (India) and the North African marinade chermoula. In Europe its use is mostly restricted to chutneys and sauerkraut, though it flavours Dutch cheeses such as Leyden and Gouda and is sprinkled on the Alsatian cheese Munster when it is eaten with bread.

Its warm scent, Elizabeth David tells us, 'pervades the souks of North Africa and of Egypt, gives the grilled lamb kebabs of Morocco their typical flavour and goes into a hundred and one Levantine vegetable, meat and rice dishes'.[155] Dry-frying brings out cumin's nuttier overtones and mitigates the bitterness that can taint the ready-ground version.

Meat-wise, cumin has a strong affinity with lamb; vegetable-wise, with carrots (witness that Moroccan staple, raw carrot, garlic and cumin salad) and, more surprisingly, beetroot: Hugh Fearnley-Whittingstall's 'raw assembly' of beetroot, walnuts and cumin in *River Cottage Veg Every Day!* (2011) achieves a wonderful balance of earthy sweetness and warmth echoed in similar recipes dating back as far as Apicius' *De re coquinaria*. The debate about whether or not it should be added to hummus rages on, matched in ferocity only by the parallel one about whether hummus was invented by Arabs or Jews. Claudia Roden's hummus bi tahina recipe from the original edition of *The Book of Middle Eastern Food* (1968) features paprika rather than cumin as a garnish. But cumin is there in the version in her later *Arabesque* (2005). Yotam Ottolenghi, in the chapter in *Jerusalem* (2012) devoted to the 'hummus wars', regards cumin's inclusion as optional; but it is there in the similar breakfast dish musabaha (hummus, but with warm whole chickpeas piled on top).

Mexican food without cumin is unthinkable. But the spice is a recent arrival, brought to South America by Spanish conquistadores who had themselves been converted to its use by the Muslim Moors, and is used sparingly. What is more, there are regional variations within regional variations. As the Mexican chef and writer Roberto Santibañez explained in an interview with the website splendidtable.org:

> Some people cook with more spices, some people cook with fewer spices. Some states have more pronounced cumin, some states don't use cumin at all ... What you see today, like me or like many others such as urban Mexican people with more of a pan-Mexican vision of our foods, we are starting to say, 'Okay, how much cumin goes into a salsa verde?' Some people will tell you, 'Oh, no, no, no, no, we don't put cumin in salsa verde at all.' But come on, you taste the salsa verde that has a little cumin and then you say, 'It's exactly what it needed to be, more "wow".'[156]

Cumin is indigenous to Egypt – it was one of the many spices used in embalming – but is cultivated in Iran, Turkey, India (the world's largest producer and consumer of the spice), China, Japan, the US and African countries such as Somalia and Sudan. It has purple and white flowers and weak stems, which cause it to sprawl. The hairy, tapered seeds, between 3 and 6 mm long, come as paired or separate carpels. Their resemblance to caraway seeds has caused all manner of culinary and etymological confusion – the Hindi word *jeera* is used for both; likewise the German *kümmel*, as in the cumin-flavoured liqueur. The more refined Iranian black cumin, *Bunium bulbocastanum*, is often mistaken for nigella. Cumin requires threshing: it must, says Theophrastus, be 'cursed and abused while sowing if the crop is to be fair and abundant'. If this is done properly, cumin will produce 'the most fruits of any plant'.

Cumin's medical uses are a mixture of the curious and the predictable. Pliny tells us that students ate it to make their skin pale and so trick their teachers into believing they were working hard. It stimulates appetite and works reliably as a carminative. Greg

Malouf says that in the Middle East today it is usual to add a pinch of ground cumin to beans.

Pliny never tired of it – it 'remained welcome' when other seasonings had grown boring – which is just as well because it was ubiquitous in ancient Rome: ground to a paste to be spread on bread, or mixed with salt to make the condiment cumin-salt, still popular in North Africa.

The fact that Apicius uses cumin in over a hundred recipes, including sauces for oysters and shellfish, might lead you to suppose it was expensive. In fact, it was dirt cheap; cheaper than pepper. In ancient Greece a miser was called *kyminopristes* – literally, a 'cumin-seed splitter'. Marcus Aurelius is supposed to have been nicknamed Cumin for his avaricious ways; though in Germany it signifies loyalty: a bride carries cumin, salt and dill with her during the marriage ceremony as a pledge of faithfulness to her husband.

CURRY LEAF

Murraya koenigii

According to criteria established earlier (see *Introduction*, p. 9), curry leaf (*mitha neem* in Hindi, *karuvepila* in Tamil) is a herb rather than a spice, and has no greater claim for inclusion here than bay leaf. I have waved it through because its flavour is itself spicy – warm, with subtle citrus overtones – and because it is so good at augmenting other spices.

Largely because of their name, curry leaves (or leaflets, to be precise) are the source of a certain amount of beginners' confusion. Does adding them to a dish mean you don't have to use any other spices? Don't they do all the work? Sadly not. Frederic

Rosengarten is obliged to point out in his *The Book of Spices* (1969), a work that did a huge amount to popularise cooking with Eastern spices in the US, that curry leaves 'are but one – and by no means the most important – of the many ingredients that may be included in curry blends'.[157]

Curry leaves are the serrated leaflets of a small tropical tree in the citrus family native to Sri Lanka and India, dark green on top and pale underneath. They are sometimes confused with *M. paniculata* or orange jasmine. *M. koenigii* grows copiously in the forests of the Himalayan foothills. Tom Stobart writes that 'anyone who visits the Corbett National Park in Kumaon will notice the strong appetising smell of curry [leaf] as the elephant bursts through the thickets and bruises the leaves of this plant, which in places forms quite a proportion of the undergrowth'.[158]

Used either whole, like bay leaves in the West, or finely chopped, curry leaves are a staple of southern Indian cooking, though much less common in the north, where they are used mainly to temper lentils: you fry them in ghee with mustard seeds and asafoetida before stirring them into dhal. They are integral to Sri Lankan cuisine, enlivening dishes such as curried crab and the vegetable-and-bread fry-up kottu roti. The sun-dried fish curry (unakka meen kari) in Vijayan Kannampilly's *The Essential Kerala Cookbook* (2003) is heavy on curry leaf (and garlic and chillies). Use them in marinades for kebabs – they have an affinity with lamb – and in chutneys, pickles and relishes. Monica Bhide's *Modern Spice* (2009) has an excellent recipe for tangy curry leaf bread, a speciality of Bangalore.

Curry leaves turn up (sometimes dried and ground, sometimes fresh) in Madras-style spice mixes and pastes (see *A Directory of Spice Mixes*, p. 235). Ideally they should be bought and used fresh as they lose their fragrance quickly, though can be stored for up to two weeks in the fridge.

A similar but more potent leaf, daun salam (*Eugenia polyantha*), is used in Indonesia.

DILL

Anethum graveolens

Dill is better known for its wispy, fern-like leaves than for its seeds. They are used much as caraway is, on cakes and bread, and in the pickling of items such as cucumbers. (Like caraway, dill contains the aromatic compound carvone.) Dill-pickled cucumbers were a favourite of Charles I and feature in his chef Joseph Cooper's *Art of Cookery* (1654). Among John Evelyn's recipes for the dish are several variants, one of which begins: 'Take great Cowcumbers that are about the size of Mangoes ...' If only we could. Rosemary Hemphill emphasises the need to use small, home-grown cucumbers and chill them for twenty-four hours prior to immersing them in brine.[159] Dill seed vinegar is a popular addition to fish sauces in Russia and Scandinavia. In Gaza dill seed is combined with hot chillies in dishes such as kishik, a lamb and chickpea stew flavoured with crumbled cakes made from fermented yoghurt and flour, and zibdiyit gambari, or 'shrimp in a bowl'.

Just as ajowan, another carminative, is often paired with pulses or vegetables like cauliflower and cabbage, so dill combats 'dairy bloat' when added to creamy sauces, especially for fish. The dill seed in the Uzbek recipe for fried flatbread with pork crackling featured in Dan Lepard's *The Handmade Loaf* (2004) pulls what could easily be a stodgy nightmare back from the brink of indigestibility.

Its name derives from the Old Norse *dilla*, meaning 'to lull', and like ajowan it is often found in gripe water colic remedies.

SEE ALSO: *Ajowan, Fennel.*

FENNEL

Foeniculum vulgare

If Greek mythology is to be trusted, women have fennel to thank for their existence. When Zeus withheld fire, Prometheus stole it from heaven and concealed it inside a hollow fennel stalk before presenting it to man. Zeus was displeased, and as a punishment ordered the blacksmith Hephaestus to create, out of water and earth, Pandora – the first woman, of box notoriety. Why fennel? Because the stalk of the variety which grew then (and grows now) in Greece, narthex or giant fennel (*Ferula communis*), is lined inside with a slow-burning white pith, making it perfect for transporting glowing coals.

You would not, however, want to eat any part of *F. communis*, as it is poisonous: the prenylcoumarins it contains cause ferulosis, a haemorrhagic disease usually fatal to livestock. And the celery-like stalks of what we most commonly think of as fennel, the herbaceous hardy annual *Foeniculum vulgare*, would be no good for transporting fire.

In medieval pharmacology fennel's oval green seeds were prescribed to improve vision and cure eye complaints. The inspiration was Pliny's belief that snakes shedding their skins ate fennel to restore their sight, which becomes blurry during this phase and exacerbates their aggressiveness. In 1842 Henry Wadsworth Longfellow celebrated this theory in his poem 'The Goblet of Life':

Above the lowly plants it towers,
The fennel, with its yellow flowers,
And in an earlier age than ours,
Was gifted with the wondrous powers,
Lost vision to restore.

Fennel seeds were establised in English cookery before the Norman Conquest. Malcolm Laurence Cameron's *Anglo-Saxon Medicine* (1993) informs us that fennel was readily available at this time, 'a common ingredient of Anglo-Saxon remedies', under the name *finul*.[160] Many of these remedies took the form of charms – incantations designed to exorcise malignant forces from a patient's body, readying it for the application of a salve containing herbs and spices itemised in the charm.

The Nine Herbs Charm pairs fennel with chervil – they are the 'very mighty two' which 'the wise Lord created,/ Holy in heaven where he hung,/ Ordained and sent into the seven worlds,/ For poor and for rich, a cure for all'. Bald's *Leechbook*, an Old English medical manual thought to have been compiled in the ninth century, repeats the Greek medical writer Oribasius' recommendation of a decoction of celery and fennel to treat 'scanty' urine.

The Greek word for fennel, *marathon*, nods to the Battle of Marathon, fought against the Persians on a plain filled with fennel plants 42 km from Athens in the late summer of 490 BC, but derives from *maraino*, 'to grow thin': the seeds were often used as an appetite suppressant. In his *Adam in Eden, or Nature's Paradise* (1657), the botanist William Coles tells us: 'Both the seeds, leaves and root of our Garden Fennel are much used in drinks and broths for those that are grown fat, to abate their unwieldiness and cause them to grow more gaunt and lank.'[161]

The Puritans of New England called them 'meeting seeds' and brought bags of them to their lengthy church services to stop their stomachs rumbling and placate their restless children. However, fennel seeds also seem to have had an amphetamine-like alerting effect, as an 1848 edition of the *New Englander and Yale Review* makes clear: their fragrance was, it says, 'almost as ecclesiastical in the country towns in New England as frankincense in the Romish churches, though employed to stimulate the senses rather than to becloud the fancy'.

This may have something to do with the fact that anethole,

fennel's chief flavour compound, is a chemical precursor for para-methoxyamphetamine, or PMA – originally a cheap substitute for LSD, more recently a lethal adulterant in rogue batches of Ecstasy tablets. Though PMA itself is more likely to depress than stimulate, so who knows?

Warm, sweet, anise-flavoured fennel is most closely associated with Italian cooking – not just the seeds, our focus here, but also the bulbous leaf base and the leaves. The amount of anethole they contain can, however, vary markedly across varieties, of which there are several, including the bitter wild fennel popular in Eastern Europe and Russia and sweet fennel (*azoricum*), also called Florence fennel or finocchio. The taste of the seeds also differs in this way.

Classed as a sweet spice in Italy, fennel seed was popularised by the fifteenth-century Italian cook Martino da Como, who mixed it with salt before rubbing it into chops. He also used it to season veal escalopes and kebabs called copiette al modo romano, which he would then spit-roast with bacon. Fennel seeds disguised the taste of the inferior pork used in the country's poorer regions – places such as Umbria, Abruzzo and Lucania, the latter producing a spicy smoked sausage called lucanica, of which numerous variants remain: for example, the Greek loukanika, which also contains orange peel. Recipes for these sausages found their way to Rome and into Apicius, who gets very excited about forcemeat, though none of his forcemeat recipes contains fennel seed.

Gillian Riley mentions approvingly the 'ndoc 'ndoc (meaning 'crazy') of rural Abruzzo:

> a sausage made with the less noble parts left over from the pig-killing – intestines, lungs, heart, parts of the snout, ears, trotters, belly fat; highly seasoned with salt, pepper, chilli, and wild fennel seeds; hung for a few days in a warm dry place; and eaten cooked, preferably as panonta: grilled with the juices dripping onto a slice of bruschetta.[162]

British acceptance of fennel seed has been hesitant: prior to the 1990s, bafflement or indifference prevailed. 'Although fennel grows wild in England, and the leaves are well known in English cooking, the seeds are ignored', says Elizabeth David.[163] Fennel seed has long been used in French spice mixes for fish, though its inclusion in the posher commercial blends of herbes de Provence – often alongside lavender – is more recent.

Sri Lankan curry powders often contain them, but their popularity in India is region-specific. The Bengali spice mix panch phoron contains fennel seed, and like asafoetida it is a signature spice in Kashmiri Pandit cuisine, where it adds a liquorice tang to rogan josh. (As onions and garlic are not eaten by Kashmiri Brahmans, fennel seed and asafoetida are used in their place to flavour the meat. The Muslim version of rogan josh, on the other hand, uses 'lots of garlic and onion and the dried flower of the cockscomb plant'[164] – *Celosia cristata*.) It also crops up in Gujarati dishes such as the speciality pakoras dakor na gota, associated with the Hindu festival holi, and in pickles and chutneys. The postprandial breath-freshener mukhwas relies heavily on fennel seed.

Elizabeth David speculates that Athenians in ancient Greece favoured a bread made from Egyptian flour called Alexandrian, which was flavoured with fennel seed. In *The Handmade Loaf* (2004) Dan Lepard mixes fennel seed with dried cherries and rye flour to make a light, flavoursome bread that goes well with soft cheese. Less flashy but hugely comforting, Rosemary Hemphill's fennel-seed potato cake is at its most effective when paired with, yes, fish or leftover turkey:

Peel and slice 1lb potatoes thinly, butter a baking dish and put in a layer of potatoes, 1 teaspoon fennel seed, and some salt and freshly ground pepper. Dot with butter. Repeat. Finish by pouring ¼ pint thin cream over the top. Bake in a moderate oven (gas mark 4, electric 350F) for about 1 hour. If becoming too crisp around the edges, cover with a piece of brown paper.

Test with a fork: when soft in the centre, the potato cake is cooked. Serve hot.[165]

SEE ALSO: *Ajowan, Dill, Liquorice, Star anise.*

FENUGREEK

Trigonella foenum-graecum

In autumn 2005 a sinister, sickly-sweet phenomenon gripped New York. A powerful maple-syrup smell wafted across the city and parts of nearby New Jersey, delighting some but worrying others who, still recovering from 9/11, called New York's 311 information line, convinced they were experiencing a chemical attack. (Tastefully, *Wired* magazine wondered later whether such an attack might have been planned by 'the Aunt Jemima wing of al Qaeda'.[166])

The US Department of Environmental Protection investigated the smell's source, but not until 2009, after several other 'maple syrup events', did they discover what it was: a factory in northern New Jersey owned by Frutarom Industries that was processing fenugreek seeds for use in the mass of fake maple-syrup products – high-fructose corn syrup and flavourings, basically – that clog the aisles of American supermarkets.

Fenugreek seeds do smell remarkably like spicy maple syrup, with bitter overtones of burned sugar and celery for which the chemical compounds sotolon and coumarin are responsible. (The vanilla smell of freshly cut grass is down to coumarin, a bitter-tasting appetite suppressant – nature's way of stopping cattle from grazing plants into extinction.) To earlier generations of

Europeans, though, the smell would have signified nothing less than curry itself.

While not the main ingredient in the earliest forms of commercial curry powder (see *A Directory of Spice Mixes,* p. 239), fenugreek was often present in disproportionately large quantities, overwhelming the other spices in the mix. Fenugreek's connotations of Anglo-Indian inauthenticity were hard for some mid-twentieth-century food writers to overlook, and I suspect it was snobbery rather than actual dislike of the spice that prompted Elizabeth David to remark that 'fenugreek is to curry much as malt vinegar is to English salads'.[167]

Of course it isn't. Fenugreek has a noble pedigree, and is key in a variety of Indian spice mixes, including the Bengali panch phoron and Tamil sambar podi. As one of the more nutritious spices – rich in iron, copper, manganese, thiamin and vitamin B6 – its presence in cheap dhal dishes must be regarded as a life-saver. In Turkey the seeds are found in çemen, the paste that coats the air-dried beef pastirma. In Sri Lanka fenugreek complements chilli and turmeric in the coconut milk-based curry kiri hodi.

Fenugreek leaves, called methi in India, are sold both fresh and dried. They are used as a vegetable (cooked like spinach – 'exceedingly bitter and unpleasant', says Tom Stobart,[168] although this is a popular method in the Yemen, where fenugreek seeds flavour the dip helbeh) and in salads. Dried fenugreek leaves are essential to what is often described as Iran's national dish, the Persian herb stew ghormeh sabzi. Like mustard and cress, fenugreek can be grown easily to the two-leaf or cotyledon stage. 'I grew fenugreek at one stage in Cornwall, outdoors, without any problem', declares Rick Stein in *Rick Stein's India* (2013), introducing a Gujarati recipe for millet and fenugreek flatbreads or bajra thepla.

'Fenugreek' derives from the Latin *fenum graecum* – 'Greek hay'. The plant, a legume in the Fabaceae family, was cultivated in ancient Greece and Rome as animal fodder but grows wild all over Asia and the Middle East. India is one of the main exporters, and within that Rajasthan, which accounts for 80 per cent of the sub-continent's output. Fenugreek is an annual with light green leaves and tiny, clover-like, triangular white flowers – *trigonella* means 'little triangle'. Between ten and twenty seeds can be obtained from each pod. Small, hard beige stones, these are notoriously difficult to grind and for this reason are sometimes soaked until they become gelatinous before being added to spice pastes. Fenugreek seeds should always be *lightly* roasted before use. Excessive roasting makes them bitter.

Over the centuries fenugreek has been used to treat a range of ailments, from fever to baldness. Where it seems to have real value is as a galactagogue (i.e., to stimulate lactation in nursing mothers) and as a treatment for diabetes. Its seeds are high in soluble fibre and so lower blood sugar by inhibiting the absorption of carbohydrates. An amino acid in fenugreek, 4-hydroxy isoleucine, stimulates insulin production, helping to regulate glucose metabolism.

Fenugreek's most important compound, however, is diosgenin, a powerful natural steroid reputed to prevent cancer;[169] also, more controversially, to increase libido, which is why it is the main ingredient in the allegedly testosterone-boosting supplement Testofen. I say 'allegedly'. A class-action lawsuit brought against Testofen's manufacturers in May 2014 cited three studies claiming there was no clinical proof that Testofen boosted anything, and certainly the fenugreek-cures-male-impotence story – something of a perennial – has a sorry, tabloid-health-section air.

In 2011 a batch of contaminated fenugreek seeds from Egypt was responsible for a Europe-wide outbreak of *E.coli*.[170] Truly, the Lord giveth and the Lord taketh away.

Fenugreek should not be confused with the quite different blue fenugreek.

SEE ALSO: *Blue fenugreek, Turmeric.*

GALANGAL

Alpinia galanga (greater)
Alpinia officinarum (lesser)

If you know your *garde manger*, the word 'galantine' will suggest to you a deboned chicken (it's usually a chicken, although it could be anything) wrapped in its own skin, then poached in stock, pressed and served in aspic. In the Middle Ages, however, galantine was a type of sauce made from breadcrumbs, cinnamon, ginger, salt, black pepper and – the most important ingredient – galangal. Here is the recipe from *Forme of Cury* (*c.* 1390):

> Take crustes of bread and grynde hem smale. Do therto powdour of galyngale, of canel, of gyngyuer, and salt it; tempre it up with vyneger, and drawe it up thurgh a straynour, & messe it forth.

Galantine was surprisingly versatile: it worked as well with strong red meats like venison as with fish. A refinement of galantine, Sawse Madame, was specific to geese. To prepare it, you stuffed the goose with sage, parsley, hyssop, quinces, pears, garlic and grapes, then placed cooked, carved slices of goose and chunks of stuffing in a pot with pre-made galantine and fat; then you added wine, more galangal, salt and 'powdor douce', a spice mix which usually contained Grains of Paradise, ginger, cinnamon, nutmeg, galangal and sugar; boiled it up and finally arranged the goose on a plate with the sauce poured over it. Simple!

At the time, writes Paul Freeman, galangal – often written as 'galingale' or 'galyngale' – was an 'expensive but widely available spice used in sophisticated cooking, and at the same time featured in pharmaceutical handbooks'.[171] Its presence in galantine is appropriate, then, given the word's connotations of gallantry (from the Old French *galant*, meaning courteous and dashing). Though it also, like almost every other spice, found its way into the spiced wine hippocras.

The Cook in Chaucer's *Canterbury Tales* is certainly familiar
with galangal:

A Cook they hadde with hem for the nones
To boille the chiknes with the Marybones
And poudre Marchant tart and galyngale.
Wel coude he knowe a draughte of London ale.
He coude roste, and sethe, and broille, and frye,
Maken mortreux, and wel bake a pye.

This repertoire of dishes seems solid, even fashionable. ('Mortreux'
is defined in the culinary manuscript *Curye on Inglish* as a boiled
dish of finely ground food in broth. 'Poudre Marchant' would have
been another type of spice mix, though no one seems to know what
it contained.) But isn't Chaucer being ironic here? The Cook is a
low-rent character with an open sore on his leg, a shop full of flies
and the unpleasant habit of reheating his pies over and over again
so that they make his customers sick. Would such a man really
have in his larder *galangal*, a staple of the dream-gardens of medieval romance writers? Probably not. Though in Chaucer's day the
word also meant sedge, so perhaps that is part of the joke.

There are two main types of galangal: 'greater' and 'lesser', both
rhizomes in the ginger family. A third type, kaempferia galangal,
is rarely used except in East European liqueurs and bitters such
as the Polish nalewkas. It has a sweeter bouquet which some find
sickly and is sometimes called 'fingerroot' because of the way thin
tubes sprout from its central core.

Greater galangal, or laos, is native to Java and has large, knobbly
roots similar to ginger, with a reddish brown or creamy skin. The
plant is 'larger, about five palms high, and not so fragrant or aromatic as the other [i.e., lesser]', says the Portuguese physician and
naturalist Garcia de Orta, dismissing previous writers like Avicenna who, he believes, give 'confused accounts' of the spice.

The Java one has leaves the shape of a lance, and it has a white flower. It has seeds, but they are not sown [... but] used by the people as salads and in medicine, chiefly those who come from Java, who are midwives (called daias) and work as doctors. They propagate the plant from rhizomes, like ginger, and not in any other way. If you see anything written to the contrary, do not believe it.[172]

Greater galangal is used all the time in south-east Asian cuisine, in green curry pastes and, most effectively, in shellfish recipes alongside garlic, chilli and tamarind. When used with lemongrass, it subtly augments the herb's flavour, despite being apparently self-effacing. As Carol Selva Rajah puts it, in south-east Asian laksas, curries and sambals 'it is the lemongrass that hits and is recognised instantaneously, while the galangal remains in the background, but without it the dish would be lacking'.[173]

As well as enlivening the tiny but impeccably styled portions of Vietnamese Hue cuisine, it can be found in the coconut soup tom khaa, the fried rice dish nasi goreng and the beef or buffalo stew rendang, where the meat is slow-cooked in coconut milk with galangal, turmeric, bay leaves, garlic, chillies and ginger – a spice mix called pemasak in Minangkabau, the language of the nomadic West Sumatran people who invented it. Pemasak helps to tenderise but also has anti-microbial properties, forming a protective coating so that cooked rendang could last for weeks and be taken on voyages.

Lesser galangal, or kencur, has a more peppery, camphorous flavour and is used more as a vegetable than a spice – peeled and sliced before being added to stews. Native to southern China, where it grows in coastal areas around Hainan and Beihai, it is sometimes added to five-spice powder but is more popular as a medicine for stomach disorders, rheumatism and catarrh. In Bali the spice paste jangkap, rubbed on duck which is then wrapped in banana leaf and roasted, contains lesser galangal along with chilli, ginger, lemongrass and nuts.

In India galangal is used as a deodorant and to freshen breath. Hildegard of Bingen thought galangal could not be bettered for angina, even by digitalis: 'Whoever has pain in the heart area or is suffering weakness due to the heart, should immediately eat enough galangal and he will recover.'[174] Culpeper refers to 'galangae, majoris and minoris' and observes:

> They are hot and dry in the third degree, and the lesser are accounted the hotter; it strengthens the stomach exceedingly, and takes away the pains thereof coming of cold or wind; the smell of it strengthens the brain, it relieves faint hearts, takes away windiness of the womb, heats the reins [loins], and provokes amorous diseases. You may take half a dram at a time.[175]

Culpeper touches here on galangal's reputation as an aphrodisiac. Possibly he had picked this up from John Gerard, who wrote that both types 'conduce to venery, and heate too cold reines'. Maino de Maneiri's fourteenth-century lifestyle manual *Regimen sanitatis* contains a recipe for 'soft-boiled egg thoroughly mashed with cinnamon, pepper, galangal and salt', which he assures us 'truly strengthens the members, especially the sperm'.[176] (Eggs were associated with fertility, while hot spices provoked desire.) Constantine uses galangal in a restorative electuary to be taken after lunch and dinner. Ibn al-Jazzar, the Tunisian physician from whom Constantine borrowed many of his recipes, wrote that galangal could induce an 'instantaneous erection'.[177]

SEE ALSO: *Ginger, Turmeric.*

GINGER

Zingiber officinale

He walked up and down, burning four holes in a valuable carpet that lay in his path.

'Ginger!' he exclaimed imposingly, halting in front of Aladdin. 'Does that convey anything?'

'An edible seasoning?' suggested the Emperor Aladdin hopefully.

'I have it!' cried the Djinn, slapping his forehead so hard that green sparks flew in the air. 'The Land of Green Ginger! It all comes back to me now. The Land of Green Ginger,' continued the Djinn impressively, 'was built by a Magician who was very fond of fresh vegetables. The idea was that he could take the Land of Green Ginger with him like a portable kitchen-garden; only fancier, if you follow me?'

Noel Langley, *The Land of Green Ginger* (1937)

The Chinese ships that ploughed back and forth across the China Sea and Indian Ocean between the thirteenth and sixteenth centuries were 'floating cities',[178] enormous clinker-built, masted junks equipped with state rooms, dining rooms, latrines and kitchen-gardens. Under the eunuch mariner Zheng He a grand flotilla of such ships explored Asia, the Middle East and East Africa between 1405 and 1433, trading as it went. Marco Polo, who a century earlier sailed on similar junks regularly as an employee of the Mongol emperor the Kublai Khan, is never more animated in his travelogue than when he is describing them:

These ships, you must know, are of fir timber. They have but one deck, though each of them contains some 50 or 60 cabins, wherein the merchants abide greatly at their ease, every man having one to himself. The ship hath but one rudder, but it hath four masts; and sometimes they have two additional masts, which they ship and unship at pleasure ...

Each of their great ships requires at least 200 mariners, some of them 300. They are indeed of great size, for one ship shall carry 5,000 or 6,000 baskets of pepper.[179]

A year after Polo's death in 1324, the Moroccan explorer Ibn Battuta set off from his native Tangier, ostensibly on a pilgrimage to Mecca, although a combination of bad luck and a fondness for detours turned it into a twenty-four-year trek across Asia, Africa and Eastern Europe. Thanks to him we have an idea of what was grown in these junks' 'gardens' – the inspiration, surely, for the 'portable kitchen-gardens' of Langley's children's fantasy. Vast wooden tubs grew what Ibn Battuta calls 'green stuffs' and 'vegetables', suggesting an array of health-giving fare. Historians surmise that these were probably bean sprouts, given the difficulty of growing greens on a seagoing vessel.

Intriguingly, the tubs also contained another plant, one we know well: an erect perennial whose name derives from *zingiber*, a Sanskrit word meaning 'horn-shaped', and whose stem sprouts from thick, twisted, tuberous rhizomes. 'Hands', these are called in the trade, because of their resemblance to swollen, arthritic fingers. They constitute the spice, which comes to us in a variety of forms: fresh or 'green'; dried (sold as 'black' with the skin still on, 'white' with it removed); ground; as young 'stem' ginger, preserved in syrup; and crystallised: that is, steeped in sugar syrup before being dried and coated with sugar.

Is it plausible that ginger was grown on these ships? The marine historian Mathieu Torck says yes: 'The adaptation of the technique on board ships does not seem far-fetched, even though no documentation has been found to place the practice in this specific environment.'[180] It would seem that Asian seafarers did take ginger with them to consume on their voyages, if we trust a passage in

Ibn Battuta's journal describing preparations for his journey from India to Yuan China:

> She [a local princess] ordered that I should be given robes, two elephant loads of rice, two buffalo cows, ten sheep, four pounds of julep and four martabans, which are big vessels, filled with ginger, pepper, citrus fruit [lemons] and mangoes, all salted with what is used in preparing for sea voyages.[181]

Ginger contains only small amounts of Vitamin C (5 mg per 100 g), but Torck says regular doses would be enough to postpone, if not actually eliminate, the danger of scurvy. That Ibn Battuta also took citrus fruit and mangoes with him means he would have been unlikely to suffer on that score and highlights what we have long known: Eastern sailors had a much better understanding of scurvy than Western ones. Not until 1753, when the Scottish surgeon James Lind published *A Treatise of the Scurvy*, was the connection between diet and scurvy clarified in Britain.

All the ginger in the world, though, could not save Ibn Battuta's belongings when, moments before he and his party were about to board a junk at Calicut harbour, a violent storm erupted and smashed most of the ships to pieces: 'The slaves, pages and horses were all drowned, and the precious wares either sank or washed up on the beach, where the zamorin's gendarmes struggled to prevent the townsfolk from making off with the loot.'[182] The one ship that managed to get away, and which was carrying not only Ibn Battuta's luggage but also the mother of his child, left for China without him.

Ginger's origins in southern China explain its centrality to Cantonese cuisine. Think of the way the spice is used with star anise to flavour steamed or steeped chicken or fish, of watercress soup and stir-fried beef. Frederick J. Simoons writes in his *Food in China: A Cultural and Historical Inquiry* (1990) that 'ginger grown in the south [of China] is succulent and better for preserving than that of other regions in the country, and most preserved ginger sold and exported comes from that region'.[183]

Ginger has a place in other schools of Chinese cookery, notably the Western (Szechuan and Hunan) school, although this relies more on chillies and Szechuan pepper to generate heat. In the Eastern school (Fujian, Zheijiang, Shanghai etc.) it offsets the fattiness of braised pork belly and complements the sharp, sherry-like taste of the Shaoxing rice wine in which so-called 'drunken chicken' is steeped.

The reason ginger spread across the world so quickly is that it adapts well to new habitats. Some six thousand years ago the peoples known to linguistic historians as Austronesians (because their numerous languages – over a thousand – can be traced back to a single 'ancestral' language) began their migration from the coast of south-eastern China across the Malay archipelago. Andrew Dalby contends that these travellers took with them wild ginger and its relatives galangal, zedoary and zerumbet. A clue to its status as 'perhaps the most ancient' spice of all[184] is that ginger cannot propagate by seed – the rhizome must be divided, 'a sign that it has grown for so long under human control that it has lost one of the essential characteristics of the wild plant from which it derives'.[185]

Historically, ginger has been valued not just as a warm, piquant flavouring but also as a pharmaceutical necessity: most of the ginger originally exported from China and India, the two main suppliers in antiquity, was intended for medical use.[186] The tenth-century Persian physician Abu Mansur distinguished between three different types of ginger – Chinese, Zanzibar and Melinawi or Zurunbaj. Chinese was, he declared, the best.

At first Chinese ginger was traded internally and with Central Asian countries. But China's trade ambit increased in line with its maritime competence. Even though Marco Polo did not actually visit Java, he understood that it was where merchants from southern China went to offload their ginger and collect pepper, cinnamon, nutmeg et al. – the island whence they 'derived and continue to derive a great part of their wealth' and 'the source of most of the spice that comes into the world's markets'.

Dioscorides thought ginger grew mostly in Eritrea and Arabia, 'where they use it fresh, as we use leeks, boiling it for soup and including it in stews':

> It has small little roots like those of cyprus, whitish, resembling pepper in taste, and with a sweet smell. Choose those that are least rotten. Some ... are preserved and carried into Italy in ceramic jars and are fit for [use with] meat, but they are used together with their pickle. They are warming and digestive, soften the intestines gently, and are good for the stomach. Ginger root is effective against things that darken the pupils [i.e., cataracts]. It is also mixed with antidotes, and in a general way it resembles pepper in its strength.[187]

Chinese doctors valued ginger for its stomach-warming properties and ability to restore the balance of yin and yang. Confucius is supposed to have added it to everything he ate, and it remains one of the most widely prescribed substances in traditional Chinese medicine. Sometimes its use in food is itself medicinal. Consider ginger-flavoured pigs' trotters, a Cantonese and Fukienese postpartum tonic typically prepared by the expecting mother's mother-in-law about a month before the birth. The food historian Yan-kit So remembers enjoying the dish as a teenager – this would have been in the late 1940s – and witnessing its painstaking creation:

> Ginger rhizomes ... pigs' trotters and a special dark and sweet vinegar, all in cattifuls [a Chinese unit of weight] and in the correct proportions, are cooked together for hours until the

ginger is suitably tender and sweetened by the vinegar. By now, the pigs' trotters are also succulent and gelatinous and the vinegar richly flavoured by the other two ingredients. The food is then stored in clay pots in the larder, reheated from time to time to preserve it. Closer to the time of the birth, which is eagerly anticipated, peeled hard-boiled eggs are added to the pots to soak in the sauce with the other ingredients.[188]

For three months after the birth the new mother is expected to eat three large bowlfuls of this stew every day in the belief that the ginger stops any bleeding from the uterus and expels the wind which the Chinese believe finds its way into the abdomen during childbirth.

In Islamic medical systems, however, ginger's heat – it was 'hot in the third degree' – was associated with pleasure. In the Koran it is drunk in Paradise by the righteous: 'They shall be served with silver dishes, and beakers as large as goblets, silver goblets which they themselves shall measure; and brimming cups from the Fountain of Ginger.' And as an aphrodisiac it was thought unusually potent, notwithstanding the competition from black pepper, galangal etc. The Tunisian medic Ibn al-Jazzar credited it with boosting both sperm production and libido. Chapter 18 of what Jack Turner rightly calls 'the spiciest of the works on the topic',[189] the fifteenth-century Arab sex manual *The Perfumed Garden*, bears the memorable title 'Prescriptions for Increasing the Dimension of Small Members and Making Them Splendid'. The poorly endowed man is advised to rub his penis before copulation with lukewarm water, 'then anoint it with a mixture of honey and ginger, rubbing it in sedulously. Then let him join the woman; he will procure for her such pleasure that she objects to him getting off her again.'

More prosaically, ginger is excellent at relieving head colds – either drunk as a tea (infuse slices of fresh root in boiling water) or shredded over food as a garnish. Raw is best – gingerols, the anti-inflammatory compounds found in ginger, are transformed into the less effective zingerone when the rhizome is cooked.

All of this explains why Austronesian sailors, like the Chinese thousands of years later, thought so highly of ginger. When they reached their destinations – the Philippines, the Spice Islands, Madagascar, Easter Island, Sumatra – the members of this diaspora planted it there. And it flourished, because ginger flourishes wherever the climate is humid, sunshine is bright and rainfall heavy. In time ginger made its way to East Africa and, with a little help from Francisco de Mendoza, to the West Indies, where it took so successfully that by the mid-sixteenth century much of Europe's ginger came from Jamaica.

Jamaican ginger, highly regarded, is pale buff in colour and has a mild, delicate flavour. Nigerian ginger has a pungent, camphoraceous aroma, while Australian ginger is sharp and lemony because its essential oils contain more citral and citronellyl acetate. On the whole, the 'gingerness' of ginger is attributable to the compounds ß-sesquiphellandrene and ar-curcumene. Most ground ginger is derived from cheaper, low-grade African varieties. (The best African ginger comes from Kenya.) Ditto the oils used to flavour commercial ginger beer and its ilk. Elizabeth David feared that repeat exposure to such ginger had made the spice unpopular with 'those who value their palates'.[190]

One would imagine fresh ginger would have been hard to come by in medieval England, but even though accounts of its use are 'scant and confusing', the historian Lorna J. Sass says that what people called green ginger was indeed 'young and just ripe, therefore quite juicy and mild', while white ginger was 'probably the partially dried root with which we are more familiar'.[191] Minced ginger is stipulated in *Forme of Cury* (c. 1390) for 'connynges' (a type of mature rabbit) in syrup, a dish served at Henry IV's coronation feast, while the one for poached eggs in custard sauce in the French domestic handbook *Ménagier de Paris* (1393) calls for a cloche ('bell') of ginger – presumably a fresh chunk of the rhizome.

Ground ginger was, of course, used copiously in spice mixes of the period and was the one constant ingredient in jance. Chiquart's version of this egg-based sauce features ginger alongside black pepper, saffron and Grains of Paradise.

Ginger continued to be popular in British cookery well into the seventeenth century. John Evelyn's cooks added it to ale, pease pottage, veal jelly, brisket and oatmeal pudding, among much else. By the eighteenth century, however, it became less popular as a flavouring in savoury dishes as its association with sweet treats like gingerbread and ginger cake solidified. Ironically, one of the earliest recipes for 'gyngerbrede', from the British Museum's Harleian manuscript of *c*. 1430, omits ginger altogether in favour of cloves and cinnamon, but this is thought to be a mistake on the part of the scribe.

The gingerbread that Samuel Pepys eats on 28 February 1669 – 'made in cakes like chocolatte' – would have been solid not soft, the result of following a recipe similar to Ann Blencow's in her 1694 *Receipt Book*:

Take 3 quarters of a pound of sugar, an ounce and half of Ginger, half an ounce of Cinamon in fine pouder. Mingle all these with your flower, and make it up with 3 pound of Treacle, just so stiff as will keep it from running about ye board; then put in 3 quarters of a pound of Melted butter, and stirring it well together; then strow in some more flower by degrees, enough to make it so stif as will make it up in cakes. The oven must be no hotter than for manchets [a type of yeast bread], lett it stand in ye Oven 3 quarters of an hour; wash out the treacle with 2 or 3 spoonfuls of Milk, bake it on buttered papers; mince in also 2 ounces of Oringe pill, and preserved sittern 2 ounces, and 2 great nuttmegs grated.

The young root, so-called 'stem ginger', is a particular delicacy in China, admired for its thinner skin and lack of fibrousness.

Europeans like it crystallised or covered in chocolate or syrup. Rosemary Hemphill: 'Whole pieces in syrup sealed in pretty blue and white or other attractively coloured patterned jars from the Orient have been a favourite of mine since childhood.'[192] Ginger cake can be a rather dry, punitive thing *à la* seed cake, reliant on powdered rather than fresh ginger. But the fashion nowadays is either to adopt a multi-ginger approach – see Delia Smith's preserved ginger cake from her *Book of Cakes* (1977), which uses ground and stem and (important, this) several spoonfuls of syrup from the stem ginger jar – or, in a spirit of purist indulgence, use only fresh ginger, as David Lebovitz does in his fresh ginger cake from *Ready for Dessert* (2011).

Mature ginger root is stronger-tasting but more versatile. It can be grated, chopped, sliced, ground or mashed to extract juice for use in (for example) Chinese marinades, where, says Ken Hom, it 'gives a subtle ginger taste without the bite of fresh chopped pieces'.[193]

SEE ALSO: *Galangal, Turmeric, Zedoary.*

GRAINS OF PARADISE
Aframomum melegueta

Despite an array of alternative names identifying it as such – Alligator pepper, Melegueta pepper, Guinea pepper – Grains of Paradise is not a pepper at all but the seed of *Aframomum melegueta*, a herbaceous perennial in the ginger (*Zingiberaceae*) family which grows copiously in the swamplands of West Africa. While it has some of the firepower of black pepper – broadly, the two spices are

used in the same way, in rubs and marinades and as table condiments – this is softened by aromas of citrus and cardamom, which
make it a piquant addition to, say, rice puddings.

But it is more than simply a foodstuff. Melegueta pepper is
highly prized within Yoruba culture. A tiny quantity is placed on
the lips of newborn babies to welcome them to the world, and in
Nigeria not offering visitors to your house a snack of Grains of
Paradise mixed with kola nut is the height of rudeness – 'like not
offering someone a cup of tea in England', as a Nigerian friend
puts it.

Now grown mainly in Nigeria and Ghana, Grains of Paradise is
indigenous to the West African coast between Freetown in Sierra
Leone and Cape Palmas in Liberia, a stretch known to medieval
traders as the 'pepper' or 'grain' coast, and to the Portuguese a
little later as Terra de Malaguet, after Melle, the African empire
of the Mandingos. It first found its way to Europe in the fourteenth century via Saharan caravan routes whose terminus was
Mundibarca on the coast of Tripoli.

From Tripoli the spice was brought to Italy, where it was chris-
tened Grains of Paradise on account of its considerable cost – a
result of its long, fraught journey – and Italian merchants' desire
to inflate this cost still further by suggesting its source was Eden
itself: 'By the time the "grains" arrived in Europe their credentials
were burnished and their origins forgotten', observes Jack Turner.
'Paradise made for as plausible an origin as any other.'[194] The
spice's place in the heavenly, scented garden in the allegorical poem
'Roman de la Rose' (c. 1230; see Introduction, p. 14) was therefore
uniquely well earned.

And yet there was scope for confusion. Several varieties of
African pepper exist, and even another type of Grains of Paradise,
A. granum-paradisi, known locally as oburo-wawa, whose roots are
eaten rather than the seeds. The Arab geographer Leo Africanus
mentions 'Sudan pepper' being imported to Morocco. Was this
Grains of Paradise or cubeb (Piper cubeba), or Ashanti pepper

(*P. guineense*), or the lesser-known Monk's pepper or chasteberry (*Agnus castus*), traditionally employed to reduce libido? To put it another way, was Grains of Paradise, as experienced by Europeans, always the same spice? We have no way of knowing, and food historians are sceptical, for as Ifeyironwa Francisca Smith points out, 'a large proportion of the spices and condiments used by ancient West Africans were either not properly documented or were just described as medicinal plants by early geographers'.[195] Most probably 'Grains of Paradise' became a catch-all term for similar-looking spices that also included the likes of Indian black cardamom.

From the mid-fifteenth century onwards the Grain Coast trade was controlled by Portugal, specifically the merchant and explorer Fernão Gomes, who was granted the monopoly of trade in Grains of Paradise by King Alfonso V – Gomes paid an annual 'rent' of 100,000 reais for the privilege, which also obliged him to spend five years exploring the rest of the West African coastline on the king's behalf. In 1602 the Dutch traveller Pieter de Marees observed the cultivation of the spice for himself:

Grain of Manigette ... is mostly found in Africa, in an area which is named after it. It grows in Fields, like Rice, but does not become as tall. It is also sown like corn: its leaves are thin and narrow, and where the Grain grows like hazelnuts, it is as big as the cobs of Maize. It is reddish in colour. Once the shells have been removed, one finds the Grain inside, covered with husks, in separate compartments, like [a] pomegranate.[196]

Grana Paradisi are enumerated among spices sold at Lyon in 1245 and as Greyn Paradijs in a tariff of duties levied at Dordrecht in the Netherlands in 1358. England acquired a taste for Grains of Paradise as a substitute for black pepper. But then the market for the spice abruptly crashed in the late fifteenth century as black pepper flooded the European market (see *Black pepper*). Melegueta pepper could not, says John Keay, compete with black pepper 'in volume, price or piquancy. Demoted to simply "Guinea Grain", grana paradisi slumped to the status of occasional ballast and by the end of the century ... had become an irrelevance.'[197]

This might be overstating it, for Grains of Paradise continued to be used and recommended well into the sixteenth and seventeenth centuries. Elizabeth I is supposed to have liked the taste of it in her beer (although evidence for this is scarce). John Gerard's *Herball* (1597) stresses its medicinal uses: the grains 'comfort and warm the weak and cold, and rid the body of infection'. Ditto Gervase Markham's *The English Huswife* (1615), which lists it as an ingredient in an ointment 'to put out the French or Spanish pox'. Just over a decade earlier, Pieter de Marees had witnessed African women who had just given birth taking Grains of Paradise to restore their energy, and wrote about it in his memoir of his trip to the Gold Coast.

But Grains of Paradise had been used medicinally for hundreds of years – or, should we say, 'medicinally'. Absalom chews 'grein and licorice' as an aphrodisiac in 'The Miller's Tale' in Chaucer's *Canterbury Tales* (*c.* 1387–1400): a common application, and possibly a valid one – recent research suggests Melegueta pepper boosts levels of testosterone production in mature male rats.[198]

The mystery of why western lowland gorillas have been dying in captivity from the heart condition fibrosing cardiomyopathy was solved once scientists worked out what was absent from their diet: *A. melegueta*, which they consumed with gusto in their natural African habitat, as well as using it to build night-time nests. '*Aframomum* contains a potent antibacterial, antiviral, antifungal and anti-inflammatory "natural drug",' says primatologist Michael Huffman of Kyoto University. 'The plant may be as much a source of preventive medicine for gorillas as it is of food.'[199]

Grains of Paradise was an essential ingredient of the medieval spiced wine hippocras and was valued for its ability to revitalise stale wine and ale. Indeed, its use in brewing, where it gave an illusion of strength to weak beer and whisky, became so wide-spread that it was banned by George III: any brewer or publican caught in possession was fined £200.

Although it has always featured in some blends of ras el hanout (see *A Directory of Spice Mixes*, p. 251) and has never stopped being used in either its countries of origin or areas with large African populations, there are signs that Grains of Paradise is becoming fashionable once again in mainstream Western cooking. This might be down to its attractive name: there are scores of other African peppers, little known in the West outside their specific communities. In *The Africa Cookbook* (1998) Jessica B. Harris lists a spice mixture for traditional Nigerian peppersoup which she admits 'reads like Martian'.[200] Two of the spices it calls for, atariko and uda, are alternative local names for Grains of Paradise and Grains of Selim, respectively. The others are more obscure: gbafilo (the ground egg-shaped fruit of the tree *Uapaca guineesis*), uyayak (also called Aidan fruit, from the flowering plant *Tetrapleura tetraptera*) and rigije (brown, flat seeds whose botanical identity I cannot pinpoint).

For Westerners such spices represent what Harris calls a 'world of new tastes that are yet to be discovered'.[201] That they can do this and yet play a major part in the daily diets of millions of people is as extraordinary as it is vaguely shameful.

SEE ALSO: *Black pepper, Grains of Selim.*

*
**

GRAINS OF SELIM

Xylopia aethiopia

Visit Senegal and you will soon see street-side stalls selling Café Touba, a strong, sweet blend of coffee and a peppery substance the locals know as *djar* but which tends in the West to be called Grains of Selim. (Presumably it was named after one of the three Ottoman sultans called Selim. Which one, however, is not clear.) Café Touba was invented as a medicine in the 1880s by Cheikh Amadou Bamba, the founder of the Mouride Brotherhood, a Senegalese branch of Sufi Islam. Typically, when you buy it today, it is dispensed from a large metal urn, then poured at some height from one cup to another in order to aerate it: a cute ritual, although improving the poor quality of the beans – cheap robusta, mostly, from the Ivory Coast – would have a more tangible impact on the taste.

During the recession huge numbers of Senegal's coffee-drinkers switched from imported coffee such as Nescafé to the cheaper Café Touba in what the World Bank described as a 'social phenomenon'.[202] Nestlé watched, alarmed: sales of instant coffee in the all-important 'out-of-home' market were crashing. So in March 2010 it launched its own version of Café Touba, Nescafé Ginger & Spice. (The addition of other spices like ginger and cloves is a nod to the mostly East African habit of flavouring coffee with ginger.) To take on Dakar's ubiquitous Touba stands it hired over 300 'roaming sales people' and charged them with selling seventy cups each per day, thus 'backing Nestlé's concept of "Creating Shared Value" in the region'. According to Alain Diop, Nestlé Professional manager for Nestlé Senegal, the 'creative concept' of the roaming sales people 'symbolises our permanent efforts to anticipate the needs of our consumers and get the closest possible to them wherever they are'.

As an example of indigenous culinary traditions being eroded by multinational opportunism this is excellent, if less blatant than the wholesale takeover of Africa by Maggi stock cubes – convenient but unhealthy little blocks of salt, hydrogenated palm oil and monosodium glutamate. The force with which Fast Moving Consumer Goods are sold to those at what marketing experts call the 'bottom of the pyramid' flattens all opposition.

Grains of Selim is derived from the berries and seed pods of *Xylopia aethiopia,* a shrubby tree in the Annonaceae family indigenous not just to Ethiopia but also to Kenya, Nigeria, Mozambique, Senegal, Uganda, Tanzania and Ghana. (In Senegal a slightly different variety, *X. striata*, is also used.) Its host of alternative names – Negro pepper, Guinea pepper, Moor pepper, Senegal pepper, *habzeli, kieng, kimba, kili* – overlap confusingly with the alternative names for Grains of Paradise and similar berries. This lack of what Nestlé would think of as branding uniformity may be why the spice has not found favour outside Africa since the days when, like Grains of Paradise, it was regarded as a cheap pepper substitute.

Between five and eight pepper berries are encased in curved, lumpy pods between 2 and 5 cm long. Its use and even preparation method in Africa are region-specific. In Senegal the immature green berries are smoked until they become sticky, then pounded to make a rub for fish. The flavour is sharp, musky and resinous but less pungent than 'real' pepper: Grains of Selim does not contain piperine. There are shades of nutmeg and cubeb. Almost every part of the tree is used in traditional African medicine. Tea made from the berries is used to treat respiratory disorders including asthma, toothaches and stomach problems. (The berries' essential oil, rich in sesquiterpene hydrocarbons, has been shown to have antimicrobial properties against a wide range of bacteria, including *Candida albicans*.)

In cooking, the pods are crushed and added whole to stews and soups such as the Senegalese one-pot mutton stew dakhine and Nigerian peppersoup. The pods are removed before serving and sometimes tied in a muslin bag to facilitate this. A recipe for peppersoup posted on the Kitchen Butterfly blog recommends removing the bitter seeds and toasting the pods over an open fire before crushing them and adding them to the spice mix.[203] The usual practice is to grind the seeds and pods together in a coffee-grinder.

SEE ALSO: *Black pepper, Grains of Paradise.*

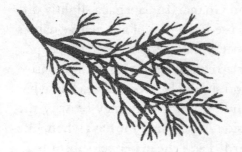

HORSERADISH

Armoracia rusticana

A bit of a pest in the garden, horseradish will flourish from the tiniest portion of root, then be very hard to eliminate if you ever want to plant something else. It is native to Eastern Europe and was popular in Germany before the British adopted it as a condiment for roast beef. Gerard sings its praises as a medicine (to kill worms and alleviate melancholia) before advising that, 'stamped with a little vinegar put thereto, [it] is commonly used among the Germans for sauce to eate fish with and such like meates as we do mustarde'.[204] Mrs M. Grieve recommends infusing sliced horseradish root in milk and using it as a cosmetic to restore lost colour to the face. She adds, bizarrely, that 'horseradish juice mixed with white vinegar will also, applied externally, help to remove freckles'.[205]

Its large green leaves, similar to dock leaves, can be used in salads. But it is normally the thick white roots that are eaten – raw, not cooked; washed and peeled; chopped or coarsely grated; then mixed with white wine vinegar and salt, then whizzed in the food processor, adding more vinegar all the while, until the mixture breaks down and becomes a coarse paste. As with wasabi (sometimes called 'Japanese horseradish') and mustard, horseradish's stimulating burn is the result of a reaction between the latent chemicals sinigrin and myrosin that occurs when the root is damaged – the plant's way of defending itself against attack.

Horseradish's hot and biting but disarmingly sweet taste divides people. In his *Theatrum botanicum* (1640) John Parkinson writes that it is popular with 'country people and strong labouring men' but is 'too strong for tender and gentle stomaches'.[206]

SEE ALSO: *Ginger, Mustard.*

JUNIPER

Juniperus communis

An evergreen coniferous tree in the cypress family, *Juniperus communis* is dioecious: it has both male and female counterparts, which must be cultivated next to each other if berries are to form. The male flowers are yellow and conical, the female ones green and rounded. The berries, which must be lightly crushed to release the piney, citrusy, turpentiney flavour so central to gin, in which they are the main flavouring agent, are not technically berries at all but seed cones, whose fleshy scales merge to create the impression of a smooth, unified surface. They ripen every two or three years but at different rates, so at any time you will find berries at varying stages of ripeness on the same bush. Should you wish to pick some, select only the blue ones and wear gloves, as the leaves are spiky. As Edmund Spenser puts it in his Sonnet XXVI: 'Sweet is the Iunipere, but sharpe his bough.'

Juniper grows across the entire northern hemisphere, but there is considerable regional variation in flavour. The best berries come from central and southern Europe, especially Croatia and Italy, although Jane Grigson felt they were 'more fragrant in the warmer limestone areas of France, where in half an hour one can pick enough to last (they keep their flavour well) for a long while'.[207]

Tom Stobart's robustly English scepticism of juniper echoes Elizabeth David's observation ten years earlier in *French Provincial Cooking* (1960) that 'the appearance of juniper berries in a list of ingredients often puzzles English people'.[208] Resurgent interest in traditional artisanal methods means few English people nowadays would be fazed by Dorothy Hartley's recipe for juniper-spiced ham pickle, or even Hannah Glasse's for veal hams (from 1774), which uses an ounce of the berries. Juniper enlivens West Country game recipes, especially marinades for venison. Its use in game-based stews is also common in Scandinavia: for instance, in the Swedish älg-gryta (moose stew). One of my favourite juniper recipes is faraona con grappa (pot-roasted guinea fowl with juniper and grappa), from Rose Gray and Ruth Rogers's *River Café Classic Italian Cookbook* (2009).

That said, juniper is most closely associated with central European and Alpine cuisine: stuffings, sauces, charcuterie and pâtés; small birds like thrush and woodcock; choucroute garnie (an Alsatian dish of sauerkraut, pork and various vegetables); pot au feu (David favours the Provençal version: 'The meat, I need hardly add, is served with olives and capers ...'); goulash (Austro-Hungarian but absorbed into Jewish cuisine – juniper and paprika go well together); and the Norwegian cheese Gammelost (literally, 'old cheese'), matured in straw soaked with the juice of juniper berries. In her *Spices, Salt and Aromatics in the English Kitchen* (1970) David approvingly includes Ambrose Heath's recipe for a dish of veal kidneys, rognons à la liégeoise: 'The kidneys are rapidly cooked in butter, and just before they are ready to serve you throw in a few crushed juniper berries, then a wineglass of gin warmed in a ladle, ignited, and poured blazing over the kidneys.'[209]

Gin, or jenever (from the French for juniper, *genièvre*), is distilled using the unripened green berries of *J. communis*. Like absinthe, it has competing creation myths. Widely thought to have been developed in the Netherlands in the seventeenth century as a herbal medicine – various inventors have been proposed – it crops up in a thirteenth-century Dutch encyclopedia, *Der naturen bloeme* (1269), as a remedy for stomachache. Juniper twigs are used in the filter bed during brewing of the full-bodied, avowedly primitivist, Finnish beer sahti, lending it a resinous, sour-sweet tang.

For such an unpromising-looking bush juniper has a large symbolic freight. In Italian religious folklore it stands for sanctuary: the infant Jesus was, it is said, placed in the branches of a juniper bush to hide him from Herod's troops. But there is no biblical source for this story, and where 'juniper' does feature in the Bible – in 1

Kings 19:4, for instance, where it shelters the prophet Elijah – its true identity is thought to be white broom.

In the Middle Ages juniper branches were burned during exorcisms and hung over doors to ward off witches. In allegorical portraiture juniper represents youth, health and constancy in marriage. The halo of juniper around the head of Florentine aristocrat Ginevra de' Benci in Leonardo da Vinci's portrait of her is doing more than punning on her name (*ginevra* is 'juniper' in Italian): on the back of the painting a sprig of juniper is flanked by a branch of laurel and a palm leaf while a scroll proclaims: VIRTVTEM FORMA DECORAT ('beauty adorns virtue').

And then, of course, there is 'The Juniper Tree', the Grimms' most disturbing tale – and that is saying something. A beautiful and pious mother gorges herself on the berries during pregnancy and is poisoned. (Juniper's volatile oils, which include the monoterpenes alpha-pinene, myrcene and sabinene, are toxic in large doses. *J. communis* seems not to affect people too much, although pregnant women are advised to avoid it. Some varietals – for example, *J. sabina* – are more toxic than others.) The woman dies shortly after the birth of her son, requesting in her final breath that she be buried beneath the juniper tree outside her house. But then the father marries again ...

The story, beside which 'Hansel and Gretel' looks irredeemably cutesy, binds together consumption and reproduction so tightly that, says Marina Warner, 'it is hard to disentangle where breeding ends and eating begins, or vice versa'.[210] The juniper tree marks a grave, but it also spews forth a phantom firebird who re-establishes something approaching the natural order, albeit one where there is no longer a place for the mother.

Nicholas Culpeper presents juniper as a grand panacea, 'scarce to be paralleled for its virtues'. There is almost nothing it can't cure, from the bitings of venomous beasts to gout, sciatica, leprosy and falling-sickness. Does juniper really, as he says, 'give safe and speedy delivery to women with child'? Possibly. Culpeper is talking here about *J. communis*, as opposed to *J. sabina*, which he calls savine and is an abortifacient – hence its nickname, used for gin too, of 'mother's ruin'. (Culpeper: 'It may be safely used outwardly, for inwardly it cannot be taken without manifest danger.'[211])

SEE ALSO: *Angelica, Silphium.*

LIQUORICE

Glycyrrhiza glabra

Liquorice – from the Greek *glyks* or *glukus* (sweet) and *rhiza* (root) – is the rhizome of a small perennial legume with purple-blue flowers. It grows wild across Europe and the Middle East and was found in Tutankhamun's tomb, although it was popular with almost all ancient civilisations going back to the Assyrians. Theophrastus calls it 'the sweet Scythian root', the Scythians being a nomadic people from the steppes of central Asia. Dioscorides advised troops on long marches to chew it to allay their thirst when water was scarce. According to Andrew Dalby, sixteenth-century English adventurers found it growing in the lower Volga valley. Christopher Burrough in 1580 reported that between Kazan and Astrakhan 'there groweth great store of licoris: the soile is very fruitful: they found there apple trees, and cherrie trees'.[212] John Gerard grew it in the garden of his London house.

The centre for liquorice production in England was Ponte-fract in Yorkshire, where it was cultivated by Dominican monks for use in herbal medicines. Pontefract's natural advantage, one it had over other liquorice-growing regions such as Surrey and

Nottinghamshire, was its clay soil. Even so, as an 1838 article from *The Penny Magazine* makes clear, enormous care had to be taken to bring the crop to perfection:

> The mode of cultivation in the liquorice-grounds at Pontefract is first to trench to the depth of three spades, the bottom to be loosened but not thrown out. Old stable-dung must then be spread on the land, in the proportion of from thirty to forty cart-loads per acre ... The land is then laid out in beds about thirty-eight inches in width, thrown up about a foot in height ... The space between each row of plants is usually sown with early dwarf or York cabbages, or early kidney potatoes ... About the third or fourth year after planting, the roots, which should be three or four feet long, are taken up some time between November and February. They are tied in bundles for sale, which is effected as early as possible, as they become dry and of less value the longer they are kept.

The yellow, fibrous sticks of its raw root have been chewed for millennia as mouth-fresheners, and still are in Italy and Spain. Liquorice can be bought ground and in dried slivers, though it is more commonly sold as hard black sticks manufactured from the boiled root extract. Its flavour, as evocative as Proust's madeleine for generations of schoolchildren, is bittersweet, slightly salty: redolent of seasides and hospital corridors.

Of all the liquorice-based sweets, Bassett's Allsorts – alternating layers of refined black liquorice and brightly coloured, marzipan-like paste – have the firmest footing in the national consciousness. They date from 1899 and were, so the story goes, inspired by an accident that befell a Bassett's sales rep called Charlie Thompson. He dropped a tray of samples he was showing a client in Leicester, mixing them up and prompting her to ask 'What have you got to show me now?' He replied: 'All sorts.' Before Allsorts, however, there were (and continue to be) Pontefract Cakes: shiny, black, coin-shaped sweets about 2 cm in diameter, stamped with an image of a castle and an owl. They are still manufactured in Pontefract, although the liquorice used to make them has been imported since the 1880s, when demand for the cakes began to exceed supply – first from Spain (hence 'Spanish' as Yorkshire slang for liquorice), now mostly from Russia.

Pontefract Cakes were developed in the early seventeenth century. At first they were marketed as a medicine. Then a local chemist called George Dunhill suggested including newly abundant sugar in the recipe to make them even sweeter. (Liquorice is already fifty times sweeter than sugar, though its initial 'hit' is less brutal and its 'delay' longer.) The sweets were hand-made and hand-stamped until the 1960s. Pontefract hosts an annual liquorice festival to celebrate the connection.

A wonderfully efficient demulcent and expectorant, especially when mixed with menthol, liquorice is commonly found in cough medicines and lozenges. Echoing Arab manuals, Culpeper recommends it for 'dry cough, hoarseness, wheezing and shortness of breath and all complaints of the breast and lung', also for consumption and bladder infections.

'In cold, damp Northern Europe, where colds, catarrh and other pulmonary problems were rife, liquorice was considered an essential commodity,' writes David C. Stuart.[213] Another popular medical use was in the treatment of gastric ulcers, glycyrrhizin being chemically similar to carbenoxolone, a commonly prescribed anti-ulcer drug. Having found its way along the Silk Road into China, liquorice became almost as important as ginseng – deployed as a pick-me-up and as an antidote to poisoning both by aconite and by a juice made from the shrub *Ephedra sinica* (ephedrine) that the Chinese were in the habit of drinking as a sexual stimulant.

Beware, though, for while it can be an effective medicine, it is poisonous in large quantities. In 2004 a fifty-six-year-old woman from Yorkshire was admitted to hospital after overdosing on liquorice. She had, admittedly, been eating a lot of it – 200 g of

Pontefract Cakes a day, ostensibly to relieve chronic constipation. She experienced catastrophic muscle failure after her potassium levels plummeted and her blood pressure soared.[214] (For the record, the European Commission advises against the consumption of more than 100 mg of glycyrrhizic acid a day.)

According to Robert Proctor, the author of *Golden Holocaust: Origins of the Cigarette Catastrophe and the Case for Abolition* (2012), as much as 90 per cent of the world's liquorice is used by the tobacco industry: blatantly in products such as pipe tobacco and Rizla papers; more covertly in cigarettes, where liquorice (and cocoa) are hidden ingredients added to prettify the scent of cheap tobacco and facilitate inhalation – liquorice is, as we have seen, an effective bronchodilator.

The addition of liquorice to Guinness complements the burned flavour of roasted unmalted barley. Generally, though, the alcohol industry prefers the similar-tasting but botanically unrelated anise.

SEE ALSO: *Fennel, Star anise.*

LONG PEPPER

Piper longum

Hotter than black pepper but otherwise similar-tasting – it contains the same alkaloid, piperine – long pepper consists of a fused mass of tiny fruits in the form of a conical spike. It grows in the north-eastern Himalayas and has largely fallen out of use except in certain Indian pickles. But it was employed widely in Ancient Greek medicine to reduce phlegm and wind and to increase semen volume.

SEE ALSO: *Black pepper, Grains of Paradise, Grains of Selim.*

MACE

Myristica fragrans

Mace is the aril of the nutmeg seed. When the fruit bursts open, the mace can be seen as the bright red webbing enclosing the shell of the nutmeg. 'Blades of mace' are dried, flattened pieces of the aril.

SEE: *Nutmeg.*

MAHLAB

Prunus mahaleb

A minor spice – some cookbooks downgrade it to a flour – little used outside Greece, Turkey and the Middle East, and then for the specific purpose of imparting a bittersweet almond flavour to cakes and pastries, mahlab (also called mahleb, mahalab, mahlep and mahlepi) is the ground seed kernel of *Prunus mahaleb*, the Mahaleb or St Lucie cherry, which grows wild across the Mediterranean, though it is farmed in Turkey and Iran.

In Greece it is used in bread and yeasty cakes such as vasilopita, often mixed with anise (see *Anise*) and mastic (see *Mastic*). Cretan Easter bread uses a powerful, delicious combination of mahlab, mastic and orange rind. In Turkey it is an ingredient in simit, bread rings rolled in sesame seeds; also pogača, traditionally baked, like Italian focaccia, in the ashes of a fireplace. It gives a fruity flavour to Nabulsi, a white, brined cheese from Palestine which in turn is used in the syrup-soaked cheese pastry kanafeh.

Often, there is a seasonal, religious theme to mahlab's use, and its availability increases in the run-up to Easter, when it is needed for the Armenian sweet bread cheoreg (sometimes chorek) and the Cypriot cheese pies flaouna. The Arabic shortbread pastry ma'amul (or mahmoul), popular in Lebanon and Syria and stuffed with nuts or dates, is eaten at night during Ramadan and on Eid holidays. Yet ma'amul are also eaten by Egyptian, Syrian and Lebanese Jews on Purim, Rosh Hashanah and Hanukkah. 'It is always a thrill to bite into them', says Claudia Roden:

> An uncle told us of a baking competition organised by a dignitary in Aleppo many years ago. The maker of the best ma'amul would get a prize, the equivalent of about £2, to be paid by the dignitary. Hundreds of ma'amul poured into his house, certainly more than £2 worth, and enough to keep him eating happily for months.[215]

Mahlab should be used sparingly or its bitterness can be over-whelming. The spice must be bought as whole kernels for the powder spoils easily, quickly losing flavour and aroma. Even the kernels go rancid after a year or so, unless kept in the freezer.

SEE ALSO: *Mastic, Orris.*

MASTIC

Pistacia lentiscus

Mastic is the resinous sap of an evergreen shrub in the pistachio family. Identifiable by its leathery leaves and clusters of red berries, which turn black when ripe, it grows throughout the Mediterra-nean but most famously and productively on the Greek island of Chios, 'so called in the Syrian language because mastic is produced there, for the Syrians call mastic *chio*'.[216] Chios's mastic trees weep a particularly aromatic resin when their bark is scored. This hardens into translucent, brittle, pear-shaped globules called 'tears', which sometimes have a dusting of white powder. Top-grade tears are *dahtilidopetres*; lower-grade ones, softer and spotted, are *kantiles* or 'blisters'. Mastic has a piney, camphorous taste and softens pleas-ingly when chewed. In fact, it was the original chewing-gum and still has its fans: witness the global popularity of the Jordanian Shaarawi Brothers' mastic gum; though it's just as easy to buy a bag of mastic tears from a Middle Eastern grocery and chew on them, ignoring the initial bitterness.

According to local legend, Chios has St Isidore to thank for its mastic trees. Isidore was an Alexandria-born officer in the Roman navy who in AD 251 dared to confess his Christianity to his commander, Numerius, while his fleet was moored at Chios. Numerius demanded he renounce his faith, and even summoned Isidore's father to help make the case, but to no avail. Isidore was tied to a horse and dragged over rocks before being beheaded and thrown into a cistern, at which point all the trees on the south side of the island spontaneously began to weep.

The co-operative of mastic-producing villages in the south of the island is known as *mastichochoria*. In 1822, during the Greek War of Independence, thousands of Chians were slaughtered by Ottoman troops, an event depicted by Delacroix in his painting *The Massacre at Chios*. Only the inhabitants of the *mastichochoria* were spared. Mastic gum was a favourite in Turkish harems, since it sweetened the breath and whitened the teeth and because chewing it gave bored concubines something to do. When Chios was under Ottoman rule, the punishment for stealing mastic was execution. The island has been part of Greece since 1913.

Mastic's uses go well beyond the merely masticatory. (The derivation, from the Greek *mastichon*, hardly needs unpacking.) In the Greek 'spoon sweet' gliko tou koutalio a confiture of mastic and sugar is dipped into ice-cold water, while in baked goods such as tsoureki and the Cretan artos, holy breads designed to be brought to church as offerings, it enhances flavour as well as lending elasticity to the texture. Mastic is added to masticha, a term that covers two different alcoholic drinks: the brandy-based liqueur Masticha Chiou and an ouzo-like spirit usually served as an aperitif. Across the Middle East mastic is pounded with orange blossom or rose water and used as a flavouring in sweets and rice puddings. (When she appeared on *Desert Island Discs* in 2004, Claudia Roden nominated mastic-flavoured ice-cream as her 'desert-island dessert'.) Before polyphosphates were used as a binding agent in meat processing there was mastic – hence its inclusion in marinades for shawarmah.

The author of the Arabic *Book of Dishes* (1226), Muhammad bin Hasan al-Baghdadi, uses mastic frequently, generally in recipes involving red meat, mixed with pepper, cumin, cinnamon and coriander – for instance, in a recipe for kid cooked with vinegar, fried celery leaves, mastic and saffron. Roden, in *A Book of Middle Eastern Cookery* (1968), cites al-Baghdadi's recipe for the meat and apricot stew mishmishiya, where the mastic works in tandem with ground almonds to create a luxuriously thick sauce. In Syria and Egypt, in dishes like the feast-day meat soup fata, it is more common to mix mastic with cardamom. Some versions of ras el hanout include it.

When William Langham suggests in his *Garden of Health* (1579) that 'the Masticke is also good against spitting of bloud', he is talking about gum disease rather than tuberculosis. Mastic really does reduce oral bacteria,[217] and the eighteenth-century remedy of plugging tooth cavities with it may well have worked. The new breed of expensive artisanal toothpastes often include it alongside such exotic ingredients as the bees' hive sealant propolis. According to an English pharmaceutical journal from 1861, an infusion of mastic was used 'in the East' to treat infantile cholera. Mixed with bread and wine, it was also applied as a poultice to the lower belly. Mastic's reputation as a reliable remedy for gastrointestinal disorders received a boost in 1998, when a study by the University of Nottingham showed it to be effective against *Helicobacter pylori*, the bug responsible for some types of stomach ulcers. In 2006 the active ingredient was identified as isomasticadienolic acid. Mastic has been used to treat high cholesterol and is the basis of the wound adhesive Mastisol, which improves the efficacy of dressings such as surgical strips.

Mastic is sometimes called Arabic gum – not to be confused with gum Arabic, resin from the acacia tree, which as E414 is found in shoe polish, printer ink and as an emulsifier in soft drinks.

MUMMIA

The word 'mummy', as in 'preserved, linen-bound Egyptian corpse', derives from the medieval Persian *mumiya*, meaning asphalt or bitumen, the tar-like resin we smear on roads and roofs but which the ancient Egyptians used in the embalming process.

Recent research by chemical archaeologists such as Stephen Buckley at the University of York has shown that bitumen was one of many antimicrobial and antifungal agents used by embalmers to preserve bodies and assist their passage into the afterlife. (Beeswax and resin from conifer and pistacia trees were also popular.) Cheaper than other resins, bitumen was mostly used in the Late Period (664–332 BC) and more often on pets than humans. But it's easier just to say 'bitumen', so …

From the Middle Ages until well into the nineteenth century, bitumen plucked from old, decayed corpses was believed to have powerful medicinal properties, especially if it came from the head. Known as mummia, it was imported, exotic and very expensive, and for these reasons listed as a spice in medieval commercial manuals.

One of the best-known of these, *La pratica della mercatura*, was drawn up in the late 1330s by the Florentine banker Francesco Pegolotti. As the historian Paul Freeman observes delightedly, mummia features in *La pratica della mercatura* alongside dragon's blood (an extract from plants of the genus *Dracaena*, employed as a dye and medicine) and tutti (the charred scrapings from the chimneys of Alexandrian zinc-smelting furnaces, also known as cadmia: popular in alchemy and as a cure for weeping ulcers, which sounds like nonsense until you realise tutti is actually zinc oxide, one of the active ingredients in ointments like Sudocrem).

Another drug handbook, Matthaeus Platearius' *Circa instans* (1166), calls mummia 'a kind of spice collected from the tombs of the dead' and advises:

You should choose that which is shining, black, bad-smelling, and firm. On the other hand, the white kind, which is rather opaque, does not stick, is not firm and easily crumbles to powder, must be refused ... If a compress is made of it and the juice of shepherd's purse herb, it stops excessive nasal bleeding ... Furthermore, to treat spitting of blood through the mouth because of a wound or a malady of the respiratory organs, make some pills with mummy, mastic powder, and water in which gum Arabic has been dissolved and let the patient keep these pills under the tongue until they have melted, then let him swallow them.[218]

Incredibly, 'corpse medicine' once verged on the respectable. James I was prescribed powdered human skull by one of Europe's most eminent doctors, Sir Theodore Turquet de Mayerne. His refusal to take it put him 'very much in the minority' according to Richard Sugg, who in *Mummies, Cannibals and Vampires: The History of Corpse Medicine from the Renaissance to the Victorians* (2011) avers that 'for well over 200 years in early modern Europe, the rich and the poor, the educated and the illiterate all participated in cannibalism on a more or less routine basis'.[219] And while it sounds like – and to some degree was – a medieval phenomenon, intellectual interest in medicinal cannibalism peaked, ironically enough, in the late seventeenth century, when a rational basis for science was being established.

Human blood was swallowed, sometimes fresh from a donor's veins. In Germany fat with the self-explanatory name *Armsünderschmalz*, or 'fat from poor executed sinners', was harvested for use in ointments. Skull moss, much of it derived from the Irish victims of English occupation, was supposed to cure epilepsy and convulsions. The preference for using material from the head over other organs reflects the belief that there dwelled the 'vital spirits' that sustained the soul. To those who complained that such practices were unholy, the Flemish scientist Jean Baptiste van Helmont responded that they were only being used 'to a good and charitable end' and that 'the remedies themselves are all mere natural means', their power 'given by God himself'.[220]

Originally, Egyptian mummies were the source of mummia. One of the earliest Egyptologists, the twelfth-century Iraqi physician Abd al-Latif al-Baghdadi, indulged in the trade himself:

> As for that which is inside [the corpses'] bodies and heads which is called mummia, there is a lot of it. The people of the country-side bring it to the city and it is sold for very little. I bought three heads full of it for half a dirham. The seller showed me a sack full of this with a breast and belly with a filling of this mummia, and I saw that it was inside the bones which absorbed it until they became part of it.[221]

But demand was so great that not only were thousands of historical human and animal remains desecrated in the rush to meet it but a grotesque mummia-harvesting industry emerged. This made the sticky most of the unwanted corpses spilling daily from prisons and hospitals. The historian Muhammad ibn Iyas (1448– 1522) mentions the trial of some Egyptian merchants accused of fabricating mummies from the recently deceased and selling them on to Europeans as sources of vintage mummia for 25 dinar per qintar. Found guilty, they had their hands cut off and hung around their necks.

Most of the mummia on the European market was imported ready-ground. But trade in the intact contents of looted Egyptian tombs was also significant. Samuel Pepys goes to see a mummy in a merchant's warehouse beside the Thames. It was obviously waiting to be chopped up and dispersed: 'I never saw any before, and therefore, it pleased me much, though an ill sight; and he [i.e., the merchant] did give me a little bit, and a bone of an arme.'[222]

Thomas Pettigrew in his *History of Egyptian Mummies* (1834) is explicit about the scale of the looting:

No sooner was it credited that mummy constituted an article of value in the practice of medicine than many speculators embarked in the trade; the tombs were sacked, and as many mummies as could be obtained were broken into pieces for the purpose of sale.[223]

The publication of John Greaves's pioneering study of the Giza complex, *Pyramidographia* (1646), ushered in a new age of ghoul tourism, and by the middle of the seventeenth century the number of curious European visitors to Egypt was high enough for a French goldsmith named Louis Bertier to open a 'cabinet of curiosities' in Cairo – an attraction he ran for twenty-two years. By the early Victorian period cities such as London and Paris were full of such cabinets, and ancient Egyptian relics central to the collections of people like the architect Sir John Soane, who in March 1825 held a three-day party at his house at 13 Lincoln's Inn Fields to celebrate his acquisition of the sarcophagus of Pharaoh Seti I.

There were also showman-scientists like the aforementioned Pettigrew, a once distinguished surgeon turned antiquarian who drew huge numbers to private parties where he would 'unroll' (i.e., perform autopsies on) mummies, quite blind to the similarities between himself and the tomb-raiders he raged against in his book.

Few, nowadays, would disagree with the philosopher Sir Thomas Browne's opinion that mummia use was a form of 'dismal vampirism'. What were people *thinking* when they swallowed or smeared it? Were they not put off by the fact that 'many who took the black powder immediately vomited it back up again'?[224] (In the opening scene of John Webster's 1612 play *The White Devil*, Gasparo tells Count Lodovico, banished from Rome for his awful behaviour, that his followers 'have swallowed you, like mummia, and being sick/With such unnatural and horrid physic,/Vomit you up i' th' kennel'.) Philip McCouat contends there was a 'long-held belief that mummies contained a mysterious life force that could be transferred to a sufferer to aid them in recovery'. This had its roots, he says, in the teachings of the Swiss-German physician Paracelsus, who believed that 'when we eat the flesh of an animal, we also attract that animal's special qualities'.[225]

Yet mummia had another, less emetic, application – as a pigment in paint-making. Mummy Brown, a compound of ground mummy, raw asphalt and myrrh, was a rich brown pigment with a colour between burnt umber and raw umber. The chemist Arthur H. Church, advising on its manufacture, wrote that it was

> usual to grind up the bones and other parts of the mummy together, so that the resulting powder has more solidity and is less fusible than the asphalt alone would be. A London colour-man informs me that one Egyptian mummy furnishes sufficient material to satisfy the demands of his customers for twenty years.[226]

While it is hard to pinpoint individual pictures where Mummy Brown was used, it was definitely on the palettes of Eugène Delacroix and the Pre-Raphaelite painter Edward Burne-Jones. Some critics liked the way it behaved on the brush. Others felt its unnatural composition worked against it. *Adeline's Art Dictionary* (1905) sounds almost disappointed when it concludes that Mummy Brown 'cannot be recommended to the painter, as, although it is a rich colour, it dries with difficulty, is not permanent, and may contain ammonia and particles of fat'.[227]

Burne-Jones used Mummy Brown for years, apparently ignorant of its true ingredients. The shock when his fellow artist Lawrence Alma-Tadema broke the news to him – unwittingly, in the course of an innocent post-prandial chat about their preferred paint colours – must have been immense and explains what happened next, which his wife, Georgiana, describes beautifully in a biographical sketch published after his death:

Edward scouted [rejected] the idea of the pigment having anything to do with a mummy – said the name must be only borrowed to describe a particular shade of brown – but when assured that it was actually compounded of real mummy, he left us at once, hastened to the studio, and returning with the only tube he had, insisted on our giving it decent burial there and then. So a hole was bored in the green grass at our feet, and we all watched it put safely in, and the spot was marked by one of the girls planting a daisy root above it.[228]

(One of those present at this bizarre funeral was Burne-Jones's nephew Rudyard Kipling, then a boy of about ten. Kipling remembered how his uncle had 'descended in broad daylight with a tube of Mummy Brown in his hand, saying he had discovered it was made of dead Pharaohs and we must bury it accordingly. So we all went out and helped ... and to this day I could drive a spade within a foot of where that tube lies.'[229])

Perhaps surprisingly, Mummy Brown continued to be sold into the mid-1960s, production ceasing only when it became impossible to source the necessary raw materials. As Geoffrey Roberson-Park, managing director of the London-based artist colour-makers C. Roberson's, told *Time* magazine in 1964: 'We might have a few odd limbs lying around somewhere, but not enough to make any more paint. We sold our last complete mummy some years ago for, I think, £3. Perhaps we shouldn't have. We certainly can't get any more.'[230]

MUSTARD

Brassica nigra, B. alba et al.

The word 'mustard' reflects the method of preparation. It derives from the Latin *mustum* or *must*, the grape juice that the Romans mixed with honey and the ground seeds of a plant they called *sinapi* to create *mustum ardens*, or 'burning must'. In 334 BC, Darius III of Persia is supposed to have sent Alexander the Great a bag of sesame seeds to symbolise his vast army. Alexander sent back a sack of mustard seeds: not only did his troops exceed Darius' in number, but their fiery vigour was unmatchable. As a condiment, mustard's virtues are well summed up by John Gerard: 'The seede of Mustard pounded with vinegar is an excellent sauce, good to be eaten with any grosse meates, either fish or flesh, because it doth help digestion, warmeth the stomache and provoketh appetite.'[231]

But which type of mustard? There are three main ones: white (*Brassica alba*), brown (*Br. juncea*) and black (*Br. nigra*), all members of the family Cruciferae on account of the cross-shaped flowers they produce. The seeds vary slightly in size but are always tiny, between 1 and 2 mm in diameter. And yet the plants can grow to be tall, 8 feet or so for *Br. nigra*, which supports their starring role in the parable of the mustard seed (Matthew 13:31–2), even if some biblical botanists suspect that Jesus' mustard may not have been a *Brassica* of any sort but rather the crooked-trunked shrub *Salvadora persica* or 'toothbrush tree':

> Another parable he put forth unto them, saying, The kingdom of heaven is like to a grain of mustard seed, which a man took, and sowed in his field: Which indeed is the least of all seeds: but when it is grown, it is the greatest among herbs, and becometh a tree, so that the birds of the air come and lodge in the branches thereof.

White mustard seeds are sand-coloured rather than white, and slightly larger than the other varieties. Their pale outer husk is removed before the seeds are used. *Br. albus* is a native of the Mediterranean but now grows across Europe and America. Its bright yellow flowers form seed pods which grow horizontally, each holding about six seeds. Its taste is mild with some initial sweetness – not very mustardy. For this reason white mustard seeds tend to be used for pickling in Europe, although they form the basis of classic American radioactive-yellow mustard, where sugar is added, and turmeric for colour. A related type is *Br. cernua* from China, although as far as I can tell its culinary use is limited.

Black mustard seeds have been eclipsed in popularity by brown ones for reasons to do with harvesting efficiency. Because *Br. nigra* grows so tall, it drops its seeds very easily when ripe. This makes harvesting by machine difficult, so it is now only grown where harvesting by hand using sickles is the norm. Erect pods close to its central stem contain twelve seeds. In some parts of India, especially Bengal and Goa, the seeds are dry-fried until they acquire a greyish hue, then used as a garnish: the frying removes their pungency and gives them a nutty, smoky taste. They turn up in the Bengali spice mix panch phoron and the south Indian sambar powder (see *A Directory of Spice Mixes*, pp. 250, 251).

Native to and grown throughout India, *Br. juncea* has larger seed pods than *Br. alba* and *Br. nigra*. (There is also a European variety known as Romanian Brown.) They feature in some regional subtypes of garam masala and in spiced ghee (baghar or tadka). Like *Br. nigra* seeds, they are often cooked in hot oil until they pop or turn grey before being stirred into vegetable or dhal dishes. Oil extracted from the seeds, called sarisar tel, is used in Kashmiri, Goan and Bengali cuisine but is illegal as a foodstuff outside India – it contains erucic acid, a fatty acid known to damage the heart.

Mustard seeds have little or no smell. Their pungent heat is released only when they are crushed and mixed with water. This activates allyl isothiocyanate, the compound responsible for the flavour of mustard (and radish, horseradish and wasabi). In its activated state it would be harmful to the plant, so it is stored latently as two chemicals, sinigrin and myrosinase, which react with each other on contact with water.

'Mustard gas', as used in the trenches with such horrible results, is chemically dissimilar despite having a mustardy smell, although mustard is an ingredient in some biofumigants. Mustard oils are, says John Kingsbury in *Deadly Harvest* (1967), 'only mildly irritant except when concentrated; then they can produce quite severe injury to the delicate membranes of the digestive system'.[232]

English mustard powder – the fine yellow stuff – needs to stand for ten minutes to develop its flavour before it is eaten and loses potency after as little as an hour. It must always be made up fresh and should never be mixed with boiling water or vinegar as these stop the chemical reaction. (It can be mixed with vinegar after the essential oils have had time to develop: the acid 'fixes' the heat. It isn't clear from Gerard's remark above whether he added water before or after pounding the seeds with vinegar.)

Mustard is thought to have been introduced into England in the twelfth century. The habit then was to grind the seeds at the table using a pestle and mortar and sprinkle it on food like black pepper. In the 1480s monks on the Farne Islands were using quern stones. By the seventeenth century differences in the way mustard was prepared in England and France were pronounced. Here is Robert May explaining the English method in *The Accomplishd Cook* (1660):

> Have good seed, pick it, and wash it in cold water, drain it and rub it dry in a cloth very clean; then beat it in a mortar with strong wine-vinegar; and being fine-beaten, strain it and keep it close covered. Or grind it in a mustard quern, or a bowl with a cannon bullet.[233]

For French mustard, on the other hand, you steeped the seed

overnight in vinegar before pounding it in a mortar with more vinegar, honey and cinnamon, keeping it 'close covered in little oyster barrels'.

Nowadays Dijon mustard is prepared from brown seeds (formerly black seeds) with the seed husks removed. It is blended with wine or verjuice, salt and spices to create a sour, blond-coloured paste which goes superbly with roasted meats and adds kick to classic French sauces such as remoulade. It has been a controlled appellation since 1937. Tom Stobart: 'Dijon mustards have an exceptionally clean taste and are the kind of French mustard that may be eaten with steak and anything else in which the taste of the dish must not be masked.'[234] Bordeaux mustards, made from black and brown seeds with the husks retained, are darker and stronger; mixed with vinegar and sugar and tarragon, among other herbs and spices. This is the type of mustard you spread on croutons for beef carbonnade.

There is, of course, a plenitude of sub-types, among them Meaux, which deploys part-crushed and part-ground black seeds to create a crunchy texture, and more exotic concoctions such as Violette from the Limousin region – violet-coloured and clove-scented, made from reduced grape must and whole black seeds. Stobart commends a mustard called Florida, made with (and in) Champagne – 'I would describe it as a ladies' mustard'[235] – though I can't find any evidence that it is still produced.

Famous German mustards, designed to be eaten with sausage, include Löwensenf – 'lion's mustard', made from pure black mustard seeds – and Weisswurstsenf, a coarse-grained, pale, mild mustard for use with white veal sausages like Bratwurst.

For a time Tewkesbury was the centre of English mustard production: see Falstaff's comment about Poins in Shakespeare's *Henry IV, Part 2*, that 'his wit's as thick as Tewkesbury mustard'. John Evelyn recommends 'best Tewkesbury' and the herbalist William Cole, writing in 1657, tells us that 'in Glostershire about Teuxbury they grind Mustard seed and make it up into balls which are brought to London and other remote places as being the best that the world affords'.

For hundreds of years these balls, in which coarsely ground seeds were bound with honey, vinegar and other spices, were the usual delivery mechanism. But the quality was variable. In his *Delightes for Ladies* (1600) Sir Hugh Plat complains that 'our mustard which we buy from the Chandlers at this day is many times made up with vile and filthy vinegar, such as our stomack woulde abhorre if we should see it before the mixing thereof with the seeds'.[236] The invention of finely powdered mustard is usually credited to a Mrs Clements of Durham, who in the early eighteenth century went from town to town on a packhorse selling her wares, becoming quite wealthy in the process – even more so once she ventured as far as London and secured the patronage of George I.

For its classic English mustard powder, Colman's, synonymous with mustard in Britain, uses mostly black mustard, finely ground and sieved, a little white mustard, and wheat flour to improve texture. Both the recipe and production method, which involved sieving the pulverised seeds through superfine bolting silk, were devised by the miller Jeremiah Colman, who founded the company at Stoke Holy Cross Mill on the River Tas, 4 miles south of Norwich.

East Anglia remains England's main mustard-growing area, but poor weather has affected yields badly in recent years – 2006 and 2007 saw some of the worst on record – causing many farmers to switch to more reliable crops such as wheat and oilseed rape. A fourteen-strong co-operative of East Anglian farmers is dedicated to growing enough mustard for Colman's to be able to call its premium product 'English mustard'.[237]

Random literary aside: Dorothy L. Sayers, creator of Lord Peter Wimsey, worked on the account for Colman's Mustard in the late 1920s during her stint as a copywriter at Benson's advertising agency. 'The Mustard Club' was Benson's most successful campaign ever:

Colman's mustard boomed and the Mustard Club was a house-hold joke all over the country. London buses sported the fascia: 'Have you joined the Mustard Club?' Hoardings queried, 'Where's Father? At the Mustard Club.' 'What is a canary? A sparrow that has joined the Mustard Club.' [...] Dorothy's humour and love of wordplay can be spotted in the creation of such characters as Miss Di Gester, Lord Bacon of Cookham, the Baron of Beef.[238]

Elizabeth David says that 'at one time good English mustards were made from a judicious mixture of the two varieties (approximately 37 per cent of brown to 50 per cent of white mustard flour), plus spices, such as pepper, chilli pepper, and even ginger, and about 10 per cent of rice flour.'[239] (I love that 'approximately'.) Sometimes turmeric is added too. Dorothy Hartley observes that 'medieval mustard seems to have been more like a creamy white sauce than the present yellow gum. We have made it to serve with brawn, then, following medieval directions, poured it like thick cream over the thin slices as they lay in the dish.'[240]

Mustard's association with beef is strong and surely has some-thing to do with the way its sharpness and heat make fattier cuts more palatable. It is also excellent in salad dressings and sauces such as hollandaise and mayonnaise, where it helps to emulsify egg yolk and oil. It is essential in Welsh rarebit and generally, as Stobart says, works well with 'vegetables of its own family' such as cauliflower and cabbage. (Try adding it to cauliflower cheese, if you don't already.)

Mustard seed is said to relieve muscular aches and to be an effective emetic, while the oil is used in India as a massage oil and hair conditioner. Pythagoras recommended mustard as an anti-dote for scorpion bites. 'When in the leaf,' writes John Evelyn, 'mustard, especially in young seedling plants, is of incomparable effect to quicken and revive the spirits, strengthening the memory, expelling heaviness ... besides being an approved antiscorbutic.'[241]

Mrs Grieve's *Modern Herbal* (1931) tells us that white mustard seeds 'were at one time quite a fashionable remedy as a laxative, especially for old people ... but from the danger of their retention in the intestines, they are not very safe in large quantities, having in several cases caused inflammation of the stomach and intestinal canal'.[242] Culpeper suggests '[rubbing] the nostrils, forehead and temples [with mustard seeds] to warm and quicken the spirits'. A decoction of the seeds 'resists the malignity of mushrooms', cures toothache and arrests hair loss.[243]

SEE ALSO: *Horseradish.*

MYRRH

Commiphora myrrha

> Your plants are an orchard of pomegranates
> With pleasant fruits,
> Fragrant henna with spikenard,
> spikenard and saffron,
> calamus and cinnamon,
> with every kind of incense tree,
> with myrrh and aloes,
> and all the finest spices.
>
> Song of Solomon, 4: 13–14

When some plants are damaged, they exude resin as a defence mechanism, to seal up the wound and stop destructive bacteria and fungi from finding their way in. Myrrh (from *mur*, the Arabic for 'bitter'; it comes from a small, thorny shrub native to Yemen and Somalia, *Commiphora myrrha*) is one such resin. Frankincense (from the Old French for 'good incense', *franc encens*; the resin from *Boswellia sacra*) is another. But the oleoresin family is vast and also includes Balsam of Mecca (*C. gileadensis*, not to be confused with the rare Balm of Gilead, which comes from the terebinth tree, *Pistacia lentiscus*), bdellium (from *C. wightii* and *C. africana* which grow in sub-Saharan Africa), Sweet Myrrh (or opopanax; *C. erythraea*), benzoin (from various species of *Styrax* tree – popular in Russian church incense), galbanum (from the Iranian *Ferula gummosa*, an ingredient in the 'Tabernacle' incense used in Jewish ritual and mentioned in the Book of Exodus) and ladanum. This last is the exudate of the Mediterranean plant *Cistus ladanifer*, not to be confused with that Victorian favourite, the alcohol-with-an-opium-chaser tonic laudanum. Herodotus observed that ladanum sticks like glue in the beards of he-goats.

Such aromatics have been features of religious and funerary rituals for thousands of years – mostly as perfumes, incense and unguents (although myrrh was added to wine well into the Middle Ages), but also as erotic stimulants. They were effective at neutralising bad smells, especially the smell of decay, and to this end myrrh was often mixed with the medicinal-smelling camphor. Techniques for making perfume as we think of it were crude. The most common, in Egypt at least, was enfleurage, where fragrant compounds are allowed to diffuse into oil or fat over a period of several days. There was no way of isolating essential oils as there is now, with the result that 'ancient perfumes and unguents were a good deal weaker than their modern equivalents'.[244] Steam distillation technology was invented by the Persian chemist Ibn Sinna (Avicenna). The earliest known perfumier is a Mesopotamian woman called Tapputi, who is mentioned in a cuneiform tablet from the second millennium BC.

Frankincense and myrrh will be familiar even to non-Christians. The three 'wise men from the east' who crossed the desert

to pay their respects to the infant Jesus were representatives of the
Magi, the Persian tribe founded by Zoroaster and known for their
astrological prowess. Marco Polo believed they had journeyed
from Saba – now Saveh in Iran – and were buried there in three
large, beautiful chambers, side by side, their bodies (including their
hair and beards) perfectly preserved.

Opinion differs over whether the wise men's offerings to the
Christ child were intended to be medicinal or symbolic. Polo
believed the latter: 'For, said they, if he take the Gold, then he is an
earthly King; if he take the Incense he is God; if he take the Myrrh
he is a Physician.'[245] In the end Jesus receives all three and gives the
men in return a closed box which turns out to contain a stone. Not
understanding that this stone is supposed to symbolise firm faith,
the wise men throw it down a well on their way back to Saba. But
just as they are doing this, fire pours down from the heavens and
fills the well. Shaken, the kings resolve to take some of this fire
home with them, so they do, and put it to work illuminating Saba's
finest church.

The Egyptian Book of the Dead calls frankincense 'the sweat of
the Gods fallen to earth'. It smells of citrus and pine, and has a
smoky, dusty quality, especially when tears of resin are burned on
charcoal – broadly how it would have been used in Ancient Egypt
when, if Plutarch is right, it was burned in the mornings. (Myrrh
was burned at midday and a compound incense called *kyphi* in the
evenings. *Kyphi* contained juniper and spikenard, which explains
why Howard Carter found a calcite vase of the stuff in Tutankhamun's tomb.) Myrrh, its scent a rich compound of wood and
liquorice, was part of the cargo that Queen Hatchepsut's sailors
brought back from their expedition to the Land of Punt (probably
Somalia and Eritrea).

From the Song of Solomon to Greek and Roman myth, perfume
has been associated with the sexual sublime. Not only did Aphrodite, goddess of love, smell gorgeous, but she used perfume to bend
feeble men to her will. To persuade the ferryman Phaon to take

her on board his vessel, Aphrodite gave him as a present an *alabastron* (vase) containing a myrrh-based ointment which, when Phaon rubbed it over himself, made him overpoweringly attractive to all the women on the island of Lesbos. Unfortunately, as Aelian tells us, Phaon suffered a violent death after he was 'surprised in the act of adultery'.

The mother of Aphrodite's one-time lover Adonis was called Myrrha (sometimes Smyrna). There are different versions of the myth, but according to the one sung by Orpheus in Ovid's *Metamorphoses* she is the daughter of King Cinyras of Cyprus. Myrrha harbours a passion for her father and, aided by her nurse, tricks him into sleeping with her – under cover of darkness so that her identity is concealed. Several nights into the affair, Cinyras can bear the suspense no longer. Desperate to know who his lover is, he turns a lamp upon her ...

Predictably, Cinyras flies into a rage. Myrrha escapes but wanders in exile for nine months, pregnant with her father's child. 'Tired of living, but scared of dying', she begs the gods for help and they oblige by turning her into a myrrh tree: 'The myrrh that drips from the bark keeps its mistress's name, and, about it, no age will be silent.' When the time comes for Myrrha to give birth, the goddess Lucina appears and stands beside her 'speaking words that aid childbirth': 'At this the tree split open, and, from the torn bark, gave up its living burden, and the child cried. The naiads laid him on the soft grass, and anointed him with his mother's tears' – those tears being, obviously, pearls of myrrh resin.

The identification of myrrh with another human exudation is bracingly graphic in the Song of Solomon when the bridegroom tells us:

> I rose up to open to my beloved; and my hands dripped with myrrh, and my fingers with sweet smelling myrrh, upon the handles of the lock ... My beloved is to me a sachet of myrrh, that lies between my breasts.

In early Christian tradition priests and other holy people emitted a sweet swell in accordance with St Paul's statement that 'we are in the aroma of Christ to God among those who are being saved' (2 Corinthians 2:15). Angels are supposed to make their presence known in the human realm by leaving a trail of perfume. And as Marina Warner has pointed out, 'the Virgin Mary, as the conqueror of sin, smells ambrosial':

> She is addressed as the 'lily of the field', the 'rose of Sharon', the 'bundle of myrrh'. In pictures of the Annunciation, Gabriel greets her with a lily staff, and its heady perfume, filling her chamber, symbolises her incorruptibility.[246]

The medieval Christian West's attitude to exotic aromatics was the same as its attitude to spices generally: that they owed their magical, aromatic, health-giving properties to their sacred provenance. Their scent was the scent of Eden, believed to be a real place in eastern Asia and shown as such on the Hereford Mappa Mundi of 1285. (This map has the Holy City of Jerusalem at its centre and the British Isles on its south-western rim. Helpfully, the Red Sea is coloured red.)

Nice-smelling things had a particularly high value in medieval times, when most things smelled awful: dwellers in the Middle Ages, says historian Paul Freedman, 'experienced a wider spectrum of olfactory sensations than we are familiar with, both good and bad. What tended to be missing was the neutral nonsmell of modernity.'[247]

What aromatics delivered was something close to the 'odour of sanctity' emitted by dead saints, especially dead saints who would have smelled very bad when they were alive – like Simeon Stylites, the ascetic who lived for thirty-seven years on a platform at the top of a pillar in Aleppo in Syria, cutting himself with ropes and allowing his wounds to fester and become worm-ridden. The best account of Stylites' gruesome contortionism comes from Edward Gibbon:

[Simeon] sometimes prayed in an erect attitude, with his out-stretched arms in the figure of a cross, but his most familiar practice was that of bending his meagre skeleton from the fore-head to the feet; and a curious spectator, after numbering twelve hundred and forty-four repetitions, at length desisted from the endless account. The progress of an ulcer in his thigh might shorten, but it could not disturb, this celestial life; and the patient Hermit expired, without descending from his column.[248]

Just before his death, when Simeon was taken ill with a fever, an unimaginably sweet fragrance is said to have drifted down from his pillar.

Not all cultures and religions value aromatics. They are used only rarely in Islam, and although we associate them with ancient Greek ceremonial, the Greeks 'probably became acquainted with resin-incense through their settlements in Egypt and Asia Minor, or from the Phoenicians of the Levant'.[249] They were absorbed into Western Christian ritual from Eastern Coptic traditions. China, however, was an enthusiastic consumer of Middle Eastern resins. It was kept supplied by Persian and Indonesian traders and in return yielded substances such as gharuwood – better known as agarwood: resin from two species of south-east Asian evergreens – and waxy camphor from the camphor laureal tree (*Cinnamomum camphora*).

SEE ALSO: *Cinnamon, Spikenard.*

NIGELLA

Nigella sativa

A loaf-top scattering of caraway, poppy or nigella seeds looks pretty and coaxes out the flavour of wheats and cereals, especially rye. But like most other seeds, *Nigella sativa* has powerful carminative properties, aiding digestion by reducing bloat, so it best complements cuisines that favour starchy, heavy-on-the-stomach dishes – East European ones, for instance.

Nigella seeds are found in recipes for: Jewish challah bread; German pumpernickel – a word which, pleasingly, translates as 'devil's fart'; Iranian Barbari flat bread – a long, oval-shaped bread usually served with a feta-like ewe's milk cheese; Greek daktyla – the 'finger bread' whose segmented look is created by slashing the dough before baking; Turkish pitta bread; the Moroccan semolina bread khobz mzaweq; some types of Indian naan including, usually, the sweet Peshawari naan; and others too numerous (and similar to the above) to list here.

The small black grains have a rough surface and an oily white interior. They are roughly triangular, with two flat sides and one curved. Their similarity to onion seeds means the two are often confused. As for bouquet, nigella's is minimal unless the seeds are rubbed, when they produce a herby aroma suggestive of carrots and oregano. To taste they are bitter and peppery, slightly smoky, with an undertone of burned onion.

In Indian cookery nigella is found in mildly spiced braised lamb dishes such as korma; also vegetable and dhal dishes, pickles and chutneys. It counteracts the windy effects of cauliflower in kalonji gobi aloo and black-eyed beans in lobia. Some garam masalas contain it, and it is one of the five spices in Bengali panch phoran (see *A Directory of Spice Mixes,* p. 250). Nigella seeds can be used instead of sesame seeds in either the sweet or savoury version of the Moroccan biscotti fekkas.

This spice is known by many names: in English sources, black caraway, black cumin and wild onion seed; in the West Indies, mangril; in India, kalonji, from the Hindi; in France, *cheveux de Vénus*; and in the US, charnushka, a corruption of the Russian *chernushka*. (Semi-relevant aside: Chernushka was the name of the dog launched into space for a single-orbit mission aboard Sputnik 9 on 9 March 1961. He was accompanied by a dummy cosmonaut, some mice and a guinea pig.) In Hebrew nigella is called *ketzah*, in Arabic *kazha*. It is mentioned in Isaiah but erroneously translated as 'dill' in some versions of the Bible.

Nigella refers to its host plant's genus, which encompasses fourteen species of flowering annuals in the buttercup family. The grey-green leaves of *N. sativa* are wispy and thread-like; its flowers, either blue or white, measure an inch or so across and have small blue veins. Nigella is native to western Asia and southern Europe, where it grows wild and in cultivation. India and Egypt are key producers. *N. sativa* arrived in Britain in the late sixteenth century and was first grown at Syon House on the banks of the Thames in west London.[250] An ornamental relative, *N. damascena*, is common in European gardens, where it is better known as love-in-a-mist on account of what Charles Dickens called its 'dense entanglement of finely divided bracts'.[251] (Its other name is the decidedly less romantic devil-in-the-bush.) The seeds of other varieties including *N. damascena* can be used in cooking but lack the power and distinctiveness of *N. sativa*.

The oldest archaeological evidence of its use comes from the Old Kingdom necropolis at Saqqara, about 20 km south of Cairo: traces of nigella were found in the 'beer jars' designed to hold ashes. The *Baghdad Cookery Book* (1226) has a recipe for 'hasty bowl bunn', a condiment produced by taking one part budhaj flour and nine parts flour of rotted bread, mixing them in a vessel, adding water, nigella, fennel and salt, then leaving it to mature for a week. In ancient Mesopotamia nigella was used in a rich pastry called mersu with dates, pistachios, garlic and coriander. Bakers who specialised in this treat were known as *episat mersi*: mersu-making was, we are told, 'an involved and respected process'.[252]

Hippocrates mentions something called melanthion which was thought for a time to be the same as nigella, but his description of the flowers as black is clearly wrong: possibly he was talking about the toxic fungus ergot. Dioscorides, writing much later, also alludes to melanthion, but this is more likely to have been nigella as we know it. Like Pliny, who calls it git, he remarks on its smell and use on bread but warns in alarmist fashion against the lethality of the seeds when consumed in excess. Nigella does contain the poisonous chemical melanthin, but you would have to eat a lot of it for the effect to be fatal. Note, incidentally, that git was the name by which corn cockle, *Agrostemma githago*, was known in the Middle Ages; John Gerard in his *Herball* (1597) actually calls corn cockle 'bastard nigella'.

In Arabic cultures nigella is known as *habbatul barakah*, meaning 'seed of blessing'. The prophet Muhammad called it 'a remedy for all diseases except death'. In Indian medicine nigella is used as a carminative and stimulant. Ayurvedic practitioners believe it induces post-natal uterine contractions and promotes lactation. Galen recommended nigella as a failsafe cure for colds and it became what Dr Caroline Petit, of the University of Warwick's Classics Department, calls 'the Vicks Inhaler of Ancient Greece'. Finding herself in Morocco recently with a bad cold, Petit visited a spice market in Marrakesh and bought a packet of the black seeds – *sanouj*, as they are called in Moroccan Arabic.

Galen recommends cold sufferers wrap a teaspoon of nigella seeds in a small square of linen, briefly rub the little parcel in their hands to warm it up, bring it to one nostril while they block the other, and inhale deeply. The operation should, he says, be repeated as often as necessary until the nose is unblocked. Petit followed Galen's instructions and was amazed by the treatment's effectiveness – and its continuing popularity two thousand years on:

Moroccans buy the seeds in the souk by the weight for a moderate price, together with small squares of linen in which they wrap a spoonful of seeds. The fact that [they] continue this practice shows that the use of nigella seeds hasn't fallen out of fashion. Indeed, many countries, especially in the Islamic world, use them and they are a particularly prized remedy to treat children with a cold.[253]

In medieval England nigella seeds were burned, mixed with pork grease and combed through hair to kill head lice – a treatment that would probably have worked well, melanthin being a potent insecticide: witness the Indian habit, outlined in Mrs Grieve's *A Modern Herbal* (1931), of 'putting [it] among linen' to prevent moth and other insect damage.

In the kitchen nigella seeds should be dry-fried before use. They are hard to grind, so a coffee-grinder or spice mill will work better than a pestle and mortar.

SEE ALSO: *Coriander, Fennel, Poppy seed.*

NUTMEG

Myristica fragrans

One May morning in the early 1880s Anna Forbes and her husband, Henry, stood on the deck of their steam-tender as it neared the Bandas, an archipelago of nine islands about a thousand miles east of Java, in what was then the Dutch East Indies.

Henry, an esteemed Scottish botanist and ornithologist, was researching the book that would become *A Naturalist's Wanderings in the Eastern Archipelago* (1885). He had been touring Sumatra alone but had looped back to the commercial and transport hub of Batavia, now Jakarta, to collect Anna so that she could accompany him to Timor.

Resilient and headstrong, Anna was no mere appendage. She was planning a book of her own, mindful that while she and Henry 'shared for the most part the same experiences', they looked upon them 'from an entirely different standpoint'. Her observations of their genteel nomadism were published as *Insulinde* (an archaic maritime term for south-east Asia) in 1887 and intended, as Anna explains in the preface, for women who might be bored by the 'admixture of scientific matter' in Henry's more scholarly effort. In fact, *Insulinde*'s focus on the everyday dislocations endured by Westerners who have packed the wrong sort of clothes for the climate lends it charm and immediacy. It has, you might say, travelled well.

The Bandas were a picturesque stopping-off point en route to Timor. As a thin breeze cut through the humidity, the Forbeses had the sensation of approaching not land as such but rather a floating mass of brilliant green vegetation. Almost the whole surface seemed to be covered in nutmeg trees – tropical evergreens that can grow to around 65 foot. But as Anna explains, the area left uncovered was significant, and fearsome indeed:

As though to form an offset to this luxuriance and fertility, towers the terrible fire-mountain Gunung Api, which reeks eternally from its shapely cone, like a fierce guardian of these gardens of Paradise ... How strange it was to lean on the ship's rail, and gaze down into the tranquil harbour, whose waters are so transparent that living corals ... are plainly seen on the volcanic sand at a depth of seven or eight fathoms; then to lift the eyes to the smoking mountain, and picture the terrible tumult in the fiery caverns within![254]

Until the early nineteenth century the Bandas, so small that they are absent from many atlases, were the sole source of the world's nutmeg. And nutmeg, which nowadays we associate with eggnog and rice pudding and Christmas, was for hundreds of years the most valuable commodity in the world – more valuable even than gold.

In the early seventeenth century ten pounds of nutmeg cost less than a penny in the Bandas. Back in Europe, it sold for just over £2: a price hike of 60,000 per cent. As Giles Milton remarks in his gripping account of England's brief involvement with the Bandas, *Nathaniel's Nutmeg*, 'a small sackful was enough to set a man up for life, buying him a gabled dwelling in Holborn and a servant to attend to his needs'.[255]

Nutmeg trees are dioecious, meaning that each tree has a specific gender. Male and female trees must be planted next to each other. Both produce bell-shaped flowers with yellow, waxy petals, but only the female trees produce the distinctive fruit, similar to an apricot, with a groove running along the side which splits to reveal a large seed with a bright red cage-like covering called the aril.

This aril is carefully removed from the kernel and left to dry in the sun. When it turns brown and brittle, it can be ground and used in cooking as mace. ('Blades' of mace are broken up bits of the aril.) A nutmeg tree takes around twenty years to reach its full potential, although the first harvest can be carried out seven to nine years after planting.

One day, starting at sunrise, Anna and Henry climbed the sloping path overhung with bamboos that led to the nutmeg woods. They wandered for miles until they reached a plantation house where a group of indigenous Bandanese was preparing nutmegs and mace for export. The couple met the brightly dressed 'gatherers' and admired the jointed poles tipped with claw-like prongs which they used to nip the stalks of the ripe nuts.

Afterwards, they walked down to the shore and toured the warehouses on the wharf and the wood-yards where the packing-cases were made.

The cases are all of one size and are carefully finished and caulked [made watertight]. The produce of the nutmeg tree forms as cleanly an article of cargo as could be wished. A box measuring about three feet by two by one contains £20 worth of nutmegs, and such a box will hold £30 to £40 worth of mace.[256]

Reading this, you might conclude that the nutmeg trade was still buoyant. In fact, the archipelago was in decline by the time the Forbeses came visiting, and not just because of the damage wrought by the monsoon winds and regular volcanic eruptions. Shortly before leaving Neira, the only island in the group flat enough to permit a decent-sized town, Anna witnessed a revealing scene:

It was the sunset hour, and in front of a house in the street parallel with the shore, a comely Chinese matron, seated behind a strong grating, was serving a dark syrup to the most emaciated, weary-looking human beings I have ever seen. It was opium. What a miserable infatuation![257]

Such was life for the less fortunate Bandanese. Meanwhile, the Dutch islanders whose families had grown rich on the nutmeg trade frittered away their fortunes while their bored children hankered for a Europe they had never known. Giles Milton describes how 'vast sums of money were squandered on grandiose waterfront mansions' and how, each evening, 'the burghers of Banda would dress in their finery and stroll up and down the promenade to the rousing music of a military brass band'.[258]

This ludicrous pomp masked a growing internal dissatisfaction with the colonial state of things. 'We're idiots here, we Europeans in this country', declares a character in the Dutch novelist Louis Couperus's *The Hidden Force* (1921), set in Java in around 1900. 'Why do we bring all the paraphernalia of our costly civilisation with us, considering that it will never last?'[259]

To answer this question we need to go back to the beginning

of the world's obsession with nutmeg – assuming, that is, we can identify that point with any confidence.

⁂

Nutmeg, from the Latin *nux*, meaning 'nut', and *muscat*, meaning 'musky', has been known to Europeans since the first century AD. Pliny and Theophrastus mention *macis* (i.e., mace) in their writings, although this may be a case of mistaken identity. Pliny was probably thinking of cinnamon, which he believed came from Syria, and Theophrastus cubeb, the bitter West African pepper.

The first authenticated nutmegs appeared in the Byzantine court in the sixth century. Their source, a closely guarded secret of the Arab merchants who supplied them, was identified in around 1000 by the Persian physician Ibn Sinna (Avicenna): he refers to *jansi ban*, or 'nut of the Bandas'.

Nutmeg as we know it had certainly reached Europe by the twelfth century. When, in 1191, Emperor Henry VI entered Rome for his coronation, the streets were fumigated with nutmeg and other aromatics. An obscure joke in the romance satire 'Sir Thopas', one of Chaucer's *Canterbury Tales* written in the late fourteenth century, is that the hero hails from Flanders, better known for its hard-bargaining merchants than for its errant knights. This may be why, on his quest for the elf-queen, Sir Thopas rides through one of the Magical Spice Forests we encountered earlier (see *Introduction,* p. 2):

> There springer herbs grate and smale,
> The lycorys and the cetewole
> And many a clowe-gilofre;
> And notemugge to put in ale,
> Whether it be moyste or stale,
> Or for to lye in cofre.

That nutmeg would be placed in a *cofre* or clothes chest as a deodorant is not so surprising. More intriguing to us is the idea of nutmeg
being mixed into ale. Not only was this quite routine, however, but
the benefits extend further than improving the flavour (which it
undoubtedly did, medieval ale being made from water and malted
grains fermented with yeast and therefore tasting, in the words
of one modern brewer who attempted to recreate it, like 'liquid
bread'): nutmeg extended its life.

Nutmeg has a strong antimicrobial effect against twenty-five
genera of bacteria including *E. coli*: hence its popularity as a food
preservative and as an ingredient in Ancient Egyptian embalming oils. Likewise, mace works against *Staphylococcus aureus* (a
common cause of both boils and food poisoning) and *Candida
albicans* (thrush). In his *Dyetary of Health* (1562) Andrew Borde
wrote that nutmegs were 'good for them which have cold in their
head and dothe comfort the syght and the brain'. But the medicinal claims made down the centuries for nutmeg and mace are so
broad that they almost cancel each other out.

Borde claimed nutmeg dampened sexual desire. Its widespread
use as an aphrodisiac suggests otherwise. The seventeenth-century
doctor William Salmon rubbed nutmeg oil on his penis before
sex to increase its size, while a recent study by researchers at the
Aligarh Muslim University in Aligarh, India, found that admin-
istering a 50 per cent ethanolic extract of nutmeg for seven days
caused 'significant and sustained increase in the sexual activity of
normal male rats without any conspicuous adverse effects'.[260]

'The nut is like a small gall nut', wrote Garcia de Orta in the
sixteenth century:

> The delicate skin which encircles it is the mace. We need not refer
> to the thick outside rind except that it is very good made into a
> conserve with sugar, and it has a pleasant scent. This conserve is
> very good for the brain and for nervous complaints. It comes from
> Banda in jars of vinegar, and some people eat it as a salad.[261]

This 'candied' nutmeg was favoured by Elizabethan chemists as a dietary supplement. In modern Indonesia the fruit's flesh is still eaten in a similar way, mixed with palm sugar and left in the sun to dry.

An Ayurvedic name for nutmeg is *made shaunda*, or 'narcotic fruit', and a medical directory published in Bombay in 1883 states that local Hindus used it as an intoxicant. Women on Zanzibar and Pemba chewed it as an alternative to smoking marijuana. The saxophonist Charlie Parker stirred spoonfuls of it into milk and Coca-Cola and encouraged his fellow musicians to do the same. Parker bought it from the grocer's shop opposite the club where he played regularly. One day the grocer walked over and said to the club owner, 'I know you do all this baking because I sell between eight to ten nutmegs a day.' The club owner was baffled until he looked at the bandstand and saw, behind it, a pile of nutmeg boxes.[262]

Malcolm X, too, used nutmeg as a substitute for cannabis when his supplies had run out. Remembering his imprisonment in Charlestown in 1946, he wrote:

> My cellmate was among at least a hundred nutmeg men who, for money or cigarettes, bought from kitchen worker inmates penny matchboxes full of stolen nutmeg. I grabbed a box as though it were a pound of heavy drugs. Stirred into a glass of cold water, a penny matchbox full of nutmeg had the kick of three or four reefers.[263]

For this reason nutmeg was banned in the 1960s from the kitchens of US federal prisons. Its alleged psychotropic effects may sound far-fetched, but they are real: nutmeg contains the phenylpropenes elemicin and myristicin, which are metabolised by the body into amphetamine-like compounds.

It also contains safrole, once used to induce abortions. Medieval abortionists were sometimes called 'nutmeg ladies'. The

Renaissance botanist Matthias de l'Obel, writing in 1576, describes an unhappily pregnant English woman who became 'deliriously inebriated after eating ten to 12 nutmegs'. She was lucky: three is generally held to be the most a person can eat without dying, although the Victorian neuroscientist J. E. Purkinje consumed three in 1829 and lived to tell the tale. Purkinje was a compulsive self-experimenter who ingested a range of poisons to test their effects, including belladonna, camphor and turpentine. Alfred Stillé in his *Therapeutics and Materia Medica* (1860) supplies the details:

> Purkinje took a nutmeg fasting, piecemeal and with sugar. The whole day long his senses were dull and his limbs heavy. His mind was not disturbed, but a glass of wine after breakfast affected him unusually. One afternoon, after he had taken three nutmegs, he immediately fell asleep and passed between two and three hours in a dreamy but pleasant state. At the end of this time he went out, and, although he had full command of his muscles, his dreamy, half-unconscious state continued. For several days afterwards wine excited him in an unusual degree.[264]

Nutmeg was used so frequently to relieve flatulence and dyspepsia that it must have done *some* good. Possibly it was added to rich foods to aid digestion as well as improve flavour. As for mace – 'If given three or four times during the twenty-four hours, in a dose of from eight to twelve grains, crushed, or powdered, mace will prove serviceable against long-continued looseness of the bowels', advises William Thomas Fernie in *Herbal Simples Approved for Modern Uses of Cure* (1897), 'but this dose should not be exceeded for fear of inducing narcotism'.[265]

A nutmeg pomander was supposed to cure 'bloody flux' and bubonic plague. During a plague outbreak in Milan in the early seventeenth century, the city's Public Health Magistracy distributed a powder made of arsenic, sulphur, Palestinian incense, carnations, orange peel, peony leaves, mastic, rue seeds and nutmeg. These ingredients were crushed and placed in a red damask bag to be hung around the neck.

As prophylactics go, it was no worse than the others on the market. In his account of Elizabeth I's death and the coming of the plague *The Wonderfull Year* (1603), the playwright and pamphleteer Thomas Dekker lambasted physicians and their crude plague remedies, finding that 'their Phlebotomies, Losinges, and Electaries, with their Diacatholicons, Diacodions, Amulets and Antidotes, had not so much strength to hold life and soule together, as a pot of Pinders Ale and a Nutmeg'.

This was the beginning of nutmeg's status as what Elizabeth David calls a 'civilised fad'. It needs to be grated; hence the popularity in the eighteenth and nineteenth centuries of pocket-sized nutmeg-graters – cylinders or half-cylinders of metal, usually silver, the surface perforated with rasped holes. Often there was a compartment for storing the seed between uses. (Mace, on the other hand, is impossible to grate and should be ground in a coffee-grinder.)

A scattering of fresh nutmeg was deemed essential in wine as well as ale, and in negus (sugared and spiced port), hot toddy and custard. In her collection of essays *Is There a Nutmeg in the House?* (2000) David tells the story of the eighteenth-century sculptor Joseph Nollekens, who was so partial to nutmegs that he would steal them from Royal Academy dinners. His wife, meanwhile, would scrounge free spices from the grocer, requesting, just as she was about to leave, a bit of clove or cinnamon to take away a funny taste she had in her mouth. Between the two of them they managed to accumulate a substantial stock of spices without paying for any of them.

Silver graters were often intricately decorated, complementing other gentlemanly paraphernalia such as hip-flasks and snuff-boxes. Casually producing one from your pocket during a meal cemented your status as a wealthy, cosmopolitan man about town.

Dickens carried a monogrammed nutmeg-grater in his waist-coat pocket. They crop up often in his writing. In *David Copper-field* (1850) Peggotty's fingers are compared to nutmeg-graters, while Mrs Joe in *Great Expectations* (1860) has 'such a prevailing redness of skin' that Pip 'used to wonder whether it was possible she washed herself with a nutmeg-grater instead of soap'.

Writing in the 1980s shortly before her death, Elizabeth David lamented the passing of this tradition and wished to revive it:

> It is far from silly to carry a little nutmeg box and grater around in one's pocket. In London restaurants, such a piece of equip-ment comes in handy. Here, even in Italian restaurants, I find it necessary to ask for nutmeg to grate on to my favourite plain pasta with butter and Parmesan, and for leaf spinach as well.[266]

Modern microplane graters give good results, or you can buy cheap nutmeg-graters made from acrylic or stainless steel – they look a bit like pepper-mills.

Nutmeg's popularity in Europe must have raised eyebrows back in the Bandas, where its use was more limited. Most commonly it was crushed to produce a scented butter which would be used as an ointment. Betel nuts were flavoured with camphor and nutmeg and chewed to make the breath sweet-smelling.

The first Westerner to visit the Bandas was the Venetian travel-ler Ludovico di Varthema, also the first non-Muslim European to enter Mecca as a pilgrim. His account of his adventures, *Itinerario de Ludouico de Varthema Bolognese*, caused a sensation on publica-tion in 1510. He called the islands' inhabitants 'beasts', 'pagans' who had 'no king nor even a governor' and were 'so stupid that if they wished to do evil they would not know how to accomplish it'.

Inspired by Varthema, the Portuguese commander António de Abreu set off for the Bandas the following year with three small vessels. Cunningly, he recruited Malay pilots to guide them, and he knew they were sailing in the right direction when, 10 miles from the islands, he began to smell nutmeg on the wind. Abreu stayed for over a month, filling every inch of the ships with nutmeg and mace.

An English party under James Lancaster, one of the founders of the East India Company, arrived in March 1603, planting flags on the islands of Ai and Run, the latter a tiny atoll avoided by most spice-seekers because of the razor-sharp sunken reef that ringed its harbour. These were England's first overseas colonies: James I called himself 'King of England, Scotland, Ireland, France, Puloway [Ai] and Puloroon [Run]'. But in 1621 the Dutch, having grown in the words of one merchant 'starke madde' at having to share nutmeg and other spices with rival powers, destroyed the English-built warehouses and processing plants on Run before cutting down all the nutmeg trees.

Thereafter the Dutch had the monopoly, fixing prices and either enslaving, massacring or transporting the local population. The notoriously ruthless Dutch governor-general Jan Pieterszoon Coen killed forty-four of the Bandas' native chiefs or *orang kayas* and brought in *perkeniers*, or planters, to run the nutmeg plantations.

After the second Anglo-Dutch war, of 1665–7, the English renounced their claims in the Moluccas under the Treaty of Breda. In return they received acknowledgement of their sovereignty over an insignificant island they had seized from the Dutch on the other side of the world: New Amsterdam – or, as it came to be known, Manhattan.

England watched the Netherlands grow rich on the back of nutmegs. Then it decided enough was enough. On the night of 9 August 1810 a group of English commandos led by one Captain Cole stormed Neira and forced the Dutch to surrender all their local territories.

England held on to the Bandas for seven years. Then, quite suddenly, it handed them back to the Dutch. Which sounds like a nice thing to have done, except that before they did it they asset-stripped as ruthlessly as any corporate financier, uprooting hundreds of nutmeg seedlings and transplanting them to other English colonies such as Ceylon, Singapore and Grenada, where, unfortunately for the Dutch, they flourished.

Today nutmegs are still grown in the Bandas, but also throughout the tropics, wherever it is sufficiently hot, humid and shady: Java, Sumatra, Bengal, Colombia, Brazil, Madagascar and Grenada, where it was introduced in 1843 after the abolition of slavery triggered a decline in sugar-cane cultivation. Annual world demand has been estimated at 9,000 tonnes. Grenada currently produces over 40 per cent of the world's supply and even has a nutmeg on its flag; but it is still recovering from the devastating effects of Hurricane Ivan in 2004. Only now are the trees that were planted in its aftermath starting to mature and yield fruit.

For export, nutmegs are graded by size – large, uniformly coloured ones are the highest quality. In Indonesia, lower-grade nutmegs that are broken or bruised are graded 'broken, wormy and punk', or BWP. It's these nutmegs that will be used for oil or cheap commercial nutmeg powder or snuff. The colour of mace blades is usually a clue to their origin. Orange-red blades tend to be from Indonesian nutmegs, orange-yellow blades from Grenadan ones.

In European cooking, nutmeg is used mainly in cakes, puddings and sauces, and in meat products from haggis to mortadella. Mace, too, works well in cakes and sauces, and with fish and poultry: it can be infused while intact, or tied up as part of a bouquet garni. Nutmeg is popular in custards, cheesecakes and lemon curd tart, also with baked or stewed fruit. In Indonesia and Malaysia the fruit pulp is used in jellies and pickles. In Italy nutmeg is commonly found in ravioli and sprinkled on pasta, and goes especially well with spinach. It peps up cauliflower cheese, omelettes, mashed potato and milk-based sauces such as Béchamel. Indeed, it is a vital ingredient in the Italian version of Béchamel, though not the French one, which uses cloves alone. It is a component of biriyanis and bhuna gosht as well as Indonesian dishes dating from the colonial era, such as semur and kue kering biscuits.

Nutmeg is still added to alcoholic drinks, especially punches, grogs and eggnog. Non-alcoholic ones, too: it is purported to be one of the secret ingredients in Coca-Cola and features in the 'original' recipe found in a diary for 1888 belonging to Coca-Cola's inventor, John S. Pemberton.

Warm, pungent and sweet, nutmeg oil is found in soaps and perfumes, where it blends well with bergamot, sandalwood and lavender. One of Jo Malone's first creations was a ginger and nutmeg-scented bath oil. Nutmeg oil is used in aromatherapy as an anti-inflammatory, to treat rheumatism and to promote digestive and reproductive health. Mace oil is stronger and spicier and generally used for soaps rather than perfumes, although it can be found in Secret Obsession, by Calvin Klein, and Penhaligon's Elixir.

SEE ALSO: *Cinnamon, Cloves.*

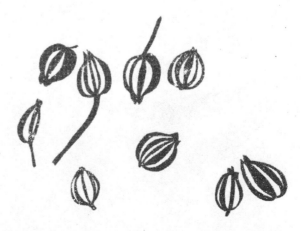

ORRIS

Iris germanica florentina

The desiccated, ground roots of *Iris germanica florentina* have a woody, bitter aroma with strong overtones of violet. Orange pomanders – perfumed balls for carrying around, fashioned from oranges studded with cloves and coated with spices 'fixed' by powdered orris root – were popular in the Middle Ages and revived by the Victorians as Christmas decorations. In Tudor kitchens, comfits similar to our 'hundreds and thousands' were made by coating the powder in layers of sugar syrup (see also *Caraway*).

Orris root can sometimes be found in blends of ras el hanout (see *A Directory of Spice Mixes,* p. 251) but is mostly used to flavour gin (Bombay Sapphire, for instance) and in perfumery (Y, by Yves St Laurent). Rosemary Hemphill includes it in her pot pourri spice blend. To forty roses' worth of dry petals she adds oils of geranium and lavender, cinnamon sticks, cloves, nutmeg, coriander seed and orris root powder. The oils are added first to the orris, which 'takes them up'. The resulting powdery mixture is stirred until it has lost its moistness, then added to the rest of the pot pourri.[267]

SEE ALSO: *Caraway, Mahlab, Mastic.*

PAPRIKA

Capsicum annuum

Paprika, a Magyar word derived from the Slavic term for pepper *paparka*, is a finely ground powder made from varieties of the chilli pepper *Capsicum annuum* with the core and seeds removed. Usually mild and sweet rather than hot – though hot varieties, such as the Hungarian erös, do exist – it offers a very different taste experience from chilli peppers, being as important for the bright red colour it imparts. Paprika is most closely associated with the cuisine of Central and Eastern Europe, especially Hungary, where it was introduced by Ottoman Turks in the sixteenth century. Despite poor harvests in recent years and competition from Spain, China and Latin America, Hungary is still a major producer. Its climate is mild – it is at the northern limit of where peppers can be brought to maturity – and some Hungarian peppers are so sweet that they can be used in cakes.

The best-quality Hungarian paprika is grown south of Budapest, near the towns of Kolocs and Szeged. In the 1920s, before breeding programmes had produced less powerful strains, the peppers were so hot that they could only be used once the pith had been removed. This was a horrible task, which only unmarried or older women were allowed to perform: 'Women with little babies couldn't do the job because they'd have to touch the children afterwards', explains Anita Molnar, CEO of paprika manufacturer Paprika Molnar.[268]

Hungarian dishes such as the meat stew goulash would be unthinkable without paprika. But the food writer Raymond Sokolov says that, in fact, Hungary was 'slow to work paprika into its everyday cuisine':[269] the first two Hungarian recipes to include the spice did not appear in print until 1829, in the third edition of a hugely popular cookbook by the Hungarian chef Istvan Czifrai. These were chicken paprikash, served with noodles, and the fish soup halaszle, traditionally prepared by fishermen in kettles over open fires. (Halaszle should be prepared immediately after the catch and should include carp, bass and the small sturgeon sterlet.)

Spanish pimentón, as used in chorizo sausage, is almost identical to paprika.

SEE ALSO: *Chilli pepper.*

PINK PEPPERCORNS
Schinus terebinthifolius

Pink peppercorns were a bit of a thing in the 1980s, when they prettified many a *nouvelle cuisine* contrivance. But they have nothing to do with pepper, being the unripe berries of a completely different plant, the Brazilian weed *Schinus terebinthifolius*. And they are toxic in large doses:

> These peppercorns can cause symptoms similar to those caused by poison ivy, as well as violent headaches, swollen eyelids, shortness of breath, chest pains, sore throat, hoarseness, upset stomach, diarrhea and haemorrhoids ... Birds who eat [*S. terebinthifolius*] are said to act intoxicated.[270]

SEE ALSO: *Black pepper, Grains of Paradise, Grains of Selim, Long pepper.*

POPPY SEED

Papaver somniferum

> O soothest Sleep! If so it please thee, close,
> In midst of this thine hymn, my willing eyes,
> Or wait the Amen ere thy poppy throws
> Around my head its lulling charities.
>
> John Keats, 'Sonnet to Sleep'

Papaver somniferum, better and more rakishly known as the opium poppy, is the source of the innocent seeds on your daily bagel as well as Thomas de Quincey's 'assuaging balm'. A tall, robust annual with bluish-green stems, it is indigenous to south-west Asia but was domesticated thousands of years ago in the coastal areas of the western Mediterranean as what the geographer Jared Diamond calls a 'founder package' – an imported plant or animal that triggered a new food production capability – then re-exported eastward. This is why poppy seeds are absent from excavated sites of the earliest farming communities in eastern Europe and south-west Asia, and appear first in farming sites in western Europe.[271]

Somniferum means 'sleep-bearing', a nod to the plant's soporific properties. 'Opium' derives from *opion* ('juice' in Greek) – in this case the milky sap, rich in the alkaloids morphine and codeine, that is obtained by making incisions in the almost ripe poppy capsules around a fortnight after flowering has occurred. Opium has been used medicinally for thousands of years. Poppies are listed in the ancient Egyptian Ebers Papyrus as medicinal plants and were cultivated by the Cretans.

The terracotta figurine of a Minoan 'poppy goddess' found in a sanctuary at Gazi in Crete has her hands raised in greeting and poppy seeds on her head. In Greek myth poppies are associated with Demeter, who, in despair over the seizure of her daughter Persephone, ate them in order to fall asleep and forget her grief.

Robert Graves says that their scarlet colour 'promises resurrection after death'.[272]

Morphine's extraordinary effectiveness as a painkiller ensured opium was a mainstay of medicine cabinets until relatively recently – as laudanum (mixed with alcohol) and as the camphorated tincture paregoric. Both were used not just for pain but also as antitussives and for diarrhoea. Barely regulated, they were horribly abused – especially laudanum, which contained 10 per cent powdered opium and was often prescribed spuriously to treat 'hysteria' in women.

For years opium's addictiveness was Western medicine's dirty open secret. The historian Wolfgang Schivelbusch believes it was the anti-bourgeois ambitions of avant-garde artists, many of whom used the drug recreationally, that drew attention to opium's habit-forming properties: no longer, thanks to them, could it be regarded as an innocuous household remedy. By the time heroin was synthesised in 1874, it had become clear that opiates were responsible for 'an escalation of toxicity with considerable consequences for society', although the widespread use of morphine in the American War of Independence, the Crimean War and the First World War eased its passage from military into civilian life in a process similar to the one Schivelbusch charts for tobacco during the Thirty Years' War.[273]

Quite how much alkaloid material is present in the tiny, kidney-shaped, slate-blue (though creamy-white in India) seeds is not clear. Frederic Rosengarten thinks none at all, because the seeds are not formed until after the capsule has lost its ability to produce opium: 'Although the tissues of the ovary are richly laced with opium-containing lactiferous vessels, there are no lactiferous ducts between the ovary and the ovules or immature seeds.'[274] Dioscorides is with him on this: poppy seeds, he says, 'contain no opium and are used extensively in baking and sprinkling on rolls and bread'.

Yet anecdotal evidence suggests otherwise. Ten minutes of googling, in fact, makes it abundantly clear that poppy-seed tea is widely drunk, if not actually enjoyed (it tastes 'grassy, dirty and bitter'[275]). In Tennessee Williams's play *The Night of the Iguana* (1961), the spinster painter Hannah is an enthusiastic brewer of poppy-seed tea. She makes it for the minister Lawrence Shannon and her frail grandfather Nonno – 'Only a good night's sleep could make it possible for him to go on from here tomorrow' – adding sugared ginger to increase its palatability.

The tea's popularity is predicated on a belief, deeply held by its fans, that poppy seeds are coated in active alkaloids which can be washed off. To make the tea, you place a quantity of seeds – one recipe suggests 300 g – in a bottle, add cool or room-temperature water and shake the bottle vigorously for between one and three minutes. The seeds must be strained out before the tea is consumed. After all this, as one authority admits, the result may not be up to much: 'If the seeds are "dirty" or covered with a large amount of morphine and codeine, the brew will be dark, bitter and euphoric. If they were prewashed, like most of the seeds sold in the spice aisle of grocery stores, the tea may be useless.'[276]

It is more usual, and more effective, to make tea from the seed head and other redundant parts of the plant – 'poppy straw', as it is known – which do contain some opium alkaloids. This has been done since ancient times. Dioscorides recommends poppy-straw tea as a cure for insomnia; also mixing the decoction with hulled barley to make a poultice for treating boils and bacterial infections such as erysipelas, although its effect would have been mostly analgesic as opium has few bactericidal properties.[277]

In 2009 eBay banned the sale of poppy-seed heads after two American students died from drinking poppy-straw tea (sometimes called doda) made using materials bought through the website. More recently, in 2013, a twenty-seven-year-old DJ from Wales, Paul Dalling, died after drinking a pint of the stuff.[278] The similarity of doda to the home-made versions of heroin popular among intravenous drug users in Eastern Europe – for example, the Polish *kompot*, supposedly invented in the early 1970s by a chemistry student at Gdansk University and also derived from poppy straw – is worth bearing in mind.

The urban myth that you can fail a drugs test if you eat too many poppy-seed muffins must have *some* truth in it, then. Except that a properly rigorous test will do more than just detect the offending alkaloids. It will also pinpoint their origin by testing for traces of thebaine, also called paramorphine, an opium alkaloid isolated in 1834 by the French chemist Pierre-Joseph Pelletier which is present in poppy plant materials but not in heroin or morphine.

Not that countries with more draconian approaches to drug possession can be bothered to discriminate. According to the BBC, one Swiss national served a four-year jail term in Dubai after customs officials found three poppy seeds on his clothes from a bread roll he had eaten at Heathrow before boarding his plane.[279]

Most opium comes from southern and eastern Afghanistan. But most poppy seeds come from the Netherlands. They have a crunchy texture and pleasantly nutty flavour, which is augmented by toasting or baking. And they can be crushed to produce an oil, called *oeillette* in France, which is used in cooking – it takes ages to go rancid – and as a drying oil in painting. For ancient farmers this oil would have been as important a reason to cultivate poppies as opium: they selected poppies, sesame, mustard and flax, whereas 'modern farmers have done the same for sunflower, safflower and cotton'.[280]

In Petronius' first-century novel *Satyricon* the wealthy freedman Trimalchio throws a lavish banquet at which he serves a row of dormice, glazed in honey and rolled in poppy seeds. Nowadays we associate the seeds with more mundane fare: bread and other baked goods, especially from Central and Eastern Europe – bagels, muffins and rolls such as Polish bialys and cozonac, the sweetbread eaten at Easter in Romania and Bulgaria. The seeds are finely ground and mixed into a sugary paste in the famous Polish poppy-seed cake makowiec and the Jewish hamantaschen, a triangular pastry eaten at Purim. Anne Applebaum and Danielle

Crittenden's *From a Polish Country House Kitchen* (2012) contains an excellent recipe for tort makowy or poppy-seed torte which requires the seeds to be soaked in advance to make them softer.

Poppy seeds' position on the cusp of sweet and savoury is the key to their versatility. For they also work well as a simple condiment, sprinkled over baked vegetables, especially root vegetables like butternut squash. In India, where they are called khus-khus, they are used a bit like arrowroot or ground almonds, as a thickener, though you also find them on naan bread.

SEE ALSO: *Nutmeg, Wormwood.*

QUASSIA

Quassia amara

Quassia is small, yellowish-white chips of wood from a tree native to South America and named by Carolus Linnaeus after a former slave, Graman Quassi (*c.* 1690–*c.* 1780), who became a healer and botanist of some repute. The tea Quassi brewed from the quassia chips worked extremely well as an antihelminthic (i.e., to kill tapeworms).

The spice is also effective at repelling insects. It contains terpenoids such as isoquassin and 'bitter principles' (as they are known in chemistry) fifty times more bitter than quinine, including quassin and 18-hydroxyquassin. No wonder a syrup made by mixing quassia chips with molasses makes 'a harmless fly-poison … with which cloth or filtering-papers are moistened'.[281] In Central America quassia wood boxes are made to protect clothes and linen from insects.

Tom Stobart claims quassia is 'a common ingredient of the tonic wines and aperitifs used so much on the Continent to bolster flagging livers'.[282] Not for me, thanks.

SAFFRON

Crocus sativus

The value of some spices has fluctuated over the years. But saffron, its name derived from the Arabic for yellow, *za'faran*, has always been reliably expensive. Elizabeth David tells the story of Eleanor, countess of Leicester, wife of Simon de Montfort, who over a six-month period in 1265 paid between 10 and 14 shillings a pound for saffron, compared to a maximum of 2 shillings and 4 pence for pepper, and only 4 pence for coriander.[283] As I write this, a single gram of Persian Sargol saffron – one of the finest cultivars, admittedly – costs nearly £13.

The reasons for its high cost are straightforward. Saffron threads are the bright, orange-red stigmas of *Crocus sativus*, a bulbous, autumn-flowering perennial in the iris family (*Iridaceae*). Each flower has only three stigmas. These must be picked by hand on the morning the flowers come into blossom, before they have had a chance to wilt or be damaged by the elements: heavy rain or frost around this time can ruin an entire harvest. Around 150 flowers will produce one gram of dried saffron.

To make matters worse, *C. sativus* is a triploid plant, which is to say it has an odd number of chromosomes and so cannot grow wild or reproduce on its own. Its survival depends on careful nurturing by humans, who must not only plant the bulbs or 'corms' but also tend them: ensure the bed is well drained, in a sunny location, protected from the predations of animals and from fungal infections such as violet root rot (also known as *mort du safran*).

A single 'mother' corm will produce six 'daughter' corms the following year. These grow on top of the mother corm, which dies. With each subsequent year new corms develop closer and closer to the surface. To prevent overcrowding, growers need to lift, divide and replant regularly, sometimes as often as every year, though generally every two to five years. Once picked, the stigmas are dried in sieves over a low heat. They must be stored immediately in airtight tins and protected from sunlight.

C. sativus originated in Bronze-Age Crete and is a natural hybrid of *C. cartwrightus* – wild saffron from the Attica region of Greece, the Cyclades and Crete – and *C. hadriaticus* from the Ionian islands. Nowadays saffron is grown throughout Europe and Asia. For thousands of years Kashmir has been renowned for its saffron, first planted by invading Persians, but consistently poor harvests and the inevitable popularity of cheaper saffron from Spain and Iran have hit its industry hard. ('None of our sons want to be saffron farmers', one Kashmiri farmer told the journalist Jason Burke in 2010. 'They want to be doctors and engineers. It's a shame but I cannot really blame them.'[284])

At one time England was a powerful force in the saffron world. The chalky soil and sunny climate of Chipping Walden in Essex (the word 'Saffron' gradually replaced 'Chipping', reinforcing the connection between town and crop) meant that, even though saffron grew elsewhere in the country, it particularly flourished there – and was evidently still flourishing in the 1720s, when James Douglass surveyed 'all that large tract of ground that lies between Saffron Walden and Cambridge, in a circle of about ten miles diameter' for the journal *Philosophical Transactions* and found saffron growing 'most plentifully'.[285]

The region's saffron farmers became known as 'crokers'. In the second edition of the *Holinshed Chronicles* (1587) we find the Revd William Harrison watching them at work as they harvest and dry the threads before packing them into leather pouches for sale at the St Ursula Fair on the saint's feast day of 21 October:

> The flowers are gathered in the mornyng, before the rising of the Sunne, whych would cauce them to welke; and the chives are picked from the flowers, these latter are throwne into the dung hill, the [chives] being dryed upon little kelles [kilns] covered wyth straigned canvasses over a soft fire; whereby, and by the waight that is layed upon them, they are dried and pressed into cakes, and then bagged up for ye benefite of theyr owners.[286]

Exactly how *C. sativus* came to this country is not known. It probably arrived with the Romans. One of the most popular, if least likely, stories is told by the geographer Richard Hakluyt in *Principal Navigations, Voyages, Traffics and Discoveries of the English Nation* (1598), of a lone Crusader bringing back a single corm from the Holy Land:

It is reported at Saffron Walden that a Pilgrim, purposing to do good to his countrey, stole an head of Saffron and hid the same in his Pilgrim's staffe, which he had made hollow before of purpose, and so he brought this root into the realme with venture of his life; for, if he had bene taken, by the law of the countrey from whence it came, he had died for the fact.[287]

Surprisingly, given the buoyancy of France's own saffron industry, English saffron more than held its own as a continental export. In a price list of spices sold by apothecaries in northern France in the 1560s, 'safren d'Engleterre' is the most valuable.

Perhaps the English were simply good and careful where others were not, and the result was a premium product. In her extended love letter to the spice *Secrets of Saffron* (2001) the American writer Pat Willard marvels at the British tendency to 'collect and draw and at seemingly inexhaustible length ponder a plant's habits, residence, character and manner'.[288] But tenacity did not, in this case, guarantee longevity. Saffron Walden's habit of presenting visiting royalty with threads of saffron in a silver cup continued until the reign of George III, in the course of which saffron fell spectacularly out of fashion in Europe. A string of poor Essex summers killed off the struggling industry and by the 1770s the town had channelled its energy into growing malt and barley instead.

Saffron is still grown today in the east of England, but on a more 'boutique' scale. Norfolk-based agricultural botanist Sally Francis started growing it in 1997, after her mother bought her twenty corms for her birthday. By 2009 she was producing more than she could use and decided to sell it through her own company, Norfolk Saffron. Another grower, the geophysicist David Smale, is based in Saffron Walden. Like Francis, he does everything by hand – planting, picking and processing – and supplies direct to chefs and shops.

'Last year's harvest wasn't great', Smale admitted to *The Guardian* in 2013.

Like most English farmers, the weather was against us – and we got only about 350 g of saffron strands. But you've got to remember saffron isn't cheap, and also I cultivate only an acre or so: our premium product sells for £15 for 0.2 g [30–40 strands' worth] at one grand London department store, though that comes in a designer tin …

I just wish people would use it properly. Even some top chefs don't seem to know what to do with it. I saw one on telly the other week who just put in a big handful of unprepared saffron at the end. That's madness – no one could afford to do that in real life, and you don't get any of that unique aroma and flavour which is the whole point.[289]

Not everyone likes the taste. Elizabeth David, ever plain-speaking, concedes that saffron can be 'most wonderfully attractive' but warns that 'incautiously used, that penetrating smell, that pungent, bitterish taste can turn the same dish into something quite repellent'.[290]

Saffron owes its rich yellow hue to the carotenoid dye crocin, and its honey-like, subtly metallic taste to the chemicals safranal and picrocrocin. Since ancient Sumer at least it has been prized as a flavouring, a medicine and a dye – albeit an unstable one – for textiles.

Frescos found at Knossos and at Akrotiri on Thera (Santorini) suggest the importance of saffron to Minoan culture. *The Saffron-Gatherer*, from the Lotus Lamp Sanctuary at Knossos, shows a blue monkey – evidently a pet, as it is wearing a red leather harness – gathering saffron into a pot. (This fresco was erroneously restored by Sir Arthur Evans to show a boy.) Saffron was used to dye the woollen bolero jackets worn by Minoan women; also in cosmetics, where it was mixed with red ochre, tallow and beeswax to make lipstick. A perfume recipe found at Knossos states simply: 'Saffron pounded in a crucible with myrrh until soft; mix with oil. Strain three times.'

Cretan saffron was exported to Egypt, where it freshened bed-clothes and was mixed into the cones of scented ox tallow that courtiers wore on their wigs and which were designed to melt delectably over the course of the day. Cleopatra is supposed to have bathed in saffron-scented mare's milk as a prelude to sex.

The Romans used saffron to deodorise public spaces, scattering it about like miniature hay. Metrodora, a Greek physician who in around AD 500 wrote what is thought to be the oldest surviving medical text by a woman, recommended it as a cure for haemorrhoids when mixed with ground pine cones, spikenard and wine-soaked dates.

Medieval monks found that if saffron was infused with glair – a glue made from egg white – it could be used as a transparent yellow glaze that made an effective substitute for gold in manuscript illumination. Its popularity as a hair dye lasted well into the sixteenth century as Venetian women mixed it with sulphur, alum and rhubarb in an attempt to create Titian-esque effects. Medieval 'bleaches' contained saffron along with henna, gorse flowers, eggs and mashed-up calf kidneys.

Saffron's use in cooking dates to Persia, home of pilau – the dish of scented, coloured rice that subsequently travelled across the Muslim world to become pilav in Turkey, paella in Spain and risotto in Italy. In India, as the food historian Lizzie Collingham explains, Persian and central Asian culture fused with that of Hindustan to create biryani. Meat was marinated in a spiced yoghurt paste, fried briefly and transferred to a pot, whereupon partially cooked rice was heaped over the meat: 'Saffron soaked in milk was poured over the rice to give it colour and aroma, and the whole dish was covered tightly and cooked slowly, with hot coals on the lid and around the bottom of the pot, just like pilau.' [291]

In some parts of Spain the rice in paella is braised, as in pilau, but not in Valencia, despite the fact that paella is considered by most Spaniards to be a Valencian dish. The Valencian chef Llorenç Millo has observed that 'paella has as many recipes as there are villages, and nearly as many as there are cooks', but saffron features in all of them. The best-known use of saffron to scent risotto is risotto *alla Milanese*, usually served with ossobuco – braised, crosscut shanks of veal. Again, risotto *alla Milanese* has a local creation myth that effaces its Muslim roots: in 1574, so the story goes, a painter called Valerius who was working on Milan's Duomo accidentally dropped some of the saffron he was using as a colourant into his risotto lunch ... But Claudia Roden has an alternative theory – that risotto *giallo*, a speciality of Jewish communities in Ferrara and Venice served on the Sabbath as a first course or side-dish, is the origin of risotto *alla Milanese*: 'The Jews dealt in saffron and other spices and used them more than the general population.'[292]

Saffron's widespread use in fish stews such as bouillabaisse and brodetto has been credited to the Phoenician traders who distributed it around Europe, including Cornwall, where they traded it for tin. Hence Cornish saffron cake, made traditionally at Easter and Christmas and special events like weddings, and served with clotted cream. This recipe for Cornish saffron cake comes from Hannah Glasse's *The Art of Cookery Made Plain and Easy* (1708):

> You must take a quarter of a peck of fine flour, a pound and a half of butter, three ounces of carraway seeds, six eggs and beat well, a quarter of an ounce of cloves and mace beat together very fine, a pennyworth of cinnamon beat, a pound of sugar, a pennyworth of rose water, a pennyworth of saffron, a pint and a half of yeast, and a quart of milk; mix it all together lightly with your hands thus: first boil your milk and butter, then skim off the butter, and mix with your flour, and a little of the milk; stir the yeast into the rest and strain it, mix it with the flour, put in your seed and spice, rose water, tincture of saffron, sugar, and

eggs; beat it all up well with your hands lightly, and bake it in a hoop or pan, but be sure to butter the pan well. It will take an hour and a half in a quick oven. You may leave out the seed if you choose it, and I think it rather better without it; but that you may do as you like.

The fact that hot cross buns originally contained saffron confirms their line of descent from the saffron crescent cakes made by the Phoenicians as offerings to Ashtoreth, the goddess of fertility and war.

During the fourteenth and fifteenth centuries demand for saffron reached a peak. As the Black Death swept across Europe, saffron was believed to be an effective antidote. Gerard's *Herball* advises that

> the weight of ten grains of Saffron, the kernels of Walnuts two ounces, Figs two ounces, Mithridate one dram, and a few Sage leaves stamped together with a sufficient quantity of Pimpernel water, and made into a mass or lump, and kept in a glass for your use, and thereof 12 grains given in the morning fasting, preserveth from the pestilence, and expelleth it from those that are infected.[293]

In 1482 the Nuremberg barber Hans Folcz published some remedies in his *On the Pestilence: A Nice, Useful, and Concise Little Tract* – for instance, saffron mixed with other spices and vinegar and applied to the buboes as a salve. Other Germanic sources mention a potion called *latwerge*[294] – a mixture of saffron, treacle and mustard which had to be fried in an eggshell.

But saffron's modishness in the Middle Ages was also linked to the fashion for 'endoring' or colouring food (see *Introduction*), especially on grand occasions. At a two-day feast held in around 1420 by the Savoyard master cook Chiquart, 25 lb. of saffron were required – which sounds a lot, and is; but not *quite* so much when you consider what it was intended to spice: 100 fat oxen, 130 sheep, 120 pigs, 200 piglets, 60 fat pigs (for larding), 200 kids and lambs, 100 calves and 2,000 poultry. 'Accounts of this kind tend to leave the reader with a sense of numerical fatigue', deadpans Roy Strong, who must have been constantly tired while writing his history of grand eating *Feast* (2002).[295]

This recipe for Golden Swan, a dish likely to have been served at a feast such as the one described above, comes from the medieval cookbook *Le Viandier de Taillevent* (c. 1300):

Take the swan and inflate it between its shoulders as with stuffed poultry and slit it along its belly. Then remove the skin together with the neck cut off at the shoulders and with the legs remaining attached to the body; then fix it on a spit, interlarded as poultry, and glaze it with saffron; and when it is cooked, it should be redressed in its skin, with the neck either straight or flat. Endore the feathers and head with a paste made of egg yolks mixed with saffron and honey. It should be eaten with poivre jeunet [yellow pepper sauce, which also contains saffron].

Perhaps because it is so expensive, saffron has always been one of the most adulterated spices – and continues to be. As recently as 2011 the Food Standards Agency (FSA) asked its counterparts in Spain to test the saffron being exported from that country after being tipped off that supposedly 'pure and genuine' saffron on sale in the UK was of poor quality, and failed to supply the usual colour and aroma.[296]

In the Middle Ages anyone who adulterated saffron or even *possessed* adulterated saffron was punished severely. At Pisa in

1305 the *fundacarii* or keepers of public warehouses were required by oath to denounce the owners of falsified saffron consigned to their custody. In Nuremberg strict laws were passed, called the Safranschou Code. In 1444 a trader found to have breached the code called Jobst Findeker was burned alive with his sacks of fake saffron heaped up around him.

For those reluctant or unable to spend the money, saffron substitutes are available, the most common of which is safflower or, as it is sometimes known, 'bastard saffron'. Note that 'Indian saffron' is not saffron at all but another name for turmeric.

There are two main methods of preparing saffron for culinary use. The first is to dry-fry the stigmas to make them brittle, then crush them into a fine powder that can be distributed evenly. The second is to steep the stigmas in hot water for at least half an hour. The resulting liquor is added to the dish towards the end of the cooking process.

SEE ALSO: *Annatto, Turmeric.*

SANSHO

Zanthoxylum piperitum

The Japanese version of Szechuan pepper, sansho is the dried and ground seed pods of the Japanese prickly ash tree. It is tangy and citrusy rather than hot (although it slightly numbs the tongue) and goes well with grilled meat and fish, especially eel (kabayaki unagi) and chicken (yakitori). The plant's leaves, called kinome, are used as a garnish. Sansho is one of the spices used in schichimi-togarashi or Japanese seven-flavour spice mix (see *A Directory of Spice Mixes*, p. 252).

SEE ALSO: *Szechuan pepper.*

SESAME SEED

Sesamum indicum

In 'Ali Baba and the Forty Thieves', one of the best-loved of the Arabian folk tales collected under the title *One Thousand and One Nights*, a poor wood-cutter discovers a thieves' den whose door springs open when the phrase 'Open, sesame!' is uttered. Ali Baba uses his knowledge of this password to steal a bag of gold coins, which he rushes home to weigh.

His greedy brother is less lucky. Cassim manages to get *into* the cave, but then forgets the password so is unable to get out again. He is found there by the returning thieves, who kill him and chop his body into four pieces, leaving it at the entrance *pour décourager les autres*.

The idea that herbs and spices have magical properties is enshrined in the earliest encyclopedias of medicine and natural history. In magic, as in medicine, Western and Middle Eastern traditions clashed benignly to generate a kaleidoscopic array of new possibilities.

As discussed earlier (see *Introduction*, p. 18), Arabic translations of Pliny (and Dioscorides, Hippocrates, Galen et al.) would go on to inform medieval Islamic scholars like Avicenna, who laid the foundations for modern scientific medicine. But intellectual traffic flowed in the other direction too. Some of the most influential was the work of Arab Spaniards such as the mathematician Maslama al-Majriti. His *The Aim of the Sage* – it is usually attributed to him, anyway – is better known in Europe as the *Picatrix*. The *Picatrix* and another book of spells, *Illumination of Knowledge*, by the Egyptian Sufi magician Ahmad bin Ali al-Buni, were duly translated into Latin and so absorbed into European Renaissance patterns of thinking about astrology, alchemy and sorcery.

A controversial figure whose work was later denounced as heretical by more conservative Islamic scholars, Ahmad bin Ali al-Buni was especially interested in *simiya* or 'letter magic', a form of mysticism based on the belief that the letters of the alphabet are obscurely entangled with the physical world. In one of his works al-Buni namechecks Chaldean magicians from ancient Mesopotamia – a priestly caste who, so the elderly occultist Agliè tells us in Umberto Eco's novel *Foucault's Pendulum* (1988), 'operated sacred machines by sounds alone'. What is more, says Agliè, 'the priests of Karnak and Thebes could open the doors of a temple with only their voice – and what else could be the origin, if you think about it, of the legend of Open Sesame?'[297]

What indeed? Though the significance of 'sesame' is not clear. Is it some sort of code or symbol? What is so special about sesame?

The answer lies in the reason that sesame – an upright annual indigenous to tropical Africa and India, with veined, oval leaves and white or pink flowers – was domesticated in the first place: its oil. 'Sesame' comes to us from the Greek *sesamon*, which derives via the Phoenician *ššmn* from the Akkadian *šamaššammu*, meaning 'oily plant'.[298] In modern Arabic it is *simsim* – and one finds 'Open, simsim!' instead of 'Open, sesame!' in some editions of *One Thousand and One Nights*.

Sesame seeds' extraordinarily high oil content (50 to 60 per cent) means they have always been important in cooking, especially as their oil (still popular, especially in China, and the basis for many margarines) is both polyunsaturated and keeps well in hot conditions. Herodotus wrote of the Babylonians that 'the only oil they use is made from the sesame plant'. The flattish, oval seeds, ranging in colour from pearly-white to black, were popular too. In his play *Acharnians* Aristophanes mentions a party where, alongside whores and dancing girls, there are 'cakes made of nice white flour and sesame seeds and honey'. Apicius includes them in a recipe for roast flamingo. Dioscorides thought the seeds both harmed the stomach and caused bad breath, by sticking to the teeth. Ripened seeds have a tendency to burst out of the pods and scatter: perhaps 'Open, sesame!' alludes to some ancient association with spontaneous release?

Before we get carried away, we should remember that 'Ali Baba and the Forty Thieves' has an uncertain relationship to the rest of the tales in *One Thousand and One Nights*. It seems to have existed only in oral form before it was added by its first European translator, Antoine Galland, to his *Les Mille et une nuits*, published in France in twelve volumes between 1704 and 1717. Galland heard the tale from a Maronite monk he met in Aleppo and jotted down six pages of notes in his diary.

In the early nineteenth century the Grimm brothers wrote a Germanic version of 'Ali Baba' called 'Simeliberg'. In this version a mountain opens to reveal a cave of riches when addressed thus: 'Berg Semsi, Berg Semsi, thu dich auf.' The echoes of 'simsim' are hard to ignore. But the Grimms, who were after all philologists and lexicographers, explained that 'semsi' was an ancient German word for 'mountain'.

Whether the phrase 'Open, sesame!' occurred in Galland's diary is not clear – it may even have been his invention – but when the critic Aboubakr Chraïbi compared 'Ali Baba and the Forty Thieves' to other similar folk tales from around the world he found it echoed a Japanese narrative tradition in which a falling pellet of food must be caught: 'If one calls [i.e., names] the pellet – as if using a magical formula – it leads to an underground cave in which other creatures live that endow the Good with riches, while envious characters go there to their disadvantage. This structure could help explain the formula "Open Sesame" as if it were an offering of food.'[299]

Sesame seeds' lack of an aromatic essential oil means that, in the eyes of some, they are not a 'proper' spice. But nor are they nuts, although many people with nut allergies are also allergic to sesame. (According to Allergy UK, 'the most common type of allergy to seed is due to sesame'. Reactions can be severe and life-threatening.) For any sort of aroma to emerge you have to toast them – preferably in a cast-iron frying pan on a medium-low heat, stirring them gently and trying to stop them from jumping around. This causes pyrazines to form and, when the toasting temperature is raised to 200°C, furans, the compounds found in roasted coffee.

With the exception of ground-sesame pastes such as the Middle Eastern tahina and the Chinese zhi ma jiang, sesame seeds are used as much for their texture as for their delicate but bitter taste: on dishes like the Chinese sesame prawn toasts; in spice mixes like the Egyptian dukka, Jordanian za'atar and the Japanese gomashio; on pies like the Cretan skaltsounakia; and in biscuits and cakes such as the Middle Eastern barazek (where the sesame blends beautifully with honey and pistachio), the Cretan nut-filled pastry gastrin, the Moroccan pancakes righaif and the Egyptian pretzels semit.

Colette Rossant remembers experiencing these for the first time when she docked at Alexandria as a five-year-old in 1937. As she descended the gangplank, she saw a 'young boy in a dirty grey robe with a large basket filled with pretzels perched on his head and hiding his face'. She asked her governess if she could have one but was told: 'Never! They're disgusting ... too dirty.' But then her grandfather, who was meeting the boat, handed her one: 'I had been right to insist on trying one', Rossant decided. 'The semit was hot, sweet and crusty like a fresh baguette, and covered with toasted sesame seeds that crackled under my teeth.'[300] Probably these would have been black sesame seeds – tastier than the standard (unhulled) beige and off-white (hulled) seeds. In fact, a spectrum exists from black to dark brown to cream. Seed colour is genetically determined. Differently hued seeds are bred for different markets: Japan and the Middle East prefer black, while India tends to favour white.

Sesame oil, too, has a similar number of taste and shade gradations to olive oil. The light varieties, nutty and good for frying, are made from cold-pressed, untoasted seeds. The darker Asian types, made from roasted seeds, have a stronger, smokier flavour and are used sparingly, to season rather than to fry.

Varieties of tahina, made from ground, hulled sesame seeds, are popular across the Middle East, Greece, Turkey, Armenia and North Africa. Tahina can be added to sauces and dips to accompany grilled meats and kebabs, and is a treacly treat when mixed with honey, say, in salad dressings. Adding chickpeas, lemon juice, garlic and olive oil to tahina creates hummus. Hummus's origins are controversial. According to Yotam Ottolenghi and Sami Tamimi, 'most people agree that it was Levantine or Egyptian Arabs who first made hummus, though even this is debatable ... But when push comes to shove, nobody seriously challenges the Palestinian hegemony in making hummus, even though both they and the Jews like calling it their own. The arguments never cease.'[301]

A hummus-like recipe from a thirteenth-century Egyptian cookery book whose title translates as *The Treasure of Useful Advice for the Composition of a Varied Table* contains no tahina at all; the chickpea purée is flavoured with vinegar, pickled lemons and an assortment of herbs and spices. Carolyn Heal and Michael Allsop say that 'the Romans made a kind of hummus from sesame and cumin, and the ancient Persians knew of it'.[302] Possibly they mean moretum, the herby cheese spread for bread described by the Roman agriculturalist Columella, which sometimes had ground nuts and seeds added to it. Sesame seeds would have been eaten in ancient Rome as part of the *tragemata*, the final course of a meal, when chewy foods like dried fruits and nuts were the focus and wine was served.[303]

The hard, biscuit-like nut fudge halva is usually made from sesame paste and hot sugar syrup. In Western Europe it is associated with India and the Middle East. But local versions exist across Eastern Europe and the Balkans, some of which use semolina, cornmeal or rice flour rather than tahina. This is true to halva's roots in ninth-century Arabia, when the word ceased to mean date paste kneaded with milk, and elements of the Persian sweetmeat afroshag were absorbed into the recipe. Some Indian versions require semolina or zedoary flour to be fried in ghee then mixed with raisins and spiced syrup, but there are pronounced regional variations: for example, 'Madras' halva uses poppy seeds.[304]

Sesame-based halva is very much a Levantine phenomenon, although, as Alan Davidson points out, it happens to be the type best known in Europe and North America.[305] In tekoua, a dish originating in sub-Saharan Africa, sesame seeds are pounded and mixed with confectioners' sugar to form small balls.[306]

SEE ALSO: *Caraway, Fennel, Nigella, Poppyseed.*

SILPHIUM

Ferula tingitana

In 631 BC a severe drought on the Greek island of Thera (Santorini) triggered an exodus that resulted in the founding of five cities in northern Africa. One of them, Cyrene, stood not far from what is now the town of Shahhat in eastern Libya, an area still known by its classical name of Cyrenaica. In its pomp Cyrene was a bustling, important place with the requisite array of temples and a port, Apollonia, 10 miles down the road. It even had its own school of philosophy. The hedonistic Cyrenaics, established by Socrates' disciple Aristippus, taught that physical pleasure was the only intrinsic good.

After becoming a Roman province in 74 BC, however, Cyrene fell into decline. Two calamitous earthquakes in AD 262 and 365 destroyed key buildings like the Library of Celsus, and by the fourth century it was a ghost city. Its ruins are a UNESCO World Heritage Site, but the local situation remains so unstable that attempts to excavate and preserve them have been on hold since 2011.

In truth, things had been shaky for Cyrene long before nature finished it off. The city owed its status as a commercial centre to a single export, a species of giant fennel (*Ferula*) called silphium, which was so highly valued as a medicine and flavour-enhancer by the Greeks – and, later, the Romans, who called it *laserpitium* – that at one point it was worth its weight in silver. A Laconian cup from around 565 BC shows Cyrene's then ruler, King Arcesilas II, sitting in a chair, overseeing the weighing and packing of silphium ready for shipment. The plant's image adorned the city's coins – a stylised rendering that would seem to corroborate Theophrastus' description of silphium as having 'a big thick root, a stem as long as giant fennel and just about as thick, and a leaf similar to celery'. The most valuable product was its resin, as Theophrastus explains:

The harvesters cut in accordance with a sort of mining-con-
cession, a ration that they may take based on what has been cut
and what remains, and it is not permitted to cut at random;
nor indeed to cut more than the ration, because the resin spoils
and decays with age. Exporting it to Piraeus [for Athens] they
prepare it as follows: after putting it in jars and mixing flour
with it they shake it for a long time – this is where its colour
comes from; and thus treated it remains stable ... It is found
over a large region of Libya, more than five hundred miles, they
say. Its oddity is to avoid cultivated land, and to retreat as the
land is gradually brought under cultivation and farmed – obviously as it, far from requiring husbandry, is essentially wild.[307]

The fact that attempts to transplant silphium to Attica and Ionia
failed wasn't such a problem as long as Cyrene's strict harvesting
quotas were respected. However, the 'large region' Theophrastus
mentions was actually a narrow band 30 miles long and 250 miles
wide. The crop was picked illicitly to feed the black market centred
on the Carthaginian port of Charax and, despite being fenced off,
was grazed by sheep belonging to Libyan shepherds frustrated by
how little of the wealth generated by the silphium trade was trick-
ling down to them. Strabo in his *Geography* mentions a 'spiteful
incursion' of local Berber nomads who deliberately uprooted the
plant as a protest against punitive taxation.

As it grew scarcer and scarcer, Cyrenaic silphium became pro-
hibitively expensive. 'Don't you remember when a stalk of silphium
sold so cheap?' wonders the sausage-seller Agoracritus in Aristophanes' *The Knights*, before going on to highlight an unmissed
aspect of its one-time abundance: 'The jurymen in the Courts were
almost asphyxiated from farting in each others' faces.'

Eventually Cyrenaic silphium was over-harvested to extinction.
The Romans substituted so-called 'Syrian silphium', the similar
though nastier-smelling species of *Ferula* known to us as asafoetida (see *Asafoetida*). According to Pliny, the last surviving stalk of

Cyrenaic silphium was sent to Emperor Nero as a gift, although he allows for the possibility that there may still be some out there somewhere and even supplies a handy tip for identifying it:

> If an animal does come upon a promising shoot, the sign will be that a sheep after eating it rapidly goes to sleep, whereas a goat sneezes rather loudly.[308]

(Actually, it's true that when they are alarmed by something goats do stamp their feet and make a noise that sounds very like a sneeze.)

The Hypatian philosopher Synesius of Cyrene claimed as late as the fourth century that there was some growing on his brother's farm. One thing is certain: few, if any, of the writers who discourse so confidently on silphium's virtues had seen the plant, and most of the time they were relying on hearsay.

Fast-forward to the sixteenth century and we find John Gerard in his *Herball* (1597) ticking off the ancients for their sloppy vagueness – 'Now then seeing the old writers being imperfect herein, it behooves us in this case to search with more diligence'[309] – before giving an account of silphium cobbled together from Pliny and Theophrastus. Interestingly, Gerard is under the impression that silphium still exists: 'The best groweth upon the high mountains of Cyrene and Africa and is of a pleasant smell.'

Silphium was used in ancient Greek and Roman cooking to lend a rich, garlicky flavour to sauces. Archestratus recommends its use with tripe and boiled sow's womb marinated in cumin and sharp vinegar, and it turns up frequently in *De re coquinaria*, the compilation of recipes attributed to the Roman gourmet Apicius. Not that your average Roman cooked in this manner. These recipes were mocked at the time for their no-expense-spared flamboyance. (Juvenal in his *Satires* asks: 'What greater joke tickles the ear of the people than the sight of a poor Apicius?') So it is ironic that even Apicius seems to have felt the need to be prudent with his supply of silphium. *De re coquinaria* contains a good tip for eking it out:

How You Can Always Have an Ounce of Laser: Put the laser into a small but ample glass cask; count out and add about twenty pine nuts. When laser is required for a recipe, grind the nuts. You will be amazed at the flavours [the pine nuts] will give to food.[310]

Apicius uses silphium in a ragout of pork and forcemeat dumplings named after the poet Matius and in a similar sweet citron ragout, in a basic recipe for lentils alongside coriander seed, mint and rue, in a soup to be made with either spelt or barley and in sauces for crane, duck, wood pigeon, chicken, guinea hen, dove, goose and flamingo. It is essential in *vulvae steriles* (sterile sow's womb) and the accompanying skin, crackling, spare ribs and trotters. It adds pungency to his *ius in elixam omnem* (sauce for all boiled meats) and – my favourite – pig's stomach stuffing:

> Take the paunch of a pig and empty it scrupulously, first washing it with a solution of vinegar and salt, and then with water. Then fill the stomach with these ingredients: pounded and ground pork mixed with three brains with the membranes removed, raw eggs, nuts and peppercorns. Blend this stuffing with a sauce made of these ingredients: ground pepper, lovage, silphium, anise, ginger, and a little rue, the best stock [to moisten], and a little olive oil. Fill the belly with the stuffing, taking care to leave a little empty space lest the stomach burst asunder during cooking. Bind up the two openings with twigs and put it into a pot of boiling water.[311]

Silphium is alleged to have cured fevers, sore throats, indigestion, seizures and leprosy, to have halted hair loss and obliterated warts and growths. Soranus in his *Gynaecology* prescribes it, applied as a balm, for thrush. But it was as a contraceptive and abortifacient that Cyrenaic silphium was most valued: Cyrenaic 4-drachma coins show a naked woman gesturing to the plant with one hand and pointing at her genitals with the other.

One option was to take silphium like the pill. Soranus advises that the monthly consumption of a chickpea-sized quantity 'not only [prevents] conception but also destroys any already existing'. Angus McLaren notes in *A History of Contraception* (1990) that 'references to abortion are far more common in the ancient world than references to contraception',[312] and it is likely that silphium had greater efficacy as an abortifacient than as a prophylactic. Yet Dioscorides, too, lists it as both. Presumably it worked, or it would not have been so popular.

Without knowing exactly what silphium was, it is hard to identify active agents, but in *Eve's Herbs* (1997) the medical historian John Riddle quotes a study showing that crude alcohol extracts of asafoetida and the related *Ferula orientalis L.* inhibited implantation of fertilised ova in rats at rates of 40 and 50 per cent respectively. This would explain why asafoetida is often found as a stand-in for silphium on medieval *quid pro quo* lists of substitute drugs; also why another recognised abortifacient, the Mediterranean weed *Thapsia garganica*, or 'death carrot', is believed by some to be silphium's true identity.

The association of silphium with love and sex is reinforced in contemporary writings such as Catullus' poems to his lover Lesbia. The poem known as Catullus 7 begins:

> You ask how many kissings
> Of yours, Lesbia, would be enough and more for me.
> As great as the number of Libyan sands
> That lie in laserpicium-bearing Cyrene.

Catullus' point is that he and Lesbia can make love for as long as they have access to contraception. The similarity of the shape of silphium seed pods to the traditional heart symbol is remarkable, though use of this scalloped ideograph to denote love dates only from the fourteenth century.

Interest in silphium waned during the Middle Ages as the likes

of pennyroyal, marjoram and angelica formed the basis of contraceptive remedies, but spiked again in the early eighteenth century,
when the German naturalist and explorer Engelbert Kaempfer
mentioned it in *Exotic Pleasures* (1712), his book of 'curious scientific
and medical observations' made in the course of his travels through
Russia, Persia and Japan as ambassador to Charles XI of Sweden.

John Laurence reproduces Kaempfer's account of watching the
asafoetida harvest in his *Complete Body of Husbandry and Gardening* (1726), adding his own clarion call to explorers to seek out the
original and best silphium, which he has heard is 'a wonderful
restorer of lost appetite, a sweetener of the blood, and a strength-
ener of the stomach and masculine vigour', and declaring himself
'far from discouraged in my hopes of getting ... the noble silphium
among us alive':

> [Silphium] was so highly esteemed for its delicate and rich
> flavour in sauces and salads, and so prized for its sovereign use
> in physic that it was dedicated to Apollo and ordered to be hung
> up in his temple at Delphi ... I am persuaded, if some curious
> persons of the East India Company would but search and bring,
> we might soon be possessed of a better treasure than is perhaps
> known at present in the whole [*materia medica*] ... A few years
> since, who would have thought (for it was thought impossible)
> that we could have brought the fruit of the pineapple to perfec-
> tion in England? And have we not now oranges, lemons, pome-
> granates, coffee, capers and what not familiar among us?[313]

Kaempfer thought that there was no difference between
Persian and Syrian silphium, that the resins were in all probability
the product of a single species, *F. assa-foetida*, however differently
adulterated they might have been. (The level and type of adul-
teration could explain the variation in flavour.) Recent botanical
studies suggest Cyrenaic silphium may have been a variant of *F.
tingitana*, which still grows across the Mediterranean and has a

ribbed stem and flowering stalk similar to silphium as depicted on Cyrenean coinage.

SEE ALSO: *Asafoetida, Fennel, Mummia.*

SPIKENARD

Nardostachys jatamansi

Another biblical aromatic, spikenard (or just nard) is produced by crushing the rhizomes of a flowering plant in the Valerian family to release an amber-coloured essential oil. Mary Magdalene uses nard to wash the feet of Jesus in John 12:1–10, angering Judas Iscariot, who asks whether it would not have been better to sell the expensive ointment and give the money to the poor: 'Then took Mary a pound of ointment of spikenard, very costly, and anointed the feet of Jesus, and wiped his feet with her hair; and the house was filled with the odour of the ointment.' (Later, of course, Jesus' dead body is spiced with myrrh and aloes before being placed in the tomb.) Nard is still used in modern aromatherapy, often as a remedy for insomnia.

SEE ALSO: *Cinnamon, Myrrh.*

STAR ANISE

Illicium verum

Despite the large Chinese populations of cities such as New York and Los Angeles, the quintessentially Chinese spice star anise took a while to gain traction in the US. Its importation was permitted only in 1971, when Richard Nixon lifted a twenty-one-year embargo on trade with the Chinese mainland, and at first it was used mainly to flavour pet food. For some reason I thought of this when, the other day, I noticed it was an ingredient in an upmarket brand of supermarket-readymeal beef lasagne. There the effect was cloying and gimmicky and somehow un-Italian, notwithstanding Italians' love of fennel, which contains the same essential oil as star anise, anethole. The subtle differences between similar-tasting spices are hugely important: spices are rarely, if ever, interchangeable.

Star anise is the seed and seed pod from an evergreen tree native to south-western China, *Illicium verum*, whose striking yellow flowers resemble narcissus. The hard brown fruits open out in the form of an eight-pointed star and are harvested just before ripening. Its Chinese names, *bat gok* (Cantonese) and *ba jiao* (Mandarin), both mean 'octagonal'. The points of the star are the carpels, which contain glossy brown seeds. The tree comes into production in its sixth year and can be active for over a hundred years.

Ground, it is the dominant flavour in five-spice powder and used as a rub for meat, especially pork, although whole stars are used to infuse soups and stews much as bay leaves are used in Western cuisine. Tea eggs – eggs boiled in Chinese tea with salt, star anise and soy sauce – also use the whole star. As an individual spice, it is more common in sweet Shanghai or Hu cuisine, with its emphasis on red cooking, the slow-braising technique that imparts a red colour to the finished dish.

Star anise's use in Malaysian cooking dates from the sixteenth and seventeenth centuries, when Indian merchants took Gujarati and south Indian food to Malaysia. There, writes Lizzie Collingham, 'Indian spice mixtures were leavened with star anise which Chinese traders had brought with them to the peninsula'.[314] Its addition to biryani is specific to south India, especially the area around Andhra Pradesh – most recipes for the Hyderabadi version contain it – although it finds its way into some blends of garam masala: for example, the one used in London's upmarket Cinnamon Club restaurant.[315] Star anise is essential to the broth for the Vietnamese beef and noodle soup pho.

Willem Schouten, a navigator for the Dutch East India Company who was the first person to round Cape Horn (which he named after his birthplace, the Dutch city of Hoorn), encountered star anise – or badiane (its Persian name), as he called it – in 1616 on his first trip to Java and the Spice Islands:

> It tastes like anise, whence some call it 'anise of the Indies', though its appearance and structure are quite different.[316]

The spice first found its way to Europe in 1588, in the cargo of the buccaneering English explorer Sir Thomas Cavendish's ship *Desire* – the only one of the three ships he had taken with him on his Drakean circumnavigation two years earlier to make it back to England.

It docked at Plymouth on 9 September, stuffed with plunder: Cavendish's star anise came not from China directly, but from shipping he had attacked near the Philippines. No one knew what to do with it, so it was used as other spices were used, to flavour wines and beers and confectionery (but not, it seems, hot dishes) – much like the sweeter, more aromatic anise, to which it was similar, if botanically unrelated. Star anise is unexpectedly delicious with fruit, especially sweet fruits such as pineapple, and adds piquancy to biscuits, cakes and creamy desserts like bavarois. Cheaper than anise, it is increasingly substituted for it in anise-based liqueurs like Anisette.

In the early 2000s star anise found another, life-saving role as the major industrial source of shikimic acid, a compound involved in the synthesis of the drug oseltamivir – better known as Tamiflu. The pharmaceutical company Roche used so much star anise in the drug's manufacture that in 2005 there was a world shortage of the spice. Farmers in southern China were baffled as their usual trading routine was bent out of shape by middlemen exploiting the fervid, goldrush climate. One farmer told the *Washington Post*: 'Before, it was pretty quiet. Now, I answer my phone all day long. People call from all over the country. It's never been like this before.'[317]

The coincidence that the area where the H5N1 avian flu virus is thought to have originated should also harbour a cure is incredible. But while star anise is used in traditional Chinese medicine to treat abdominal pain and headaches, in its raw state it has no efficacy against flu. (Since 2005 Roche has pioneered a fermentation process that uses *E. coli* bacteria rather than star anise to produce shikimic acid.)

Note well that *I. anisatum*, the Japanese varietal of star anise sometimes used to flavour tea, is highly toxic and can cause seizures and kidney failure.

SEE ALSO: *Fennel, Liquorice.*

SUMAC

Rhus coriaria

Usually sold as a coarse, slightly moist, ferrous-red powder, sumac – from the Arabic *summaq*, meaning 'red' – is ground from the peppercorn-sized dried berries or 'drupes' of *Rhus coriaria*, a shrub that grows wild across the Mediterranean and Middle East. The berries grow in conical clusters. They are harvested at the end of the summer and left on the branch to dry in the sun before being rubbed off. Once they have dried, the berries are ground and, usually, sifted to remove the stony seeds, although it is possible to buy ground sumac with the seeds left in, or indeed unground on the branch if you happen to be in, say, a market in southern Lebanon.

In Iran, Iraq and Turkey sumac is supplied in restaurants as a table-top condiment for sprinkling over kebabs and grilled meats or over onions as an appetiser. In Armenia it adds pep to missahatz, the flatbread pizzas sold by street vendors rolled and wrapped in wax paper. The berries can also be used whole: you crush them lightly, then steep them in water for around twenty minutes. The resulting juice works well in dressings, especially for the Lebanese bread salad fattoush, or can simply be added to dishes like the spicy fish stew samak el harrah. In Lebanon and Syria the habit is to mix sumac with water into a thick paste.

'Almost all houses in the Lebanon would keep a stock of sumac', wrote Tom Stobart in 1970.[318] 'I have used it myself, ever since I discovered it some years ago, for it has a rounded fruity sourness (due to malic acid as in sour apples) without the distinctiveness of vinegar or the brutality of tamarind or lemon.' As a description of sumac's subtly tart flavour, this is spot on. Stobart might have added that sumac is so mild it can be sprinkled by the table-spoonful, although take care first that it hasn't had salt added – a common practice.

Although it doesn't feature in Apicius, sumac is supposed to have been a Roman favourite. Pliny admired its astringent and cooling properties. The Romans imported it from Syria – they called it Syrian sumac. Theophrastus writes that 'tanners use this tree for dyeing white leather' and observes that 'the fruit reddens like the grape, and the appearance of it is like small lentils set close together; the form of these ... is clustering'.[319] Dioscorides recommends sumac as a hair dye and for menstrual and gum disorders.

Sumac occurs in the medieval cookbook known as *Liber de coquina*, in recipes for chicken and for something called Lombard Compost, a sweet-and-sour relish made with turnips, parsnips, figs, apples, pears, carrots, radishes, parsley and fennel, and seasoned with saffron and anise as well as sumac. A Chinese variant, *R. chinensis*, grows in the Himalayas and is used in Nepal to make chutney.

Despite its ubiquity in Middle Eastern cooking since at least the thirteenth century – it is mentioned in al-Baghdadi's *Baghdad Cookery Book* (1226) – sumac was little known in northern Europe until the 2000s, when a new wave of popularisers led by Yotam Ottolenghi and Greg Malouf picked up the baton from Claudia Roden. Roden's pioneering, exquisitely detailed *Book of Middle Eastern Food* (1968), while it demystified the cuisine for Westerners, was hampered in some of its ambitions by the unavailability of key ingredients. Roden has said that when she moved to London from Cairo in the 1950s, sumac and other staples such as pomegranate syrup were almost impossible to obtain. This explains why sumac is absent from the original edition, surfacing only in the revised edition published as *A New Book of Middle Eastern Food* in 1985, which contains a recipe for fatayer bi zahtar, or thyme and sumac pies.

Nowadays, of course, sumac is everywhere, part of a broader trend of Middle Eastern foods formerly regarded as exotic gaining mass acceptance (see *Introduction*, p. 1). In the case of sumac, Ottolenghi rightly takes some of the credit: 'I knew something was achieved when I recently spotted sumac in the spice section of my local Waitrose', the London-based chef writes in *Plenty* (2010), introducing a recipe for fried butter beans with feta, sorrel and sumac. 'I know Waitrose is up-market, but who had even heard of sumac or za'atar [the spice mix of which sumac is a component; see *A Directory of Spice Mixes*, p. 253] a couple of years ago?'[320]

Sumac may not have been known in the West as a foodstuff, but it was popular as an industrial dye in the nineteenth century, when sumac bark was imported into Britain from Sicily for the purpose. In the 1860s the Scottish orientalist Sir Henry Yule went to Celli, near Palermo, where *R. coriaria* grows plentifully, to watch it being ground. He observed: 'There is nothing peculiar in the process of pulverising sumac except the very extraordinary atmosphere produced in the mill. The interior is dark as the most intense London fog, and one comes out saturated with fine powder. The odour is not unpleasant, something between snuff and chamomile.'[321]

Over twenty varieties of sumac grow in North America, including *R. typhina* (or staghorn sumac), *R. glabra* (smooth sumac) and the poisonous *R. vernix* (poison sumac) and *R. toxicodendron* (poison ivy). All parts of the poison sumac plant contain the resin urushiol, which can irritate the skin and, when released in smoke from burning the wood, inflame the lining of the lungs, with sometimes fatal results. Both smooth and staghorn sumac have been used by indigenous Americans as remedies for diarrhoea, asthma, colds and rashes. The Natchez tribe used the root of *R. aromatica* (fragrant sumac) to treat boils. The leaves are mixed with tobacco and smoked, while juice from the crushed berries is sweetened with maple syrup to make sumac tea or cold 'sumac-ade'.

SEE ALSO: *Amchur, Tamarind.*

*
**

SZECHUAN PEPPER

Zanthoxylum piperitum

Szechuan pepper (*Zanthoxylum piperitum*), sometimes called anise pepper because of the resemblance of its ripe seed pods to star anise, isn't poisonous, but, like pink peppercorns, it isn't pepper either. It is the berry of the prickly ash tree, native to the region of China it is named after and one of the spices in both five-spice powder and Japanese seven-flavour spice mix (see *A Directory of Spice Mixes*, pp. 239, 252). Its botanical name derives from the Greek *xanthon xylon*: 'blond wood'.

Szechuan pepper is used extensively in hot, pungent Szechuan cooking, often alongside star anise and ginger, and is mixed with salt to create the condiment hua jiao yen. In isolation its citrusy notes and tendency to numb the mouth come to the fore. Andrew Dalby remarks that one eighth-century emperor used to take his tea with Szechuan pepper and clotted cream.[322] Its ground, dried leaves are the source of the Japanese flavouring sansho, sometimes called Japanese pepper despite the fact that its relationship to pepper is even flimsier than that of the berries.

There are scores of different species of *Zanthoxylum*, the seeds of which are used as spices across China, northern India, Thailand and even Africa: uzazi, the fruit of *Z. tessmannii*, is used sparingly in Nigerian stews. The Tibetan variety of Szechuan pepper is a key ingredient in the sauce that accompanies the Tibetan dumplings momos.

SEE ALSO: *Black pepper, Grains of Paradise, Grains of Selim, Pink peppercorns.*

TAMARIND

Tamarindus indica, syn T. officinalis

The popularity of souring agents such as tamarind and sumac has historically been attributed to the local unavailability of lemons. But while this may be true of sumac in ancient Rome, it can't be so in India and the Middle East, where lemons have long been commonplace. Besides, the fruit's sour-sweet taste is so different that it would be hard to accept lemons, whose bite derives from citric rather than tartaric acid, as an adequate substitute.

Tamarind means 'date of India' (from the Arabic *at-tamr al-hindi*), and the drooping, wind-resistant evergreen, with its grey bark and small clusters of yellow flowers, grows wild across the subcontinent, although it originated in East Africa and was introduced to India by Arab traders and Jewish settlers in the Keralan port city of Cochin. Easy to grow, it became a mainstay of colonial gardens. In Alice Perrin's story 'The Rise of Ram Din' (1906) an Indian father escorts his son to 'where the sahibs dwell beyond the city', hoping to secure him menial work: 'Here it was all open space and broad roads, with trees of mango, teak and tamarind, and the gardens were very beautiful.'[323] When, on the other hand, the British needed to visit the Indian territories in Goa, they protected themselves from harassment by placing a tamarind pod in one ear, exploiting a local belief that fresh tamarind pods were inhabited by demons. This earned them the nickname *lugimlee* or 'tamarind heads'. Mrs M. Grieve expands on the superstition in her *A Modern Herbal* (1931):

> The natives of India consider that the neighbourhood in which tamarind trees grow becomes unwholesome, and that it is unsafe to sleep under the tree owing to the acid they exhale during the moisture of the night. It is said that no plant will live under the shade of it, but in the author's experience some plants and bulbs

bloomed luxuriantly under the tamarind trees in her garden in Bengal.[324]

The spice comes from the tree's curved bean-pod, dark brown when ripe. Inside, a sticky pulp encloses between one and ten shiny black seeds. Usually tamarind is sold either as a paste, a juice concentrate or a compressed block of dried, broken pods, seeds and pulp. To prepare the latter, tear off a tablespoon's worth and soak it in 150 ml of warm water for ten minutes, swirling it occasionally with your fingers. The resulting juice should be strained through a nylon sieve – not a metal one, as this will react with the acid. Syrian Jews cook down this liquid further with salt, lemon juice and sugar to create the dressing and marinade ou'. Similar concentrates exist across the Middle East and are often diluted with ice-cold water to make a tart, refreshing drink, rather as sumac is by Native Americans.

In India tamarind flavours a broad range of foodstuffs from pulses to pork and fish and jellies, from the ginger chutney pulinji to sour vegetable curries and sambar and the rice-based lentil dish bisi bele bath. It lends astringency to okra and aubergine, hence its presence in the Iranian okra stew khoresh bamieh khuzestani and the Egyptian aubergine stew which is one of the highlights of Allegra McEvedy's *Leon: Ingredients and Recipes* (2008). In Iran tamarind is sold in plastic wraps and eaten by children like confectionery. Within Gernot Katzers's observation that 'the sour and fruity taste of tamarind merges well with the heat of chillis' lies the secret of the British curry-house speciality vindaloo.[325]

Vindaloo is not really an Indian curry at all, but a Goan version of the Portuguese carne de vinho e alhos – meat, usually pork, cooked in wine vinegar and garlic. ('Vindaloo' is a mispronunciation of *vinho e alhos*.) Unable to procure wine vinegar, Portuguese colonists mimicked the flavour with tamarind, black pepper and a crude vinegar derived from fermented palm tree sap. The seeds of its colossal popularity in Britain were sown in 1797, when the

British invaded Portuguese-controlled Goa and discovered that the region's Catholic cooks were not bound, as Hindus and Muslims were, by religious rules forbidding the cooking and eating of beef and pork. This led to Goan cooks being highly prized across British India and commanding disproportionately high salaries. (Dane Kennedy, in his introduction to the 2003 Penguin reissue of the explorer Richard Francis Burton's *Goa and the Blue Mountains* (1851): 'Goa was an imperial backwater in the mid-nineteenth century, notable mostly for its export of servants, cooks, clerks, and other labourers to British India.')

You don't have to be a stickler for authenticity to feel that vindaloo has been debased by its reputation for macho hotness. Heat was never the point, and what most people assume to be vindaloo – generic curry sauce turbocharged by chillies to the point of inedibility – is nothing of the sort. 'When filming in Bangladesh a few years ago,' remembers Rick Stein, 'our guide told me that a couple of his friends from Sylhet with restaurants in the UK had been to my restaurant in Padstow, had the monkfish vindaloo and pronounced it not a vindaloo at all. I said nothing, but the recipe came from Rui Madre Deus, my friend in Baga Beach, Goa, and I reflected that I probably knew more about Goan vindaloo than they did.'[326]

Stein's beef vindaloo recipe in *Rick Stein's India* (2013) uses two tablespoons of tamarind liquid in the marinade – as you might imagine vindaloo should. However, runs the counter-argument, tamarind was only used in the first place to replicate the flavour of vinegar. So isn't it more appropriate to use wine vinegar, or malt vinegar, as in the recipe for vindaloo of pork shoulder in *The Cinnamon Club Cookbook* (2003); or even cider vinegar, as in Goan pork curry with potatoes from Madhur Jaffrey's *Curry Nation* (2012)?

As the curry historian Lizzie Collingham explains, the success of vindaloo inspired south Indian cooks to create another Indo-Portuguese fusion food, the fish curry ambot-tik ('sour and hot'), where yet again tamarind's tongue-curling tang is pivotal.

Claudia Roden has stressed the importance of tamarind in Jewish cooking. Her *Book of Jewish Food* (1997) contains a superb sweet-and-sour (and hot) recipe for lamb with red chillies and tamarind which she credits to a Mrs L. Samuel, who contributed it to a Bene Israel (Jewish Indian) cookbook.

The ingredients of Worcestershire Sauce are supposed to be a secret. But according to recipe notes found in a skip at Lea & Perrins' head office in 2009, Worcestershire Sauce contains tamarind extract – which would make sense, as the product's roots are Indian. In 1836 (or so) a retired governor of Bengal by the name of Lord Marcus Sandys went to his local druggists in Worcester, Lee & Perrins, and asked them to make up a recipe for a condiment he had enjoyed in India – a fermented anchovy sauce similar to the Roman garum. The pharmacists had a go, but the result was disappointing and they soon forgot all about it. Eighteen months later, they were clearing out a store room when they came across several barrels of the stuff. And it tasted amazing.

Tamarind is rich in vitamin C and was given to sailors to ward off scurvy. It is also mildly laxative, thanks to the presence of potassium bitartrate (or 'cream of tartar' as it is known in cookery). In Ayurvedic medicine it is used to treat bowel disorders and nausea. Tea made from the leaves is supposed to combat malarial fever, while a paste made from the seeds is painted on insect bites and styes.

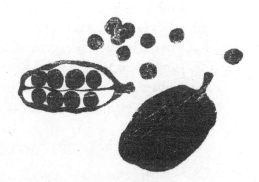

TURMERIC

Curcuma longa

Turmeric is one of the cheapest and most versatile spices. The bright yellow spice is a principal ingredient in one of world's most derided foodstuffs, curry powder (see *A Directory of Spice Mixes,* p. 239). While its acrid, woody flavour is nobody's idea of neutral, it isn't overpowering either. One book attributes its popularity to its success at 'masking the rank ammoniac smell' of decaying fish. Interestingly, though, it never took off in the medieval West as its flavour was considered unexceptional compared with the superficially similar saffron, of which Europe had plentiful, if expensive, supplies.

Turmeric is sometimes called 'Indian saffron' or 'false saffron'. When Marco Polo thought he saw turmeric growing in China in 1280 he wrote: 'There is also a vegetable which has all the properties of true saffron, as well the smell as the colour, and yet it is not really saffron.'[327] In fact, the only property turmeric shares with saffron is its yellowness, unless you count its limited application as a fabric dye. Hindu monks' robes are coloured with turmeric as Minoan tunics were with saffron. But both dyes fade rapidly in sunlight.

C. longa is a robust perennial in the ginger family with densely packed, conical spikes of light yellow flowers. Its name derives from the Latin *terra merita* – 'deserving earth'. Like ginger, it has a thick, round, yellowish rhizome out of which grow short 'fingers'. Harvesting occurs around ten months after planting and involves the whole underground 'system' of roots being lifted. The raw turmeric is then prepared for market: cleaned, cured, boiled, dried either in the sun or in hot ovens, then polished to remove its roughness. During this process the turmeric loses three-quarters of its weight.

Once cured, the turmeric is graded into 'fingers' – these are the highest quality – then 'rounds' and 'splits'. The rhizomes are rock-hard and difficult to grind at home. This is one spice you can be forgiven for buying ready-ground. Or you can peel and slice raw chunks and use them in stews or – even better – pickles.

SEE ALSO: *Fenugreek*.

VANILLA

Vanilla planifolia

For anyone whose childhood was unspent, as Philip Larkin has it, in the Britain of the 1960s and '70s, the word 'vanilla' is intimately bound up with canary-yellow slabs of Wall's ice-cream squished between brittle, sugared-cardboard wafers. Funnily enough, the 1970s especially was a boom-time for ice-cream engineering. The Cornetto, where a careful layering of oil and chocolate insulates the cone from the ice-cream and stops it from going soggy, was invented in 1976 by the Italian company Spica and had the immediate effect of making all other ice creams look rather basic.

But the simple vanilla block had a nostalgic force, harking back as it did to the less frenetic days of the 1920s when butcher Thomas Wall II finally implemented a scheme he had dreamed up before the First World War – to use his factories and staff to make ice-cream over the summer months when demand for pies and sausages fell.

Vanilla is still, for most people, the 'default' ice-cream flavour; the base-camp from which we light out for more exotic taste territories. And despite what we tell ourselves, we are a conservative breed when it comes to food. Tim Ecott, in his book *Vanilla: Travels in Search of the Luscious Substance* (2004), observes that 'British ice-cream buyers choose vanilla 90 per cent of the time'.[328]

Not that vanilla ice-cream lacks a noble heritage. Between 1784 and 1789, before he became the third president of the US, Thomas Jefferson spent time in Paris as minister to France. There, he had his first taste of vanilla ice-cream and was so bowled over that he asked the chef (possibly his butler, Adrien Petit) for the recipe. Jefferson's handwritten copy can be found at the Library of Congress. It begins:

> mix the yolks & sugar
> put the cream on a fire in a casserole, first putting in a stick of
> Vanilla.
> when near boiling take it off & pour it gently into the mixture
> of eggs & sugar.
> stir it well …

The claim, sometimes made, that Jefferson introduced ice-cream into America is false. It was being made by colonists as early as the mid-eighteenth century, perhaps using the recipe in Hannah Glasse's *Art of Cookery* (1751), which involves raspberries. But Jefferson undoubtedly popularised it by serving it at presidential banquets – one diner, the physician Samuel Mitchill, noted that 'ice-creams were produced in the form of balls of the frozen material inclosed in covers of warm pastry, exhibiting a curious contrast, as if the ice had just been taken from the oven'[329] – and the food orders he placed with William Short, US chargé d'affaires in Paris, contain frequent requests for the 'batons' [pods] of vanilla Jefferson was unable to source locally.

The green-stemmed, creeping vanilla orchid – from the Spanish *vainilla*, a diminutive of *vaina* or 'pod' – is indigenous to the rainforests of south-eastern Mexico, Central America and the West Indies. There are more than a hundred different species, but almost all the cultivated vanilla in the world comes from *Vanilla planifolia* (sometimes called *V. fragrans*), which in its wild state can grow to 80 feet tall. Its long, narrow pod is harvested unripe, at which stage it has no flavour at all. For the pods to have any culinary application, fermentation must be forced by dipping them in hot water, sweating them for ten days (spreading them out in the sun, then wrapping them in blankets overnight) and then drying them in the sun.

This curing process, called the 'Bourbon method' after the French Indian Ocean island (renamed Réunion in 1793) on which it was first employed, can take five or six months, over the course of which the beans lose four-fifths of their weight. It is onerous, intensive work, which requires constant vigilance: growers compare it to looking after a newborn baby. At the end of the curing, the active ingredient vanillin emerges in the form of a crystalline surface frosting called *givre* – although for some reason Tahitian vanilla pods become flavoursome without ever producing *givre*. In Uganda in the 1970s the American spice company McCormick set up a factory for the rapid, artificial curing of cut beans, but the venture was not a success.

Only in the 1990s did the Ugandan vanilla industry revive, and nowadays many smaller Ugandan producers prefer to use the Bourbon method because it gives better results. Production of cured vanilla in the French islands (Réunion, Mauritius and Madagascar) surpassed that of Mexico, the one-time centre of production, in the early twentieth century. By 1929 Madagascar was supplying over 80 per cent of the world market, and it has continued to do so ever since.

Because vanilla is expensive – demand massively exceeds supply – much of what passes for vanilla is synthetic vanilla flavouring. 'The cheap "vanilla ice-cream" of Britain, which contains very little vanilla and less cream, is surely destined for renaming', says Andrew Dalby.[330] Vanillin is a phenol with a similar structure to eugenol (found in cloves) and isoeugenol (nutmeg). It can be manufactured easily from coal tar or, more commonly, waste pulp liquor, a by-product of the paper-making process:

Waste liquor consists mainly of lignin, a substance found in and between the cell walls of land plants. Lignin contributes to the rigidity of plants and makes up about 25 per cent of the dry weight of wood. It is not one compound but a variable cross-bonded polymer of different phenolic units.[331]

The interesting thing about synthetic vanillin is that it is not fake, not an imitation, even though it is created using an artificial process. It is chemically identical to vanillin from the vanilla bean. But vanilla from vanilla beans has a richer flavour – sweet, aromatic, musky – because of the numerous other compounds present. So, ironically, the purity of synthetic vanillin counts against it, giving it a harsh odour and bitter aftertaste. That said, wood-based vanillin is considered a force for good in the wine-making world: 'When wine is stored in oak casks, vanillin molecules are leached from the wood, contributing to the changes that constitute the ageing process.'[332]

The first known use of vanilla is as a flavouring for chocolate. When the conquistadores were in Mexico in 1520, the soldier who would go on to be Hernán Cortés's historian, Bernal Díaz del Castillo, noticed the Aztec emperor Montezuma drinking chocolate flavoured with what the Aztecs called *tlilxochitl* (ground black vanilla pods) mixed with honey. Diaz noted that the Aztecs drank their chocolate cold, whipped into a froth so thick 'it must be taken with the mouth wide open'.

The first written reference to the vanilla orchid comes in 1552, when it appears in a Vatican herbal called the *Badianus Code*. Its authors list *tlilxochitl* as 'an ingredient in a nosegay, a potion to protect against infection and worn around the neck when travelling'.[333] In 1602 Hugh Morgan, the Essex-born apothecary to Queen Elizabeth I, suggested it might have wider culinary applications, and in her final years the queen came to like its flavour so much that she allegedly demanded that all her food be flavoured with vanilla (although similar stories are told of several spices and hard to verify). By 1700 the French had started using it to scent tobacco.

Nowadays, four main types of vanilla are cultivated: Bourbon, grown across the Indian Ocean islands; Tahitian vanilla, from French Polynesia, which has a floral tang and comes from the strain *V. tahitiensis*; West Indian vanilla, from the *V. pompona* variety grown mostly in the Caribbean; and Mexican vanilla, made from *V. planifolia* but sometimes adulterated with tonka bean extract.

Both Casanova and the Marquis de Sade used vanilla as an aphrodisiac. Casanova once ate a lock of a lover's hair inside a sweet flavoured with 'essences of ambergris, angelica, vanilla, alkermes and styrax'. Sade liked to serve his dinner guests a chocolate pudding containing vanilla and the urethral irritant cantharides (or 'Spanish fly'). In his letters, 'vanilla' was Sade's code word for 'aphrodisiacs intended to improve the quality of his orgasms'.[334] 'Manilla', on the other hand, was his private euphemism for masturbation. In 1784, Sade wrote to his wife from prison:

> I know full well that vanille causes overheating and that one should use manille in moderation. But what do you expect? When that is all one has ... One good hour in the morning for five manilles, artistically graduated from 6 to 9, a good half hour in the evening for three more ...

Vanilla flowers do not pollinate easily. In 1836 the Belgian botanist Charles Morren noticed that the plants could not produce fruit naturally unless melipona stingless bees specific to Mexico and Central America were present; also that the window for pollination was narrow as the orchid flower remained in bloom for only twenty-four hours. The French attempted to transplant vanilla to Mauritius, Madagascar and Réunion but did not succeed until a method of artificial pollination was invented in 1841 by a twelve-year-old slave on Réunion called Edmond Albius. Albius used the pointed tip of a bamboo stick to lift the rostellum, the flap separating the male anther from the female stigma, before pressing the sticky pollen mass into the stigma with his thumb.

Soon, Ecott explains, 'the boy Edmond was in great demand, despatched in a carriage on a tour of other plantations so that he could demonstrate the art of "orchid marriage" to other slaves. His sensational trick, *le geste d'Edmond*, was about to make many of their masters rich.'[335]

Albius himself, however, did not benefit. Freed in 1848, when France abolished slavery in its colonies, he was nevertheless convicted of stealing jewellery shortly afterwards. The ten-year prison sentence he received was commuted in recognition of his contribution to the vanilla industry.

Good-quality vanilla essence is as useful and effective as the beans, although these can last for years if kept correctly, so don't worry too much about expense. Store the beans in sugar and the sugar will take on the vanilla flavour. Veterans of school cake sales know that vanilla can be overused in baking with sickly results – the *Hummingbird Bakery Cookbook* (2009) has a lot to answer for – but Nigella Lawson's Devil's Food Cake, from *Kitchen* (2010), mixes vanilla with muscovado sugar and high-quality cocoa to create a cake that Montezuma himself would surely have appreciated.

Vanilla is an ingredient – sometimes secret – in a wide range of processed foods and (hateful word) beverages. Its presence in Coca-Cola has been rumoured for years, and it is certainly in the 'original' recipe found in the diary of its inventor, John S. Pemberton. Tim Ecott repeats an anecdote widely believed by vanilla dealers and growers – that there was more to the reformulated Coke introduced in 1985 as New Coke than a desire to take on sweeter rival Pepsi by adding more sugar. In fact, he suggests, Coca-Cola wanted to limit its reliance on vanilla, whose cost and availability fluctuate markedly, so massively reduced the quantity of vanilla in the Coke formula. This sounds plausible, but fails to explain why in 2002 the company decided to do the opposite of this by launching Coca-Cola Vanilla, which despite its spluttering take-off (it was discontinued, then relaunched) has been a global commercial hit. Real vanilla is still preferred over synthetic vanilla by high-end ice-cream manufacturers, although the addition of black vanilla seeds as a badge of authenticity is purely cosmetic: the seeds don't actually taste of anything.

Vanilla is used in liqueurs such as Galliano and is a favourite in milk-based puddings, especially cordon bleu warhorses like *crème à la vanille*. Most modern versions of the medieval drink eggnog contain it. A personal favourite, Claire Macdonald's Eggnog and Chocolate Pie, from *Celebrations* (1989), uses vanilla in the pastry rather than the filling.

In perfumery vanilla often constitutes the base note – the smell that lingers after other more impactful but volatile smells have faded.

WORMWOOD

Artemisia absinthium

Wormwood, or *Artemisia absinthium*, is a perennial with a sharp, pungent smell and greeny-grey foliage covered with fine hairs and tubular yellow flowers. Easily cultivated, it is found across Europe, North America and Asia, and often grown as an ornamental. Its preference is for wild, dry, rocky slopes.

So is it a herb or a spice? Its relative tarragon (*A. draculuncus*) is always classed as a herb, and it is wormwood's dried leafy parts that are used. But – and yes, I know this is woolly and unscientific – it feels to me more like a spice. It *behaves* more like a spice, generating the 'spice effect' discussed earlier (see *Introduction*, p. 9), having been employed since antiquity to add a bracing bitterness to infusions and alcoholic drinks, including mead and purl, a fortified beer popular with Samuel Pepys which Martyn Cornell describes as

> ale heated until almost boiling ... with a shot of gin, generally in the ration of ten parts ale to one part spirits, and flavourings of the maker's choice: usually something bitter, such as Roman wormwood (less powerful than 'standard' wormwood), with perhaps orange peel, ginger and, by the middle of the nineteenth century at least, sugar.[336]

The name wormwood, derived, like vermouth, from the Old English *wermod*, probably refers to its traditional use as a remedy for tapeworm. When, in 1996, the grave of an Iron-Age druid was discovered in the Essex village of Stanway, the tools of his trade were found to include scalpels, retractors, a surgical saw – and a strainer containing traces of artemisia pollen. The tea that was presumably strained through this would have been a remedy for something – to banish worms or venereal disease, promote menstruation or induce an abortion. John Evelyn possessed a recipe for a medicinal wormwood ale, to be drunk 'every morning at 4 or 5 of the clock', after which the imbiber is directed to go back to sleep. 'For the shortness of breath [... it] is excellent,' he tells us.[337]

Wormwood is best known to us, however, as one of the flavourings in absinthe, along with anise and fennel. This foul-tasting spirit's invention was always credited, in the murky, romantic folklore that surrounds absinthe, to one Dr Pierre Ordinaire, a political refugee from the French Revolution who settled in the Swiss canton of Neuchâtel in the 1790s. In fact, the original formula was devised by a local apothecary, Henriette Henriod, bought by one of her customers, Daniel-Henri Dubied, who had been impressed by the way Henriod's 'elixir' cured his indigestion and fired his libido, and mass-produced by Dubied's son-in-law Henri-Louis Pernod, who by 1849 was running twenty-five distilleries in and around Pontarlier in the Franche-Comté region of eastern France.

Absinthe was adopted with enthusiasm by the middle classes in the puffed-up Paris of Napoleon III's Second Empire. *L'heure verte* – the optimum time for taking absinthe as an aperitif – was between six and seven o'clock in the evening. But as France's wine industry failed, brought to its knees by the vine disease phylloxera, absinthe's status as a bourgeois tipple faltered. Cheap, often adulterated absinthe replaced wine as the drink of the poor, and the spirit's respectable reputation was tarnished. The resulting dissolute scene, which would culminate in absinthe becoming a byword for *fin-de-siècle* decadence, provided ready subject matter for writers and artists, many of whom (Verlaine, Rimbaud, Baudelaire, Van Gogh, Toulouse-Lautrec) drank the stuff to excess. Its British fans included Oscar Wilde and Aubrey Beardsley.

Manet's 1859 painting *The Absinthe Drinker* is a sombre, autumn-hued portrait of an alcoholic rag-picker called Collardet, dressed like an aristocrat in a top hat and cloak. (The half-full glass of absinthe on the ledge next to him was added much later, between 1867 and 1872.) It appalled Manet's teacher Thomas Couture, who exclaimed: 'An absinthe drinker! And they paint abominations like that!' Degas's later *Dans un Café* (1876), rechristened *L'Absinthe* in 1893, was posed by two models, the painter and etcher Marcellin Desboutin, who did not drink absinthe, and an actress called Ellen Andrée. Both paintings were initially reviled by critics because of their low subject matter.

Absinthe historian Jad Adams observes that by the time Degas painted *Dans un Café* 'all the elements of the absinthe story were in place: it was the hallucinogen for artists, the poison for the poor, and the sophisticated drink for the bourgeoisie. There was also the dreadful but unconfirmed fear that absinthe rendered its drinkers both bad and mad.'[338]

Worries about absinthe's effects were stoked by English

sensation novels such as Marie Corelli's *Wormwood: A Drama of Paris* (1890), whose middle-class narrator, Gaston Beauvais, plumbs the depths of *absintheur* hell to become 'a slinking, shuffling beast, half monkey, half man, whose aspect is so vile, whose body is so shaken with delirium, whose eyes are so murderous, that if you met me by chance in the day-time you would probably shriek from sheer alarm'.[339]

Moves to prohibit absinthe gained support, and by 1915 the liqueur had been banned in the US and across much of Europe, including France. In 1988 it was legalised in all EU countries apart from France, although a loophole meant that wormwood-based spirits could be sold there as long as they were not called absinthe. The ban was lifted in France in 2011, basically to annoy Swiss distillers who were trying to persuade the EU that the drink was a regional product, like Parma ham, and that they should be awarded sole manufacturing rights.

Whatever else absinthe's effects were – and we shall come to them presently – the main reason it wrecked lives was its high alcohol content: typically between 65 and 72 per cent proof. One function of the alcohol was to keep the oils in solution. Once water was added, as it was supposed to be before the absinthe was drunk, they were emulsified, turning the green liquid cloudy – an effect known as 'louching' which occurs in other anise-flavoured liqueurs and spirits like ouzo, pastis and raki.

The controversy over wormwood centres on thujone, the chemical compound found in the plant that is supposedly responsible for absinthe's psychoactive qualities. Even in small quantities it can cause convulsions and renal failure; but then you would expect a similar outcome in instances of extreme alcohol abuse. Historic accounts of wormwood intoxication suggest cannabis-like effects, as in Oscar Wilde's explanation of absinthe's effects to Ada Leverson:

Take a top hat. You think you see it as it really is. But if you had never heard of one before and suddenly saw it alone, you'd be frightened or laugh. That is the effect absinthe has, and that is why it drives men mad.[340]

Towards the end of the nineteenth century there was widespread pessimism in European artistic and intellectual circles about the future of civilised societies. Theories of 'degeneration' focused on organic decline – the sort of negative evolution witnessed by H. G. Wells's Traveller in *The Time Machine* (1895). The French psychiatrist Valentin Magnan (1835–1916) thought that alcohol, but particularly absinthe, was a catalyst for degeneration because the madness it induced was, he believed, hereditary. Magnan conducted extensive research into whether absinthe abusers experienced an 'absinthe effect' over and above the effect an abuser of alcohol alone might experience. Magnan decided they did, and stated confidently:

> Absinthe acts in the same way as belladonna, henbane, datura, and haschisch [cannabis] and does not require, like alcohol, to prepare its way, for, as is shown by physiological experiment, it can rapidly give rise to hallucinations and delirium before the alcohol contained in the liqueur of absinthe has had time to produce trembling in man.[341]

Unfortunately, Magnan's experiments were extremely crude. Some guinea pigs he stuck in a glass jar next to a saucer containing essence of wormwood; others he placed next to a saucer of pure alcohol. The former experienced 'epileptiform convulsions' after inhaling wormwood vapour; but then the quantity of thujone present in the vapour was exponentially greater than it would have been in absinthe, where the thujone content is actually minuscule. A study carried out in 2005 recreated three absinthe recipes from 1899, tested them using gas chromatography-mass spectrometry and found that the highest contained only 4.3 mg of thujone per litre.[342] In other words, estimates of thujone levels in pre-ban absinthe were hugely exaggerated. Absinthe is no hallucinogen.

Some modern-day absinthe manufacturers boast about their products' high thujone levels. But as the Wormwood Society's website politely points out, 'one would die of alcohol poisoning long before one could consume enough absinthe to get a substantial dose of thujone'.

The wormwood that falls as a star from the sky in Revelations, its bitterness causing men to die in great numbers, is thought to be not *A. absinthium* but 'biblical wormwood' or *A. judaica*, a species particular to Israel, Egypt and Saudi Arabia. Others have pointed to *A. herba-alba* or 'white wormwood', which grows abundantly in Israel's desert regions and is made into a tea by the Bedouin of the Sinai and the Negev. The Hebrew word usually translated as wormwood, one that features eight times in the Bible, is *laanah*. But, as Michael Zohary points out in *Plants of the Bible* (1982), there is no accurate translation for *laanah* or contextual evidence that *laanah* is a bitter plant: 'Because it is frequently coupled with rosh [poison hemlock], some scholars believe that the two words are synonymous, like other name-pairs in the Bible.'[343]

SEE ALSO: *Nutmeg, Poppyseed*.

ZEDOARY

Curcuma zedoaria

When spices fall out of fashion, it is often because they are insufficiently distinctive and so supplanted by rival spices that do a similar job more effectively. So it is with zedoary. This bitter, camphorous spice (*Curcuma zedoaria*), native to north-east India but cultivated across Asia, is a plant in the Zingiberaceae family whose brown-skinned rhizome smells faintly of mango and tastes like ginger. Zedoary bears yellow flowers with red and green bracts. Before it can be harvested it must mature for two years.

Known in Indonesia as kentjur, zedoary crops up raw in Thai salads, in Indonesian rempah meatballs and the peanut sauce for the boiled-vegetable salad gado-gado, and in Indian pickles (achar). It is often mixed with ginger and turmeric to add a pungent top note in seafood curries. It can be bought as a powder or in dried slices presenting a grey surface with a yellowish interior. A starch obtained from the root called shoti is used in India as a thickener and in Indonesia as a baby food.

Generally, zedoary is nowadays used more in perfumery and medicines than in cooking – as indeed it was when Arab traders first brought it to Europe in the sixth century. It is a component of *abir*, an Indian talcum powder sprinkled on clothes and thrown into the air by Hindus at the Holi festival. In China during the T'ang dynasty (618–906) it was mixed with saffron and camphor and strewn on paths before the emperor.

Zedoary is absent from Greek and Roman medicine directories, although interestingly it features in the *Lacnunga*, the collection of Anglo-Saxon medical texts and prayers, which suggests it was known in England before the tenth century. One use in particular stands out – as an ingredient in a 'holy drink' against elfin enchantment.[344]

The spice's heyday seems to have been the Middle Ages, although, as Andrew Dalby points out, it was often confused by both Arab and European writers with a form of wild ginger called zerumbet (*Zingiber zerumbet*): 'Both came from the East and both names percolated into European languages from Arabic (*zadwâr, zarunbâd*).'[345] He quotes Nicholas Culpeper, who believes that, although the plants look different, their effect is the same: 'They are both hot and dry in the second degree, expel wind, resist poison, stop fluxes and the menses, stay vomiting, help the colic, and kill worms. You may take half a dram at a time.'[346] In his _Medicinal Dispensatory_ (1657) the French royal physician Jean de Renou notes that zedoary is related to zerumbet but 'more vulgar and notorious'. Besides, he adds, 'neither plant have [sic] been seen whole by any almost in Europe.'[347]

Called kuchoora in India, where it originated, and lempoyang in Malaysia, Z. _zerumbet_ crops up in perfumes and soaps. The plant has leafy stems with flower heads roughly 3 inches long, which enclose small yellow-white flowers. Once these bulbous heads have matured and turned bright red, a fragrant, watery sap will gush from them when they are manipulated. This sap can be drunk, though it is also effective as a shampoo – hence another name for zerumbet, 'shampoo ginger'.

Writing at the end of the thirteenth century, the Montpellier-based physician Bernard de Gordon declares in his _Lilium medicinae_: 'Here is something new that is commonly done now: give ground zedoary seed to drink with broth or wine, and without doubt it kills all [worms].' The history of humanity is the history of human infestation with parasites. Much of the world population still carries what epidemiologists call a 'worm burden'. In the Middle Ages this burden would have been especially heavy. Gilbertus Anglicus, author of the medical encyclopaedia _Compendium medicinae_ (c. 1230), witnessed worm infestations so acute they drove patients mad:

> Sometimes they seem to be frenetic, sometimes maniacal, sometimes melancholic; sometimes they fall silent like lethargic apoplectics; sometimes they fall down like epileptics; sometimes they faint like in the suffocation of the womb; sometimes they suffer runs like in dysentery; sometimes they grind their teeth and shout like in sciatica; sometimes they beat their bellies like in colic.[348]

Bernard de Gordon is persuasive on the subject of zedoary, as he was on many others – he was one of the first medical writers to identify leprosy, scabies and anthrax as contagious – but of course there was no shortage of antihelminthics (worm remedies). The most popular was easy-to-find wormwood, but mugwort, penny-royal and mulberry bark were also used.

In humoral terms these were hot, dry medicines designed to counter the phlegmatic conditions in which worms thrived. Zedoary's scarcity means it would have been used only rarely, and the medical historian Luke DeMaitre attributes belief in its efficacy to mystique: medicines such as zedoary and ambergris, a waxy substance secreted by the intestines of sperm wales, were 'especially appreciated because they were exotic and expensive'.[349]

Yet zedoary is used extensively in traditional Chinese medicine to treat digestive disorders and promote menstrual function. Sometimes zedoary is called 'white turmeric'; sometimes the word denotes not just *C. zedoaria* but also *C. phaeocaulis Val.*, a close relative grown in the Szechuan, Guangdong and Guangxi provinces of China. Zedoary's reputation as a purgative may account for its presence in bitter tonic drinks such as Swedish Bitters. Dehydrocurdione, a sesquiterpene isolated from zedoary, has been found to be effective as an anti-inflammatory when tested on arthritic mice.[350]

SEE ALSO: *Ginger, Turmeric.*

A DIRECTORY OF SPICE MIXES

This is a round-up of some of the more common spice blends (pastes and liquors as well as dry mixtures) from around the world. Bear in mind that for most of them, particularly the ones from India, Africa and south-east Asia, there is no single, definitive recipe. Their composition is prone to massive variation according to region, family, chef and food type. Feel liberated rather than scared by this!

ADVIEH

The warm, fragrant Persian mix advieh – Persian for 'spice mixture' – almost always contains turmeric, cinnamon, cloves, cardamom, ginger and cumin. It is more commonly made in the home than bought pre-prepared, although in its more generic manifestations it is very similar to garam masala or even curry powder (see below). A cook might use one blend for hearty lamb-based dishes (where it cuts through the fattiness) and another for light sprinkling over rice. Alan Davidson distinguishes between advieh from the south of Iran – broadly the recipe above, though without the ginger – and advieh from the north-west of the country, which is more subtle and delicate and includes rose petals or buds. Najmieh Batmanglij's recipe in her book *A Taste of Persia* (2007) is simple but effective, containing two tablespoons of rose petals, cinnamon and cardamom and one tablespoon of cumin.

APPLE PIE MIX

One of those mixes it seems incredible people would rather buy ready-made than blend for themselves, this usually combines cinnamon, cloves and nutmeg. Arguably, the fashionable addition of cardamom and ginger gilds the lily. (See *Mixed spice*, below.) A similar combination called Pumpkin Pie Spice is popular in America and often contains allspice as well. Note, though, that 'pompyon-pie' was popular in England in the seventeenth and eighteenth centuries. Here is the recipe in Hannah Woolley's *The Gentlewoman's Companion* (1675):

> Take a pound of Pompion, and slice it; an handful of Time, a little Rosemary, sweet Marjoram stripped off the stalks, chop them small; then take Cinamon, Nutmeg, Pepper, and a few Cloves, all beaten; also ten Eggs, and beat them all together, with as much Sugar as you shall think sufficient; then fry them like a Froise; and being fried, let them stand till they are cold; Then fill your Pye after this manner: Take Apples sliced thin round-wise, and lay a layer of the Froise, and another of the Apples, with Currans betwixt the layers; be sure you put in good store of sweet Butter before you close it. When the Pye is baked, take six yolks of Eggs, some White-wine or Verjuice, and make a Caudle thereof, but not too thick; cut up the lid and put it in, and stire them well together whilst the Eggs and Pompions are not perceived, and so serve it up.[351]

BAHARAT

A Middle Eastern mix whose seemingly exotic name is, like advieh, a basic product description: *bahārāt* is the Arabic for 'spices', apparently derived from *bharata*, the Sanskrit word for the Indian subcontinent. Typical spices in baharat are black pepper, cassia or cinnamon, cloves, coriander seed, cumin, nutmeg and dried red chilli peppers. It is sometimes called Lebanese seven-spice mix (and fenugreek substituted for ginger). In Turkey mint is often added and in Syria allspice, while in the Gulf states adding bay leaves and dried lime powder to a basic baharat creates the mix for the rice dishes kabsa. Gil Marks says that the Iranian version is added to cheroset, the fruit and nut paste eaten by Jews at Passover Seder.

BERBERE

From Ethiopia and Eritrea, berbere contains fenugreek, ajowan, garlic, chilli peppers, rue, nigella and ginger. A common addition is the 'false' or 'Ethiopian' cardamom known as korarima (*Afromomum corrorima*). In Ethiopia its preparation is highly ritualised, the chillies being dried in the sun for as long as three days before being mixed with the other spices and left out to dry once again. The result, fiery as well as aromatic, is best appreciated in dishes like the chicken stew doro wat and the lamb dish yebeg alicha.

In 1887, at a feast to consecrate the church of Entoto Maryam in the recently founded city of Addis Ababa, Queen Taytu Bitul served an enormous feast for which over 5,000 oxen, cows, goats and sheep were slaughtered and a 'river' devised of tej (honey wine) flowing into the banquet hall on wooden troughs. The berbere, of great symbolic importance as it was supposed to reflect the scale of the country's trade networks, contained cayenne pepper, garlic, ginger, pounded shallots, rue, basil, cloves, cinnamon, cardamom, Grains of Paradise and ajowan: 'These peppers, rare and much prized in the 1600s, had become by 1887 a staple crop of the empire's lowlands and Rift Valley conquests.'[352]

BIZAR A'SHUWA

A mix from Oman, courtesy of Jill Norman in her *Herbs and Spices: The Cook's Reference* (2015), based on a recipe in *Al Azaf: the Omani Cookbook* by Lamees Abdullah Al Taie. Cumin, coriander, cardamom, chilli, turmeric and cloves are blended with vinegar and garlic to make a stiff paste for rubbing on meat.

CAJUN

Acadians – whence 'Cajun' – are the descendants of the French colonists of Acadia in the north-east of North America who settled in south Louisiana in the eighteenth century after the Great Derangement, when the British forced them out of their settlements. Cajun cuisine marries French traditions with Creole and Native American ones to create dishes such as jambalaya and gumbo. The main spices used are cayenne pepper, paprika, possibly cumin; also Tabasco sauce, invented in Louisiana in 1868. There should be some garlic in there too.

CASSAREEP

A thick, stock-like base for stews such as pepperpot, made in Guyana from cassava root, spiced with cloves, cinnamon, black pepper and cayenne pepper. Strongly antimicrobial, cassareep makes it possible to keep a stew for several days without refrigeration, even in hot weather. But if the cassava root is not boiled for long enough in the early stages of cooking, cassareep can be fatal as in its raw state the root contains hydrogen cyanide.

CHAR MASALA

A spice mix from Afghanistan – equal parts cinnamon, cloves, cumin and either black or green cardamom – used specifically to flavour rice.

CHERMOULA

A spicy marinade and/or condiment used in North African cuisine that varies in composition from dish to dish. There are countless recipes, but I base mine on Ghillie B. Başan's recipes from her book *Tagine* (2007). For her baked tagine of lamb with quinces, figs and honey the chermoula contains garlic, ginger, red chilli peppers, salt, coriander (the herb), parsley, ground coriander seed, ground cumin seed, olive oil, honey and the juice of a lemon. The mix for her fish tagine with preserved lemon and mint is subtly different, dropping the ginger, coriander seed and honey and adding saffron.

CHINESE FIVE-SPICE POWDER

This subtle, delicate mix, used throughout China and Vietnam, usually contains equal parts of cassia, cloves, star anise, Szechuan pepper and fennel seed – but some recipes also include liquorice, ginger, nutmeg and turmeric. Five-spice powder can and often does contain more than five spices. The importance of 'five' is thought to relate to the Chinese categorisation of natural phenomena into five elements (wood, fire, earth, metal, water). Taste, correspondingly, is reduced to five flavours (sour, bitter, sweet, pungent, salty), each of which is represented in five-spice. Five-spice works particularly well with fatty meats such as duck and pork.

CURRY POWDER

The word 'curry' is a second-generation derivation of the Tamil *kari* and the Portuguese *caril*, meaning 'sauce'. But in colonial India it was applied in blanket style to a mass of different region-specific dishes, becoming one of the staples of Anglo-Indian cuisine. As the food historian Lizzie Collingham explains, this cuisine was impressively pan-Indian in the way that it 'absorbed techniques and ingredients from every Indian region and was eaten throughout the entire length and breadth of the subcontinent'. But the only people doing the eating were the British, and 'no Indian ... would have referred to his or her food as a curry'.[353]

The British were aware that food eaten in Goa was different from that in, say, the Punjab. But with every attempt to categorise ('Madras curry' was vaguely hot and red) came dilution: the mighty Mughal dish korma, from the Urdu *kormah*, meaning 'to braise', became the insipid mulch of almonds and coconut milk it still is in many British curry-houses. What often passes for korma has as much to do with English spiced medieval cooking as it does with India.

The first known recipe for 'currey' in an English cookbook is in Hannah Glasse's *Art of Cookery Made Plain and Easy* (1747). The daughter of a prosperous Northumberland gentleman, Glasse made a bad marriage and wrote her way out of reduced circumstances, observing in her introduction: 'I believe I have attempted a Branch of Cookery which Nobody has yet thought worth their while to write upon.' She fixed in print recipes that until then had only been informally disseminated. Interestingly, her curry is spiced with just coriander seed and black pepper, although notice how particular are her instructions for preparing them:

> TAKE two Fowls or Rabbits, cut them into small Pieces, and three or four small Onions, peeled and cut very small, thirty Pepper Corns, and a large Spoonfull of Rice, brown some Coriander Seeds over the Fire in a clean Shovel, and beat them to Powder, take a Tea Spoonful of Salt, and mix all well together with the Meat, put all together in a Sauce-pan or Stew-pan, with a Pint of Water, let it stew softly till the Meat is enough, then put in a Piece of Fresh Butter, about as big as a large Walnut, shake it well together, and when it is smooth and of a fine Thickness dish it up, and send it to Table. If the Sauce be too thick, add a little more Water before it is done, and more Salt if it wants it. You are to observe the Sauce must be pretty thick.

The first English restaurant to serve curry was the Norris Street Coffee House, in London's Haymarket, in 1773. The first Indian-owned restaurant in the city was Sake Dean Mahomet's Hindustan Coffee House at 34 George Street, where diners could smoke hookahs filled with 'real Chilim tobacco'. By the 1860s, when Mrs Beeton was writing her recipes for an 'Indian dish of fowl', mulligatawny soup and (a fascinating colonial conflation) curried kangaroo tails, the British love affair with curry was well under way and the idea that Indian food might be cooked at home was no longer considered eccentric.

Victorian women's periodicals teemed with recipes and articles by memsahibs promoting curries as novel, exotic additions to a household menu. The middle-class housewife ignored these developments at her peril, implied Mrs Beeton, now that 'men are ... so well served out of doors – at their clubs, well-ordered taverns, and dining houses'.[354]

If curry had the advantage of cheapness, being perfect for using up leftover scraps of meat and fish, it could also, when desired, be rich and luscious. The novelist William Makepeace Thackeray, born in Calcutta where his father was secretary to the board of revenue in the British East India Company, treats the home-cooking of curry as a form of erotic revue in 'Poem to Curry', one of his *Kitchen Melodies* anonymously published in *Punch* magazine:

Three pounds of veal my darling girl prepares,
And chops it nicely into little squares;
Five onions next procures the little minx
(The biggest are the best, her Samiwel thinks),
And Epping butter nearly half a pound,
And stews them in a pan until they're brown'd.
What's next my dexterous little girl will do?
She pops the meat into the savoury stew,
With curry-powder table-spoonfuls three,
And milk a pint (the richest that may be),
And, when the dish has stewed for half an hour,
A lemon's ready juice she'll o'er it pour.
Then, bless her! Then she gives the luscious pot
A very gentle boil – and serves quite hot.
PS – Beef, mutton, rabbit, if you wish,
Lobsters, or prawns, or any kind fish,
Are fit to make a CURRY. 'Tis, when done,
A dish for Emperors to feed upon.

In Indian households spices would have been bought fresh, then

purpose-ground on a millstone, in some cases by a specially designated scullion or *masalchi*. Plainly, this was impossible for English
cooks, who lacked both the expertise and the necessary raw materials. So they resorted to what became known as 'curry powder', in
which turmeric and fenugreek were usually the dominant flavours.

Sometimes cooks would make this themselves, based on recipes
sent over from friends or relatives in India; or they would rely
on writer–popularisers such as Colonel Kenney-Herbert, whose
vast output of cookery writing was collected in 1878 as *Culinary
Jottings for Madras*. The colonel's 'stock receipt for curry powder'
is 'turmeric, coriander-seed, cumin-seed, fenugreek, mustard-
seed, dried chillies, black pepper corns, poppy-seed, dry-ginger': a
mixture very similar to the south Indian kari podi, though lacking
its all-important curry leaves. Eliza Acton's in her *Modern Cookery*
(1845) is credited to a 'Mr Arnott':

Turmeric 8 oz.
Coriander seed 4 oz.
Cummin seed 2 oz.
Foenugreek seed 2 oz.
Cayenne ½ oz.

The first commercially produced curry powder was sold at least
as early as 1784, when Sorlie's Perfumery Warehouse in Piccadilly
advertised its mixture in the *Morning Post*. Called Solander after
the Swedish botanist Daniel Solander, who accompanied Captain
Cook to the Pacific, much was made in the advert of its health
benefits: it rendered 'the Stomac active in Digestion', 'the blood
naturally free in Circulation' and 'the mind vigorous'. It was also,
apparently, an aphrodisiac, contributing the 'most of any food to
an increase of the human race'.

Other powders and pastes followed. Selim's Curry Paste,
invented by Captain William White of the Bengal Army, was
introduced in 1844 by a company that is still with us, Crosse &

Blackwell. Trompe's Curry Powder cost 4s. 6d. from Reece's
Medical Hall. In 1893, so the story goes, a salesman called James
Allen Sharwood visited Madras, sampled a locally produced range
of spice mixtures prepared by one P. Vencatachellum and was so
impressed he promptly became its export agent.

Dr Livingstone took ready-made mulligatawny paste with him
to Africa, but its use left him 'in a very exhausted condition'. In
October 1859 he wrote that his cook had used it indiscriminately,
ignoring instructions to add only a couple of spoonfuls: 'In consequence of the overdose, we were delayed several days in severe
suffering.'[355]

Curry powder encourages the idea that all curries are essentially
the same, that the only gradations that matter are to do with heat.
The way the British cooked curries, too, using flour to make a
roux to which they added curry powder – common practice until
the 1980s – was enough to raise any Indian cook's blood pressure.
Madhur Jaffrey has written, uncompromisingly, that 'if "curry" is
an oversimplified name for an ancient cuisine, then "curry powder"
attempts to oversimplify (and destroy) the cuisine itself'.[356]

On one level there is no disputing this: curry powder is *obviously*
inauthentic, *obviously* an approximation, and for this reason has
been largely supplanted by better-quality pastes as Western tastes
have become more sophisticated. But well into the 1960s it was
possible to claim that the average European and American cook
had little choice but to use it. After all, where was he supposed
to find fenugreek? 'Since most of these tropical products are not
readily available to the American housewife in a fresh state, the
most practical way for her to prepare curry is to use a blend of
curry powder that has been subdued to become more acceptable to
the average American palate', advises Frederic Rosengarten in *The
Book of Spices* (1969).[357]

Defenders of curry powder point to garam masala, which looks
like the same sort of thing. But garam masala is more like a condiment, added towards the end of cooking and intended to augment

the flavour of existing spices rather than be the sole spicing agent. Similarly, the spice powders used in dishes like the vegetable stew kolumbu are only part of the story – kolumbu requires additional tempering with asafoetida, mustard seeds and curry leaves.

Poor-quality commercial curry powder often smells strongly of fenugreek. But its main ingredient is usually turmeric, which contributes what Tom Stobart accurately calls an 'earthy flavour, redolent of an abandoned spice cupboard'.[358] Between 1820 and 1840 the popularity of curry powders caused a threefold increase in imports of turmeric to England, up to 26,468 lb. from 8,678 lb.

DUKKAH (OR DUQQA)

An Egyptian condiment which mixes herbs and hazelnuts with spices. The ingredients are crushed, not powdered – the name derives from the Arabic for 'to pound'. Claudia Roden advises that it is usually eaten at breakfast, with bread dipped in olive oil, or as an evening snack. In *A Book of Middle Eastern Food* (1968) she gives two recipes. The first, her mother's, combines hazelnuts with coriander seed, sesame seed, cumin, salt and black pepper. The second, quite different, is from Edward Lane's *Manners and Customs of the Modern Egyptians* (1836). Lane advises that dukkah is 'commonly composed of salt and pepper with za'atar or wild marjoram or mint or cumin-seed, and with one or more, or all, of the following ingredients – namely, coriander seed, cinnamon, sesame, and hummus (or chick peas). Each mouthful of bread is dipped in this mixture.'

Modern commercial versions of the mix vary wildly. Many are influenced by adaptations introduced in Australia and New Zealand, where dukkah was popular before its recent ascent into European fashion. The Dukkah Company Cornwall includes almonds, cayenne pepper and other chillis in its Hot Sand blend.

GOMASHIO

A dry condiment, used in Japanese cuisine, made from toasted unhulled sesame seeds, sugar and salt, all ground up in a suribachi

– a grooved pestle and mortar. Gomashio is popular with people on macrobiotic diets as a flavouring for rice. But it also works well sprinkled over beans and vegetables. A similar Japanese condiment is furikake, where sesame seeds are mixed with dried fish, chopped seaweed and monosodium glutamate (MSG).

GREEN CURRY PASTE

Of the three pillars of Thai *kaeng* – broadly, 'dishes with gravy' – green curry is usually (though not always) more powerful than yellow and red because of the characteristics of green bird's-eye chillies. Red can sometimes *seem* stronger because we know the colour signifies heat and taste is partly influenced by psychology. But it also depends, obviously, on how many chillies you use. Delia Smith reduces the number of green chillies needed from 'about 35' to eight in the Thai green curry with chicken from her *Winter Collection* (1995). In her *Ultimate Curry Bible* (2003) Madhur Jaffrey quotes a recipe by chef Sarnsern Gajaseni at the Oriental Hotel in Bangkok. It's the one I always use. It can sometimes be hard to find fresh coriander with the roots still attached. If so, the stems make an acceptable subsitute, or as Jaffrey recommends 'a small handful of the leaves'. To make ten tablespoons you need:

14 fresh, green bird's eye chillies
5 cloves garlic
140 g/5 oz. shallots, chopped
1 tablespoon fresh lemon grass, thinly sliced
3 thin slices peeled fresh or frozen galangal, or ginger
1 thin slice of fresh kaffir lime rind, or dried rind, soaked in
   water for 30 minutes
6–8 fresh coriander roots, washed well and coarsely chopped
freshly ground white pepper
¼ teaspoon shrimp paste or 2 anchovies from a can, chopped
½ teaspoon ground cumin
½ teaspoon ground coriander seed

Green, red and yellow curries are good examples of the way Thai cuisine has been influenced by both China (from which it derives cooking techniques such as stir-frying and steaming) and India (the heavy use of spices). But as Elisabeth Lambert Ortiz puts it, it has 'borrowed piecemeal rather than wholesale ... always making the newcomers play a Thai tune and retaining the indigenous cuisine': 'Thus, where the Chinese might steam fish plain, the Thais will add lemon grass; where an Indian curry might be flavoured with only two spices, a Thai curry may contain many, along with herbs, fish sauce and coconut milk.'[359] See also *Red curry paste,* below.

HARISSA

A hot but aromatic spice paste most closely associated with Tunisia and Algeria but widely used across North Africa and the Middle East as a condiment or mixed with water to flavour tagines, couscous and soups. It can be bought as either a paste or a powder. Or you can make your own using dried red chillies, garlic, salt, coriander (the herb), caraway seeds and olive oil. Other possible additions include smoked paprika, cayenne pepper, mint, cumin and lemon juice. It should be left to stand for several hours before using to allow the flavours to develop.

Harissa's name derives from Orissa, the old name for the east Indian state now called Odisha, where the chilli peppers used in harissa were grown. Chillies were brought from the New World to Iberia in 1514 and reached India in the early seventeenth century. Harissa should be seen in the context of other hot or sour pastes such as the Italian agresto (a sort of pesto made with juice from unripe grapes, popular in the Middle Ages) and Sephardic Jewish bagna brusca, similar to the Greek egg-and-lemon sauce avgolemono. These sauces were, as Mary Ellen Snodrass has written, products of the 'medieval ferment that brought Jews and Moors to Spain and spread eastern Mediterranean cooking throughout the region'.[360]

HAWAIJ

A Yemeni spice mix used mostly in the brewing of coffee, although also in soups, stews and as a rub for barbecued meat. Its most common ingredients are anise, fennel seed, ginger and cardamom. The soup-specific version includes cumin, turmeric and black pepper and loses the ginger and anise. Israel's large Yemenite community means hawaij is also very popular there.

KHMELI SUNELI

Literally 'dried spices', this mix hails from Georgia, where it is used as a rub for meat or in stews. Generally, its components are blue fenugreek (the ground seeds and pods), coriander seed, garlic, dried marigold flowers (known locally as 'Imeretian saffron'), chilli and black pepper. The recipe in Paula Wolfert's *The Cooking of the Eastern Mediterranean* (1994) also includes cloves, dried mint and basil.

KOCHUJANG (OR GOCHUJANG)

A hot Korean sauce made from fermented soy beans, red chilli peppers, glutinous rice and salt. It has been produced commercially since the 1970s but used always to be made at home – outdoors, over the course of many years, in earthenware pots.

LA KAMA

A Moroccan spice mix, but much simpler than ras el hanout. It's based around a mere five spices – cinnamon, black pepper, ginger, turmeric and nutmeg – and works well with lamb and chicken, though its best-known use might be in harira, the pulse-heavy Mahgrebian soup. *The Anthropologists' Cookbook* (1977) points out that this is eaten throughout the year, not just to break the fast of Ramadan, but during Ramadan the price of ingredients rises dramatically. This means there is no typical recipe because 'the quality and quantity of the ingredients of a family's harira will depend, at least in part, upon their ability to pay. Moreover, families pride themselves upon special recipes which distinguish their harira from anyone else's.'[361]

MALAYSIAN SPICE MIX

Malaysia is central to the story of spices. The Strait of Malaçca, the narrow passage between the Malay Peninsula and Sumatra, was once one of the world's busiest stretches of waterway as mer-chants from India, China and the Middle East flocked to the port of Malacca (now Melaka) to trade. Malaya, as it was called, had trading contact with India as early as the fourth century, but the relationship was catalysed in the late eighteenth century, when the British East India Company acquired Penang Island off the Malay Peninsula and designated it part of India. Indian workers, particu-larly south Indian Tamils, were imported to work on Malay black pepper, rubber, sugar and coffee plantations. All of these influences can be tasted in Malaysian cuisine. Madhur Jaffrey explains: 'One Malay-Indian fish curry may be enthusiastically seasoned with nearly all the spices used in south India, from mustard and fennel seeds to red chillies and fenugreek. Another might include a south Indian curry powder on the one hand and the very Chinese oyster sauce, dark soy sauce and rice wine on the other.'[362]

A very basic but versatile Malaysian spice mix might contain the following ingredients, infused with tamarind and lemon grass: black peppercorns, coriander seed, fennel seed, galangal, chillies, cumin seed and turmeric.

MASALA

Masala means 'spice mix', either dry or a paste, mild and aromatic or hot and pungent. Each region of India – and within that, prob-ably each family – has its own variations. The most common are the north Indian garam masala, usually added at the end of cooking, which contains cloves, cardamom, cinnamon, black pepper, mace, bay leaf, cumin and coriander seed, and chat masala, used as a condiment to flavour salads and street-stall snacks and made with cumin, dried ground ginger, mint, asafoetida, black pepper and salt.

MASSAMAN

A Thai iteration of a Persian-influenced north Indian curry, massaman (meaning 'Muslim') curries tend to be mild, their flavour a result of the combination of dry spices. Typically these might include all or some of the following: dried red chillies, white pepper, cumin seed, coriander seed, cinnamon, ginger, star anise, cloves, cardamom and turmeric, combined with shallots, lemon grass, garlic and shrimp paste. Introducing a recipe for massaman beef curry in his book *The Thai Table* (2008), Terry Tan observes that the dish is sixteenth-century Persian in origin and 'very typical of south Thailand cooking as the region nudges north Malaysia where the population is largely Muslim'; also that Malaysian cooking 'is itself heavily influenced by early Indian, Arab and Persian traders ... Certainly many Malaysian beef and mutton curries are just a whisper away from a quintessential massaman curry.'[363]

MITMITA

A hot Ethiopian spice mix whose power derives from bird's-eye chillies blended with korarima (see *Berbere,* above), ginger, cumin, cinnamon and cloves. A good example of its use is kitfo, where raw minced beef is marinated in mitmita and the clarified butter niter kibbeh (spiced with ajowan, cardamom and nigella).

MIXED SPICE

A sweet, aromatic mix of the sort of spices popular in English baking: cinnamon, cloves, nutmeg, sometimes allspice and coriander seed. It harks back very obviously to the medieval powder douce (see *Introduction*, p. 11). Sometimes called 'pudding spice', it is used to flavour custard-based desserts such as bread and butter pudding as well as Christmas cake, hot cross buns, etc. See also *Apple pie mix*, above.

PANCH PHORAN

Panch phoran means 'five spices' and is a blend of whole (never ground) seeds mostly used in Eastern India and Bangladesh. Usually it contains cumin seed, fenugreek, black mustard seed, nigella and fennel seed. The spices are left whole and should be tempered in oil or ghee until they pop in the frying pan.

PILPELCHUMA (OR FILFEL CHUMA)

A chilli and garlic paste similar to harissa (see above). The name means 'pepper garlic'. Used in Libyan Jewish cuisine, it contains red chillies, cayenne pepper, paprika, cumin, caraway seeds, garlic and salt in a base of sunflower oil. Yotam Ottolenghi recommends whisking it into eggs before scrambling them.[364] Fish cooked in the sauce, h'raimi, is eaten on Sabbath eve. Gil Marks remarks that the paste is also popular in Rome, where it was introduced by Libyan Jews fleeing Libya for Italy after the Six-Day War in 1967.[365]

QUATRE-ÉPICES

Four spices – usually ground white or black pepper, cloves, nutmeg and ginger – commonly used in French cuisine in charcuterie as well as stews and soups. A version appears in one of the earliest extant French cookery manuscripts, 'Le Menagier de Paris', from 1393. The dominant flavour tends to be pepper. There is a sweet version too which resembles the English mixed spice (see *Mixed spice,* above) – it substitutes allspice for the white or black pepper.

Jane Grigson recommends the blend in *Larousse Gastronomique*:

125 g white pepper
10 g cloves
30 g ginger
35 g nutmeg

She recommends adding it to a mustard and brown sugar glaze

for baked ham or, intriguingly, sprinkling it into mashed potatoes 'to be served with fromage de tête [terrine made from the head of a calf or pig], trotters, sausages, etc.'[366]

RAS EL HANOUT

The name means 'head of the shop' – basically 'from the top shelf', implying the best-quality spices available. Ras el hanout is a North African mix notable for its large number of ingredients (anywhere between twelve and thirty). Each shop or stall will have its own proprietary blend, or make up a batch according to a family's instructions. Typically ingredients will include cumin, cinnamon, cloves, cardamom, coriander seed, black pepper, paprika, fenugreek, turmeric, nutmeg, mace and galangal. In the past cantharides or 'Spanish fly' – a urethral irritant derived from the ground-up body of a green beetle, believed to be an aphrodisiac – was sometimes added. Ras el hanout is available in 'brut' form, with the spices left whole rather than ground. Moroccan food expert Paula Wolfert bought some brut ras el hanout forty years ago and claims it is 'still aromatic', although she says she 'just bought it for analysis'.[367] According to Alan Davidson, Tunisian ras el hanout contains rose petals and is milder than the Moroccan variety.[368]

RED CURRY PASTE

Almost identical to Thai green curry paste (see above), but with hot red chillies and possibly paprika.

SAMBAR POWDER

The spice blend for use in the south Indian and Sri Lankan soup sambar: coriander seed, cumin, black pepper, fenugreek, amchur, brown mustard seed, chilli powder, cinnamon, turmeric, curry leaf, asafoetida and besan flour. Madhur Jaffrey writes that 'early British curry powders were probably based on a similar mixture of spices and split peas, as is evident from many nineteenth-century recipes'.[369] See *Curry powder*, above.

SHICHIMI-TOGARASHI (OR JAPANESE SEVEN-FLAVOUR)

A coarse-textured Japanese condiment in which the heat of the chilli is offset by the citrus and iodine tang of, respectively, tangerine peel and nori (seaweed). A typical mix – there can be more ingredients than seven – contains sansho (*Zanthoxylum piperitum* – the Japanese version of Szechuan pepper), dried tangerine peel, cayenne pepper, flaked nori, ginger, black sesame seeds, white poppy seeds or black hemp seeds, and minced garlic.

The mix is supposed to date from 1625, shortly after red chilli peppers were introduced into Japan. A pharmacy in the medical quarter of Edo (now Tokyo) invented shichimi-togarashi as a prophylactic remedy for flu. Incredibly, the shop still exists: you can visit Yagenbori Shichimi Togarashi in Asakusa and buy their different blends of the mix – *ogara* (extra hot) or *kogara* (mild) – as well as special wooden containers for storing it.

TABIL

From Tunisia and Algeria, a blend of coriander seed (*tabil* means 'coriander' in Tunisian Arabic), caraway seed, dried chilli flakes and garlic powder, for use in lamb tagines.

TAKLIA

A simple Lebanese spice mix consisting of ground coriander seed and garlic fried in butter.

TSIRE

The spice mix for the eponymous Nigerian street food – strips of beef on a skewer, sold from roadside stands – tsire contains crushed peanuts or peanut butter, ginger and chilli powder. It can also include cloves, nutmeg and cinnamon and is great as a rub for chicken too.

ZA'ATAR

A Middle Eastern condiment made from herbs derived from local versions of thyme, oregano and basil mixed with sesame seeds, sumac and salt. One of these herbs grows wild in Israel and Palestine and is actually (just to confuse you) called za'atar. Yotam Ottolenghi and Sami Tamimi say the smell of this is 'part and parcel of the Palestinian heritage and the smell of home to anyone who grew up either in Jerusalem or elsewhere in the mountainous regions of the Holy Land'.[370] Most sources give za'atar the herb as *Origanum syriacum*, but Ottolenghi and Tamimi describe it as a type of hyssop (*Hyssopus officinalis*), native to southern Europe but popular in English kitchen gardens from the sixteenth century onwards as it was used in gargles and skin washes. Za'atar the mix, by contrast, is sprinkled over chicken, hummus, salads and the thick yoghurt labneh.

ZHUG (OR ZHOUG)

A coarse chilli paste from the Yemen introduced to Israel by Yemeni Jews. Containing hot green chillies alongside garlic, cloves, cardamom, cumin, coriander (the herb) and flat-leaf parsley, it is reputed to boost the immune system. It is typically served in pitta with falafel or shawarma.

NOTES

1. Lizzie Collingham, *Curry: A Tale of Cooks and Conquerors* (Chatto & Windus, 2005), p. 24.
2. Madhur Jaffrey, *Ultimate Curry Bible* (Ebury, 2003), p. 25.
3. Yotam Ottolenghi and Sami Tamimi, *Jerusalem* (Ebury, 2012), p. 16.
4. Jean Bottéro, *The Oldest Cuisine in the World: Cooking in Mesopotamia* (University of Chicago Press, 2004), p. 1.
5. 'Ready Happy Returns: The Instant Meal Celebrates Its 30th Birthday', *The Independent* (23 July 2009).
6. Nigel Slater, *Toast* (Fourth Estate, 2003), p. 2.
7. Alexandre Dumas, *Dictionary of Cuisine* (1873; Routledge, 2014), p. 18.
8. Jack Turner, *Spice: The History of a Temptation* (Vintage, 2004), p. xix.
9. Frederic Rosengarten, *The Book of Spices* (Pyramid, 1969), p. 16.
10. Andrew Dalby, *Dangerous Tastes: The Story of Spices* (British Museum Press, 2000), p. 10.
11. Ibid., p. 16.
12. Wolfgang Schivelbusch, *Tastes of Paradise* (1979; Vintage, 1993), p. 5.
13. John Fenn (ed.), *The Paston Letters* (Knight, 1840), p. 66.
14. Sara Paston-Williams, *The Art of Dining: A History of Cooking and Eating* (National Trust, 1993), p. 36.
15. www.godecookery.com/goderec/grec13.htm.
16. Odile Redon, Françoise Sabban and Silvano Serventi, *The Medieval Kitchen* (University of Chicago Press, 1998), p. 26.
17. Rosengarten, *The Book of Spices*, p. 61.
18. 'The Crusaders and the Diffusion of Foods', cliffordawright.com.
19. Quoted in John Block Friedman, *The Monstrous Races in Medieval Art and Thought* (Syracuse University Press, 2000), p. 166.
20. Charles Corn, *The Scents of Eden* (Kodansha, 1998), p. xx.
21. Anna Pavord, *The Naming of Names: The Search for Order in the World of Plants* (Bloomsbury, 2005), p. 21.
22. Agnes Arber, *Herbals: Their Origin and Evolution* (Cambridge University Press, 1912), p. 2.

23. Isabella Beeton, *Book of Household Management* (Beeton, 1861), p. 183.

24. Slater, *Toast*, p. 18.

25. Interviewed in Christopher Frayling, *Strange Landscape: A Journey through the Middle Ages* (BBC, 1995), pp. 12–13.

26. Ottolenghi and Tamimi, *Jerusalem*, p. 16.

27. Turner, *Spice: The History of a Temptation*, p. xiv.

28. Dalby, *Dangerous Tastes*, p. 128.

29. B. W. Higman, *Slave Population and Economy in Jamaica, 1807–1834* (Cambridge University Press, 1979), p. 25.

30. Robert Renny, *An History of Jamaica* (Cawthorn, 1807), p. 159.

31. *The Sugar Cane: A Monthly Magazine, Devoted to the Interests of the Sugar Cane Industry*, vol. 5 (Galt & Co., 1873), p. 24.

32. Carole Elizabeth Boyce Davies (ed.), *Encyclopedia of the African Diaspora* (ABC-CLIO, 2008), p. 591.

33. 'Sweet Heat: For Jamaicans, It's All about Jerk', *New York Times* (2 July 2008).

34. William James Gardner, *A History of Jamaica* (Elliot Stock, 1878), p. 322.

35. Paston-Williams, *The Art of Dining*, p. 160.

36. Ibid., p. 322.

37. Jane Grigson, *English Food* (Macmillan, 1974), p. 273.

38. P. C. D. Brears, *The Gentlewoman's Kitchen: Great Food in Yorkshire, 1650–1750* (Wakefield Historical Publications, 1984), p. 71.

39. Hugh Fearnley-Whittingstall and Nick Fisher, *The River Cottage Fish Book* (Bloomsbury, 2007), p. 418.

40. 'Beef Up your Christmas Menu', *Financial Times* (29 November 2008).

41. Mark Kurlansky, *Salt* (Random House, 2002), p. 124.

42. 'The Ultimate Corned Beef and Cabbage', epicurious.com.

43. Sue Shephard, *Pickled, Potted and Canned: The Story of Food Preserving* (Headline, 2000), p. 63.

44. Gil Marks, *The Encyclopedia of Jewish Food* (Houghton Mifflin Harcourt, 2010), p. 145.

45. Elizabeth David, *Spices, Salt and Aromatics in the English Kitchen* (Penguin, 1970), p. 22.

46. John Gerard, *Herball* (Norton & Whittakers, 1636), p. 1002.

47. Mrs M. Grieve, *A Modern Herbal* (Cape, 1931), p. 39.

48. James Nicoll, *An Historical and Descriptive Account of Iceland, Greenland and the Faroe Islands* (Oliver & Boyd, 1840), p. 387.

49. Louis Cheskin, *Color Guide for Marketing Media* (Macmillan, 1954), p. 37.

50. Dalby, *Dangerous Tastes*, p. 145.

51. Quoted in Dalby, *Dangerous Tastes*, p. 145.

52. George Don, *General History of the Dichleamydeous Plants* (Rivington, 1831), p. 294.

53. Rick Bayless, *Rick Bayless Mexican Kitchen* (Simon & Schuster, 1996), p. 66.

54. Quoted in Andrew Dalby, *Siren Feasts: A History of Food and Gastronomy in Greece* (Routledge, 1996), p. 140.

55. Garcia de Orta, *Colloquies on the Simples and Drugs of India* (1563; Sotheran, 1913), p. 44.

56. Ibid., p. 45.

57. Tom Stobart, *Herbs, Spices and Flavourings* (International Wine and Food Publishing Company, 1970), p. 29.

58. Nilanjana S. Roy (ed.), *A Matter of Taste: The Penguin Book of Indian Writing on Food* (Penguin India, 2004), p. 94.

59. William Beaumont, *Experiments and Observations on the Gastric Juice and on the Physiology of Digestion* (Maclachlan & Stewart, 1838), p. 15.

60. John Evelyn, *Acetaria: A Discourse of Sallets* (1699; Brooklyn Botanic Garden, 1937), p. 113.

61. Quoted in Ann Hagen, *A Handbook of Anglo-Saxon Food: Processing and Consumption* (Anglo-Saxon Books, 1992), p. 98.

62. Ibid., p. 99.

63. Robert Lacey and Danny Danziger, *The Year 1000: What Life Was Like at the Turn of the First Millennium* (Abacus, 2000), p. 90.

64. Jacobus Canter Visscher, *Letters from Malabar* (Adelphi Press, 1862), p. 153.

65. *Travels of Peter Mundy, in Europe and Asia, 1608–1667* (Hakluyt Society, 1919), p. 79.

66. Carolyn Heal and Michael Allsop, *Cooking with Spices* (Granada, 1985), p. 244.

67. David, *Spices, Salt and Aromatics*, p. 151.

68. 'Vietnam Pepper Output Likely to be 150,000 Tonnes, India's 45,000', *Business Standard* (19 November 2013).

69. Paul Freedman, *Out of the East: Spices and the Medieval Imagination* (Yale University Press, 2008), p. 4.

70. Tom Standage, *An Edible History of Humanity* (Atlantic, 2012), p. 65.

71. *The Roman Cookery of Apicius*, trans. and adapted by John Edwards (Rider, 1985), p. xxi.
72. Neil MacGregor, *A History of the World in 100 Objects* (Allen Lane, 2010), p. 216.
73. Pliny, *Natural History*, XII; 14, p. 29.
74. 'Grandpre's Voyage to Bengal', *Annual Review and History of Literature* (Longman and Rees, 1804), p. 49.
75. Isidore of Seville, *Etymologiae*, Book 17, ed. J. Andre (Paris, 1981), pp. 147–9.
76. Dioscorides, *De materia medica* (IBIDIS Press, 2000), Book II, p. 319.
77. Pierre Pomet et al., *A Complete History of Drugs* (J. and J. Bonwicke, S. Birt etc., 1748), p. 123.
78. Collingham, *Curry*, p. 120.
79. A. R. Kenney-Herbert, *Culinary Jottings from Madras* (1878; Prospect, 1994), p. 186.
80. Darra Goldstein, *The Georgian Feast: The Vibrant Culture and Savory Food of the Republic of Georgia* (University of California Press, 1999), p. xiv.
81. Jiaju Zhou, Guirong Xie et al., *Encyclopaedia of Traditional Chinese Medicines*, vol. 5, *Isolated Compounds* (Springer, 2011), p. 587.
82. Grieve, *A Modern Herbal*, p. 728.
83. Agatha Christie, *At Bertram's Hotel* (1965, HarperCollins, 2002), p. 8.
84. Ibid., p. 13.
85. Arabella Boxer, *Book of English Food* (rev. edn, Fig Tree, 2012), p. 200.
86. Elisabeth Ayrton, *The Cookery of England* (Penguin, 1974), p. 520.
87. Elizabeth Gaskell, *Cranford* (1853, Penguin, 2005), p. 81.
88. Postcard from Virginia Woolf to Grace Higgens, 1936, quoted in Jans Ondaatje Rolls, *The Bloomsbury Cookbook* (Thames & Hudson, 2014), p. 180.
89. Eliza Smith, *The Compleat Housewife* (Longman et al., 1727), p. 170.
90. Stobart, *Herbs, Spices and Flavourings*, p. 46.
91. Claudia Roden, *A Book of Middle Eastern Food* (Penguin, 1968), p. 397.
92. Nicholas Culpeper, *Complete Herbal* (1653; Wordsworth, 1995), p. 59.
93. Stobart, *Herbs, Spices and Flavourings*, p. 48.
94. Shihzen Li, Porter Smith and George Arthur Stuart (eds), *Chinese Medicinal Herbs* (Georgetown Press, 1973), p. 37.
95. thespicehouse.com/spices/whole-white-cardamom-pods.
96. Rosengarten, *The Book of Spices*, p. 169.

97. Stobart, *Herbs, Spices and Flavourings*, p. 48.
98. Ibid., p. 168.
99. James Baillie Fraser, *Travels in Koordistan, Mesopotamia, &c: Including an Account of Parts of Those Countries Hitherto Unvisited by Europeans* (Bentley, 1840), p. 119.
100. Ibid., p. 119.
101. Evelyn, *Acetaria*, p. 164.
102. Heal and Allsop, *Cooking with Spices*, p. 83.
103. Ibid., p. 90.
104. John Lanchester, 'Restaurant Review: Nando's', *The Guardian* (15 January 2011).
105. Paul W. Bosland and Dave DeWitt, *Complete Chile Pepper Book* (Timber Press, 2009), p. 10.
106. Harry T. Lawless and Hildegarde Heymann, *Sensory Evaluation of Food: Principles and Practices* (Springer, 1999), p. 202.
107. Ibid., p. 204.
108. Alexandra W. Logue, *The Psychology of Eating and Drinking* (Psychology Press, 2004), p. 274.
109. Ibid.
110. Heal and Allsop, *Cooking with Spices*, p. 90.
111. gernot-katzers-spice-pages.com/engl/Caps_fru.html.
112. Jason Goldman, 'Why Do We Eat Chilli?', *The Guardian* (14 September 2010).
113. Logue, *Psychology of Eating and Drinking*, p. 274.
114. Turner, *Spice: The History of a Temptation*, p. 12.
115. Collingham, *Curry*, p. 54.
116. Ibid., p. 53.
117. Rosengarten, *The Book of Spices*, p. 145.
118. Sallie Morris and Lesley Mackley, *The Complete Cook's Encyclopaedia of Spices* (Hermes House, 1997), p. 31.
119. Heal and Allsop, *Cooking with Spices*, p. 86.
120. Delia Smith, *How To Cook: Book Two* (BBC, 1999), p. 130.
121. Quoted in Dalby, *Dangerous Tastes*, p. 149.
122. Dave DeWitt and Nancy Gerlach, *The Food of Santa Fe: Authentic Recipes from the American Southwest* (Tuttle Publishing, 1998), p. 14.
123. Ibid.
124. gernot-katzers-spice-pages.com/engl/Caps_fru.html.

125. Susan Montoya Bryan, 'Chile Experts: Trinidad Moruga Scorpion is the Hottest', *Associated Press* (15 February 2012).

126. Ibid.

127. Gil Marks, *Olive Trees and Honey: A Treasury of Vegetarian Recipes from Jewish Communities around the World* (Wiley & Sons, 2005), p. 10.

128. Turner, *Spice: The History of a Temptation*, p. 4.

129. Joyce Tyldesley, *Hatchepsut: The Female Pharaoh* (Penguin, 1996), p. 145.

130. James Henry Breasted, *Ancient Records of Egypt: The Eighteenth Dynasty* (University of Illinois Press, 2001), p. 109.

131. Ibid., p. 113.

132. Quoted in Dalby, *Dangerous Tastes*, p. 37.

133. Theophrastus, *Enquiry into Plants*, IX, V (Loeb Classical Library, 1916), p. 243.

134. Malyn Newitt, *A History of Portuguese Overseas Expansion, 1400–1668* (Routledge, 2004), p. 107.

135. R. Van den Broek, *The Myth of the Phoenix* (Brill Archive, 1972), p. 169.

136. Grigson, *English Food*, p. 301.

137. Heather Amdt Anderson, *Breakfast: A History* (AltaMira Press, 2013), p. 238.

138. Dorothy Hartley, *Food in England* (1954; Little, Brown, 1996), p. 636.

139. David, *Spices, Salt and Aromatics*, p. 26.

140. Giorgio Buccellati, *Terqa: A Narrative*; http://128.97.6.202/tq/pages/10.html (January 2009)

141. Quoted in Dalby, *Dangerous Tastes*, pp. 50–51.

142. David, *Spices, Salt and Aromatics*, p. 27.

143. Turner, *Spice: The History of a Temptation*, p. 27.

144. Antonio Pigafetta, *The First Voyage around the World* (Hakluyt Society, 1874), p. 65.

145. Ibid., p. 102.

146. Ibid., p. 124.

147. Ibid., pp. 134–5.

148. Penny Le Couteur and Jay Burreson, *Napoleon's Buttons: 17 Molecules That Changed History* (Tarcher/Penguin, 2003), p. 33.

149. Turner, *Spice: The History of a Temptation*, p. 290.

150. Dalby, *Dangerous Tastes*, p. 126.

151. Ibid., p. 94.

152. Dan Lepard, *The Handmade Loaf* (Mitchell Beazley, 2004), p. 230.
153. *Leechbook III*, quoted in Peter Dendle and Alain Touwaide (eds), *Health and Healing from the Medieval Garden* (Boydell Press, 2008), p. 149.
154. *Oxford Companion to Beer* (Oxford University Press, 2011), p. 267.
155. David, *Spices, Salt and Aromatics*, p. 28.
156. http://www.splendidtable.org/story/how-the-flavors-of-the-middle-east-ended-up-in-mexico.
157. Rosengarten, *The Book of Spices*, p. 422.
158. Stobart, *Herbs, Spices and Flavourings*, p. 68.
159. Rosemary Hemphill, *Penguin Book of Herbs and Spices* (Penguin, 1966), pp. 75–6.
160. Malcolm Laurence Cameron, *Anglo-Saxon Medicine* (Cambridge University Press, 1993), p. 147.
161. William Coles, *Adam in Eden, or Nature's Paradise* (Streater, 1657), p. 53.
162. Gillian Riley, *The Oxford Companion to Italian Food* (Oxford University Press, 2007), p. 190.
163. David, *Spices, Salt and Aromatics*, p. 32.
164. Collingham, *Curry*, p. 35.
165. Hemphill, *Penguin Book of Herbs and Spices*, p. 81.
166. 'What a Hundred Million Calls to 311 Reveal about New York', Wired.com (1 November 2010).
167. David, *Spices, Salt and Aromatics*, p. 33.
168. Stobart, *Herbs, Spices and Flavourings*, p. 77.
169. 'Diosgenin, a Steroid Saponin of *Trigonella foenum graecum* (Fenugreek), Inhibits Azoxymethane-Induced Aberrant Crypt Foci Formation in F344 Rats and Induces Apoptosis in HT-29 Human Colon Cancer Cells', *Cancer Epidemiology, Biomarkers and Prevention* (August 2004).
170. 'Europe E.coli Outbreak May Have Been Caused by Egyptian Seeds', *Daily Mail* (30 June 2011).
171. Freedman, *Out of the East: Spices and the Medieval Imagination*, p. 11.
172. Garcia de Orta, *Colloquies*, p. 209.
173. Carol Selva Rajah, *Heavenly Fragrance: Cooking with Aromatic Asian Herbs, Fruits, Spices and Seasonings* (Periplus Editions, 2014), p. 144.
174. Quoted in Wighard Strehlow and Gottfried Hertzka, *Hildegard of Bingen's Medicine* (Inner Traditions, 1988), p. 37.

175. Culpeper, *Complete Herbal*, pp. 313–14.

176. Quoted in April Harper and Caroline Proctor (eds), *Medieval Sexuality: A Casebook* (Routledge, 2007), p. 119.

177. Turner, *Spice: The History of a Temptation*, p. 195.

178. Charles Corn, *The Scents of Eden: A History of the Spice Trade* (Kodansha, 1998), p. 6.

179. Marco Polo, *The Book of Ser Marco Polo*, trans. and ed. H. Yule and H. Cordier (John Murray, 1921), vol. 2, pp. 249–50.

180. Mathieu Torck, *Avoiding the Dire Straits: An Inquiry into Food Provisions and Scurvy in the Maritime and Military History of China and Wider East Asia* (Otto Harrassowitz Verlag, 2009), p. 147.

181. Quoted in Torck, *Avoiding the Dire Straits*, p. 147.

182. Ross E. Dunn, *The Adventures of Ibn Battuta, a Muslim Traveller of the Fourteenth Century* (University of California Press, 1986), p. 225.

183. Frederick J. Simoons, *Food in China: A Cultural and Historical Inquiry* (CRC Press, 1990), p. 371.

184. Dalby, *Dangerous Tastes*, p. 21.

185. Ibid.

186. Simoons, *Food in China*, p. 371.

187. *The Herbal of Dioscorides the Greek*, Book II (panaceavera.com/BOOKTWO.pdf), p. 319.

188. *Food in Motion: The Migration of Foodstuffs and Cookery Techniques*, vol. 2, ed. Alan Davidson (Oxford Symposium, 1983), p. 116.

189. Turner, *Spice: The History of a Temptation*, p. 222.

190. David, *Spices, Salt and Aromatics*, p. 34.

191. Lorna J. Sass, *To the King's Taste* (Metropolitan Museum of Art, 1975), p. 24.

192. Hemphill, *Penguin Book of Herbs and Spices*, p. 87.

193. Ken Hom, *Chinese Cookery* (BBC, 2001), p. 27.

194. Turner, *Spice: The History of a Temptation*, p. 46.

195. Ifeyironwa Francisca Smith, *Foods of West Africa: Their Origin and Use* (National Library of Canada, 1998), p. 95.

196. Pieter de Marees, *Description and Historical Account of the Gold Kingdom of Guinea* (1602; British Academy, 1987), p. 160.

197. John Keay, *The Spice Route* (John Murray, 2005), p. 150.

198. G. Y. Mbongue, P. Kamptchouing and T. Dimo, 'Effects of the Aqueous Extract of Dry Seeds of *Aframomum melegueta* on Some

Parameters of the Reproductive Function of Mature Male Rats', *Andrologia*, 44 (1) (February 2012), pp. 53–8.

199. Cheryl Lyn Dybas and Ilya Raskin, 'Out of Africa: A Tale of Gorillas, Heart Disease ... and a Swamp Plant', *BioScience*, 57 (5) (2007), pp. 392–7.

200. Jessica B. Harris, *The Africa Cookbook: Tastes of a Continent* (Simon & Schuster, 1998), p. 153.

201. Ibid.

202. *Living through Crises: How the Food, Fuel and Financial Shocks Affect the Poor* (World Bank Publications, 2012), p. 223.

203. http://www.kitchenbutterfly.com/2011/03/01/how-to-make-nigerian-pepper-soup/.

204. Gerard, *Herball*, p. 242.

205. Grieve, *A Modern Herbal*, p. 419.

206. John Parkinson, *Theatrum botanicum* (Thomas Cotes, 1640), p. 861.

207. Jane Grigson, *Charcuterie and French Pork Cookery* (Michael Joseph, 1967), p. 37.

208. Elizabeth David, *French Provincial Cooking* (1960; Folio Society, 2008), p. 73.

209. David, *Spices, Salt and Aromatics*, p. 36.

210. Marina Warner, *Monsters of Our Own Making: The Peculiar Pleasures of Fear* (University Press of Kentucky, 2007), p. 65.

211. Culpeper, *Complete Herbal*, p. 142.

212. Quoted in Dalby, *Dangerous Tastes*, p. 80.

213. David C. Stuart, *Dangerous Garden: The Quest for Plants to Change Our Lives* (Harvard University Press, 2004), p. 43.

214. 'Woman "Overdoses" on Liquorice', BBC News website, 21 May 2004.

215. Roden, *A Book of Middle Eastern Food*, p. 414.

216. *The Etymologies of Isidore of Seville* (Cambridge University Press, 2006), p. 296.

217. K. Takahashi, M. Fukazawa et al., 'A Pilot Study of Antiplaque Effects of Mastic Chewing-Gum in the Oral Cavity', *Periodontal* (April 2003).

218. Quoted in Freedman, *Out of the East*, p. 15.

219. Richard Sugg, *Mummies, Cannibals, and Vampires: The History of Corpse Medicine From the Renaissance to the Victorians* (Routledge, 2011), p. 1.

220. Ibid., p. 173.

221. Quoted in Okasha El Daly, *Egyptology: The Missing Millennium: Ancient Egypt in Medieval Arabic Writings* (Psychology Press, 2005), p. 97.

222. Samuel Pepys, *Diary 1668–69* (University of California Press, 2000), p. 197.

223. Thomas Pettigrew, *A History of Egyptian Mummies* (Longman, 1834), p. 7.

224. Joyce Tyldesley, *Egypt: How a Lost Civilisation Was Rediscovered* (Random House, 2010), p. 41.

225. Philip McCouat, 'The Life and Death of Mummy Brown', *Journal of Art in Society* (2013), www.artinsociety.com.

226. Arthur H. Church, *The Chemistry of Paints and Painting* (Seeley, Service & Co., 1915), p. 14.

227. Quoted in McCouat, 'The Life and Death of Mummy Brown'.

228. Georgiana Burne-Jones, *Memorials of Edward Burne-Jones*, Volume 2 (1904; Lund Humphries, 1993), p. 114.

229. Rudyard Kipling, *Something of Myself* (1937; Cambridge University Press, 1991), p. 10.

230. 'Techniques: The Passing of Mummy Brown', *Time* (2 October 1964).

231. Gerard, *Herball*, p. 245.

232. John Kingsbury, *Deadly Harvest* (Allen & Unwin, 1967), p. 90.

233. Robert May, *The Accomplishd Cook* (1660; Brooke, 1671), p. 156.

234. Stobart, *Herbs, Spices and Flavourings*, p. 125.

235. Ibid., p. 126.

236. Sir Hugh Plat, *Delightes for Ladies* (1609; Boles, 1630), Section D (10).

237. 'How English Mustard Almost Lost Its Name', bbc.co.uk (2 September 2012).

238. Barbara Reynolds, *Dorothy L. Sayers: Her Life and Soul* (Hodder, 1993), p. 191.

239. David, *Spices, Salt and Aromatics*, p. 41.

240. Hartley, *Food in England*, p. 93.

241. Evelyn, *Acetaria*, p. 30.

242. Grieve, *A Modern Herbal*, p. 567.

243. Culpeper, *Complete Herbal*, p. 176.

244. Turner, *Spice: The History of a Temptation*, p. 208.

245. Marco Polo, *The Travels of Marco Polo*, trans. Henry Yule (Wikisource).

246. Marina Warner, *Alone of All Her Sex: The Myth and the Cult of the Virgin Mary* (Oxford University Press, 2013), p. 102.
247. Freedman, *Out of the East*, p. 81.
248. Edward Gibbon, *History of the Decline and Fall of the Roman Empire* (J. & J. Harper, 1826), p. 431.
249. R. A. Donkin, *Dragon's Brain Perfume: A Historical Geography of Camphor* (Brill, 1999), p. 6.
250. Jane Mossendew, *Thorn, Fire and Lily: Gardening with God in Lent and Easter* (Bloomsbury, 2004), p. 34.
251. 'Popular Names of British Plants', *All The Year Round*, vol. 10 (1864), p. 538.
252. Cathy K. Kaufman, *Cooking in Ancient Civilisations* (Greenwood, 2006), p. 31.
253. www2.warwick.ac.uk/knowledge/health/nigella-seeds-the-vicks-inhaler-of-ancient-greece.
254. Anna Forbes, *Unbeaten Tracks in Islands of the Far East* (1887; Oxford University Press, 1987), p. 58.
255. Giles Milton, *Nathaniel's Nutmeg* (Hodder, 1999), p. 6.
256. Forbes, *Unbeaten Tracks in Islands of the Far East*, pp. 61–2.
257. Ibid., p. 228.
258. Milton, *Nathaniel's Nutmeg*, p. 368.
259. Louis Couperus, *The Hidden Force* (1921; University of Massachusetts Press, 1985), p. 159.
260. S. Ahmad Tajuddin et al., 'An Experimental Study of Sexual Function Improving Effect of Myristica fragrans Houtt', *BMC Complementary and Alternative Medicine* (20 July 2005).
261. Garcia de Orta, *Colloquies*, p. 273.
262. Robert George Reisner, *Bird: The Legend of Charlie Parker* (Citadel Press, 1962), p. 149.
263. Malcolm X, *The Autobiography of Malcolm X* (Grove Press, 1965), p. 152.
264. Alfred Stillé, *Therapeutics and Materia Medica*, vol. 1 (Blanchard and Lea, 1860), p. 511.
265. W. T. Fernie, *Herbal Simples Approved for Modern Uses of Cure* (Boericke & Tafel, 1897), p. 395.
266. Elizabeth David, *Is There a Nutmeg in the House?* (Michael Joseph, 2000), p. 94.
267. Hemphill, *Penguin Book of Herbs and Spices*, p. 130.

268. 'Paprika: A Primer on Hungary's Spicy Obsession', CNN.com (29 November 2013).
269. Raymond Sokolov, *Why We Eat What We Eat: How Columbus Changed the Way the World Eats* (Simon & Schuster, 1993), p. 129.
270. 'FDA and French Disagree on Pink Peppercorn's Effects', *New York Times* (31 March 1982).
271. Jared Diamond, *Guns, Germs and Steel: The Fates of Human Societies* (Norton, 1997), p. 101.
272. Robert Graves, *The Greek Myths*, Book One (1995; Penguin, 1982), p. 96.
273. Wolfgang Schivelbusch, *Tastes of Paradise: A Social History of Spices, Stimulants and Intoxicants* (1979; Vintage, 1993), p. 207.
274. Rosengarten, *The Book of Spices*, p. 353.
275. Kenaz Fillan, *The Power of the Poppy: Harnessing Nature's Most Dangerous Plant Ally* (Inner Traditions, 2011), p. 226.
276. Ibid., p. 95.
277. Roy Porter and Mikuláš Teich (eds), *Drugs and Narcotics in History* (Cambridge University Press, 1997), p. 8.
278. 'DJ Died after Drinking a PINT of Deadly Poppy Tea He Made Using a Recipe He Found Online', *Daily Mail* (31 December 2013).
279. 'Tourists Warned of UAE Drug Laws', BBC News website (8 February 2008).
280. Diamond, *Guns, Germs and Steel*, p. 119.
281. Grieve, *A Modern Herbal*, p. 67.
282. Stobart, *Herbs, Spices and Flavourings*, p. 155.
283. David, *Spices, Salt and Aromatics*, p. 48.
284. Jason Burke, 'Kashmir Saffron Yields Hit by Drought, Smuggling and Trafficking', *The Guardian* (19 July 2010).
285. James Douglass, 'An Account of the Culture and Management of Saffron in England', *Philosophical Transactions of the Royal Society* (1 January 1753).
286. Quoted in Dorothy Hartley, *The Land of England: English Country Customs through the Ages* (Macdonald, 1979), p. 354.
287. Richard Hakluyt, *The Principal Navigations, Voyages, Traffics and Discoveries of the English Nation*, vol. 5 (Cambridge University Press, 1904), p. 240.
288. Pat Willard, *Secrets of Saffron* (Souvenir Press, 2001), p. 112.

289. 'Meet the Producer – David Smale', *The Guardian* (16 November 2013).
290. David, *Spices, Salt and Aromatics*, p. 46.
291. Collingham, *Curry*, pp. 27–8.
292. Claudia Roden, *The Book of Jewish Food* (Penguin, 1996), p. 384.
293. Gerard, *Herball*, p. 152.
294. The notes to William Woys Veaver (ed.), *A Quaker Woman's Cookbook: The Domestic Cookery of Elizabeth Ellicott Lea* (Stackpole Books, 2004), explain that, during the Middle Ages, a German *latwerge* could be 'any of several thick, partially dehydrated preparations of slowly cooked fruit. Because it was generally cooked with sugar, at the time treated as an internal medicine, *latwerge* was once only available through apothecaries. By the sixteenth century, however, the concept of *latwerge* as food had become part of German folk cookery.'
295. Roy Strong, *Feast: A History of Grand Eating* (Cape, 2002), p. 72.
296. 'Something Smells Odd in the Lucrative World of Saffron', *The Independent* (10 January 2011).
297. Umberto Eco, *Foucault's Pendulum* (Picador, 1988), p. 289.
298. gernot-katzers-spice-pages.com/engl/Sesa_ind.html.
299. 'Galland's Ali Baba and Other Arabic Versions', by Aboubakr Chraïbi, in Ulrich Marzolph (ed.), *The Arabian Nights in Transnational Perspective* (Wayne State University Press, 2007), p. 11.
300. Colette Rossant, *Apricots on the Nile: A Memoir with Recipes* (Bloomsbury, 2001), pp. 17–18.
301. Ottolenghi and Tamimi, *Jerusalem*, p. 112.
302. Heal and Allsop, *Cooking with Spices*, p. 283.
303. Joan Pilsbury Alcock, *Food in the Ancient World* (Greenwood, 2006), p. 183.
304. Alan Davidson (ed.), *The Oxford Companion to Food* (Oxford University Press, 2014), p. 378.
305. Ibid.
306. Jessica B. Harris, *The Africa Cookbook: Tastes of a Continent* (Simon & Schuster, 1998), p. 320.
307. Quoted in Davidson (ed.), *The Oxford Companion to Food*, p. 742.
308. Pliny, *Natural History*, XV; 33, p. 21.
309. Gerard, *Herball*, p. 1006.
310. *The Roman Cookery of Apicius*, trans. Edwards, p. 8.
311. Ibid., p. 166.

312. Angus McLaren, *A History of Contraception* (Wiley-Blackwell, 1992), p. 28.
313. John Laurence, *Complete Body of Husbandry and Gardening* (Tho. Woodward, 1726), p. 398.
314. Collingham, *Curry*, p. 241.
315. Iqbal Wahhab and Vivek Singh, *The Cinnamon Club Cookbook* (Absolute Press, 2003), p. 31.
316. Willem Schouten, *The Relation of a Wonderful Voyage* (Nathanaell Newbery, 1619), quoted in Dalby, p. 81.
317. 'Demand for a Chinese Fruit Skyrockets', *Washington Post* (18 November 2005).
318. Stobart, *Herbs, Spices and Flavourings*, p. 197.
319. Theophrastus, *Enquiry into Plants*, III, XVIII, p. 303.
320. Yotam Ottolenghi, *Plenty* (Ebury, 2010), p. 214.
321. Giuseppe Inzenga and Sir Henry Yule, 'On the Cultivation of Sumach, *Rhus coriaria*, in the Vicinity of Celli, near Palermo', *Transactions of the Botanical Society*, vol. IX (1868), p. 14.
322. Dalby, *Dangerous Tastes*, p. 76.
323. Elleke Boehmer (ed.), *Empire Writing: An Anthology of Colonial Literature, 1870–1918* (Oxford University Press, 1998), p. 331.
324. Grieve, *A Modern Herbal*, p. 788.
325. http://gernot-katzers-spice-pages.com/engl/Tama_ind.html.
326. Rick Stein, *Rick Stein's India* (BBC/Ebury, 2013), p. 266.
327. Marco Polo, *Travels*, p. 340.
328. Tim Ecott, *Vanilla: Travels in Search of the Luscious Substance* (Michael Joseph, 2004), p. 209.
329. Quoted in Edwin Thomas Martin, *Thomas Jefferson: Scientist* (Collier, 1961), p. 15.
330. Dalby, *Dangerous Tastes*, p. 148.
331. Le Couteur and Burreson, *Napoleon's Buttons*, p. 130.
332. Ibid.
333. Ecott, *Vanilla*, p. 21.
334. John Phillips, *The Marquis de Sade: A Very Short Introduction* (Oxford University Press, 2005), p. 26.
335. Ecott, *Vanilla*, p. 125.
336. Martyn Cornell, http://zythophile.wordpress.com/2010/12/23/how-to-go-a-wassailing/.
337. Christopher Driver (ed.), *John Evelyn, Cook* (Prospect, 1997), p. 43.

338. Adams, *Hideous Absinthe*, p. 55.
339. Marie Corelli, *Wormwood: A Drama of Paris* (1890; Broadview Press, 2004), p. 363.
340. Richard Ellmann, *Oscar Wilde* (Penguin, 1987), p. 441.
341. V. Magnan, 'On the Comparative Action of Alcohol and Absinthe', *The Lancet* (19 September 1874), p. 412.
342. Dirk W. Lachenmeier, J. Emmert, T. Kuballa and G. Sartor, 'Thujone – Cause of Absinthism?' *Forensic Science International* (May 2005).
343. Michael Zohary, *Plants of the Bible* (Cambridge University Press, 1982), p. 184.
344. Wilfrid Bonser, *The Medical Background of Anglo-Saxon England* (Wellcome, 1963), p. 164.
345. Dalby, *Dangerous Tastes*, p. 100.
346. Culpeper, *Complete Herbal*, p. 320.
347. Jean de Renou, *Medicinal Dispensatory* (Streater and Cottrel, 1657), p. 272.
348. Quoted in Luke DeMaitre, *Medieval Medicine: The Art of Healing from Head to Toe* (ABC-CLIO, 2013), p. 259.
349. DeMaitre, *Medieval Medicine*, p. 25.
350. T. Yoshioka, E. Fujii and M. Endo, 'Anti-Inflammatory Potency of Dehydrocurdione, a Zedoary-Derived Sesquiterpene', *Inflammation Research*, 47 (12) (December 1998), pp. 476–81.
351. Hannah Woolley, *The Gentlewoman's Companion* (Maxwell, 1675), p. 146.
352. James C. McCann, *Stirring the Pot: A History of African Cuisine* (Ohio University Press, 2009), p. 73.
353. Collingham, *Curry*, p. 115.
354. Beeton, *The Book of Household Management*, p. 3.
355. David Livingstone, *Expedition to the Zambesi* (John Murray, 1894), p. 143.
356. Hazel Castell and Kathleen Griffin (eds), *Out of the Frying Pan: Seven Women Who Changed the Course of Postwar Cookery* (BBC Books, 1993), p. 135.
357. Rosengarten, *The Book of Spices*, p. 423.
358. Stobart, *Herbs, Spices and Flavourings*, p. 71.
359. Elisabeth Lambert Ortiz, *Encyclopedia of Herbs, Spices and Flavourings* (Dorling Kindersley, 1992), p. 150.

360. Mary Ellen Snodgrass, *Encyclopedia of Kitchen History* (Routledge, 2004), p. 256.
361. Jessica Kuper (ed.), *The Anthropologists' Cookbook* (1977; Routledge, 1997), p. 110.
362. Madhur Jaffrey, *Ultimate Curry Bible* (Ebury, 2003), p. 16.
363. Terry Tan, *The Thai Table* (Marshall Cavendish, 2008), p. 128.
364. Ottolenghi and Tamimi, *Jerusalem*, p. 302.
365. Grigson, *Charcuterie and French Pork Cookery*, p. 41.
366. 'A-Z of Unusual Ingredients: Ras el hanout', *Daily Telegraph* (20 November 2013).
367. Davidson (ed.), *Oxford Companion to Food*, p. 672.
368. Jaffrey, *Ultimate Curry Bible*, p. 326.
369. Ottolenghi and Tamimi, *Jerusalem*, p. 34.

SELECT BIBLIOGRAPHY

Jad Adams, *Hideous Absinthe: A History of the 'Devil in a Bottle'* (I. B. Tauris, 2004)

Agnes Arber, *Herbals* (Cambridge University Press, 1912)

Elisabeth Ayrton, *The Cookery of England* (Penguin, 1974)

Ghillie Başan, *Tagine: Spicy Stews from Morocco* (Ryland, Peters & Small, 2007)

Ghillie Başan, *The Food and Cooking of Lebanon, Jordan and Syria* (Lorenz, 2011)

Ghillie Başan, *The Complete Book of Turkish Cooking* (Hermes House, 2013)

Maggie Black, *A Heritage of British Cooking* (Letts, 1978)

Arabella Boxer, *Book of English Food* (Hodder, 1991)

Lesley Chamberlain, *The Food and Cooking of Eastern Europe* (University of Nebraska Press, 1989)

Lizzie Collingham, *Curry: A Tale of Cooks and Conquerors* (Chatto & Windus, 2005)

Charles Corn, *The Scents of Eden* (Kodansha, 1998)

Andrew Dalby, *Siren Feasts: A History of Food and Gastronomy in Greece* (Routledge, 1996)

Andrew Dalby, *Dangerous Tastes: The Story of Spices* (British Museum Press, 2000)

Andrew Dalby, *Tastes of Byzantium: The Cuisine of a Legendary Empire* (I. B. Tauris, 2010)

Elizabeth David, *Spices, Salt and Aromatics in the English Kitchen* (Penguin, 1970)

Elizabeth David, *Is There a Nutmeg in the House?* (Michael Joseph, 2000)

Dave DeWitt and Paul W. Bosland, *The Complete Chile Pepper Book* (Timber Press, 2009)

Jared Diamond, *Guns, Germs, and Steel* (Norton, 1997)

Bertha S. Dodge, *Quest for Spices and New Worlds* (Archon, 1988)

Christopher Driver and Michelle Berriedale-Johnson, *Pepys at Table* (Bell & Hyman, 1984)

Tim Ecott, *Vanilla: Travels in Search of the Luscious Substance* (Michael Joseph, 2004)

John Edwards, *The Roman Cookery of Apicius* (Rider, 1984)

Nichola Fletcher, *Charlemagne's Tablecloth: A Piquant History of Feasting* (Weidenfeld & Nicolson, 2004)

Nelson Foster and Linda S. Cordell (eds), *Chilies to Chocolate: Food the Americas Gave the World* (University of Arizona Press, 1992)

Christopher Frayling, *Strange Landscape: A Journey through the Middle Ages* (BBC, 1995)

Paul Freedman, *Out of the East: Spices and the Medieval Imagination* (Yale University Press, 2008)

Darra Goldstein, *A Taste of Russia* (Random House, 1983)

Darra Goldstein, *The Georgian Feast: The Vibrant Culture and Savory Food of the Republic of Georgia* (University of California Press, 1999)

Jane Grigson, *English Food* (Macmillan, 1974)

Jane Grigson, *Vegetable Book* (1978; Penguin, 1998)

Ann Hagen, *A Handbook of Anglo-Saxon Food: Processing and Consumption* (Anglo-Saxon Books, 1992)

Jessica B. Harris, *The Africa Cookbook: Tastes of a Continent* (Simon & Schuster, 1998)

Dorothy Hartley, *Food in England* (1954; Little Brown, 1996)

Carolyn Heal and Michael Allsop, *Cooking with Spices* (Granada, 1985)

Rosemary Hemphill, *The Penguin Book of Herbs and Spices* (Penguin, 1966)

Nicola Humble, *Culinary Pleasures: Cookbooks and the Transformation of British Food* (Faber, 2005)

Madhur Jaffrey, *Madhur Jaffrey's Indian Cookery* (BBC, 1982)

Madhur Jaffrey, *A Taste of India* (Pavilion, 1985)

Madhur Jaffrey, *The Ultimate Curry Bible* (Ebury, 2003)

John Keay, *The Spice Route* (John Murray, 2005)

Giles Milton, *Nathaniel's Nutmeg* (Hodder, 1999)

Yotam Ottolenghi, *Plenty* (Ebury, 2010)

Yotam Ottolenghi and Sami Tamimi, *Jerusalem* (Ebury, 2012)

Elizabeth Lambert Ortiz, *Encyclopedia of Herbs, Spices and Flavourings* (Dorling Kindersley, 1992)

Sara Paston-Williams, *The Art of Dining* (National Trust, 1993)

Anna Pavord, *The Naming of Names: The Search for Order in the World of Plants* (Bloomsbury, 2010)

M. N. Pearson, *The Portuguese in India* (Cambridge University Press, 1987)

Roy Porter, *The Greatest Benefit to Mankind: A Medical History of Humanity from Antiquity to the Present* (HarperCollins, 1997)

Maria and Nikos Psilakis, *Cretan Cooking* (Karmanor, 2003)

Odile Redon, Françoise Sabban and Silvano Serventi, *The Medieval Kitchen: Recipes from France and Italy* (University of Chicago Press, 1998)

Claudia Roden, *A Book of Middle Eastern Food* (Penguin, 1968)

Claudia Roden, *The Book of Jewish Food* (Penguin, 1996)

Claudia Roden, *Arabesque: A Taste of Morocco, Turkey and Lebanon* (Michael Joseph, 2005)

Frederic Rosengarten Jr, *The Book of Spices* (Pyramid, 1969)

Lorna J. Sass, *To the King's Taste* (Metropolitan Museum of Art, 1975)

Wolfgang Schivelbusch, *Tastes of Paradise: A Social History of Spices, Stimulants and Intoxicants* (1979; Vintage, 1993)

Marjorie Shaffer, *Pepper: A History of the World's Most Influential Spice* (Thomas Dunne, 2013)

Sue Shephard, *Pickled, Potted and Canned: The Story of Food Preserving* (Headline, 2000)

Rick Stein, *Rick Stein's India* (BBC/Ebury, 2013)

Tom Stobart, *Herbs, Spices and Flavourings* (International Wine and Food Publishing Company, 1970)

Roy Strong, *Feast: A History of Grand Eating* (Cape, 2002)

David Stuart, *The Kitchen Garden* (Hale, 1984)

Richard Sugg, *Mummies, Cannibals and Vampires: The History of Corpse Medicine from the Renaissance to the Victorians* (Routledge, 2011)

Jack Turner, *Spice: The History of a Temptation* (Vintage, 2004)

Ivana Veruzabova, *Czech and Slovak Food and Cooking* (Aquamarine, 2012)

Pat Willard, *Secrets of Saffron* (Souvenir, 2001)

Sami Zubaida and Richard Tapper (eds), *Culinary Cultures of the Middle East* (I. B. Tauris, 1994)

ACKNOWLEDGEMENTS

Lots of people were exceptionally generous to me while I was researching *The Book of Spice*: offering tips and stories that opened up new avenues; buying, lending or recommending books; or just cooking me interesting meals (that's you, Stephen Heath and Martin Brookes). I particularly want to thank: Ruth Taylor, who gave me the run of her enormous library of historical cookery books, thus ensuring I didn't have to spend every single day in the British Library picking up colds and drinking overpriced coffee; Matthew Horsman, for posting me Jared Diamond's *Guns, Germs and Steel* (1997) all the way from Canada; Blessing Ohanusi, for help with the entry on Grains of Paradise; Joe Luscombe, for help with the entry on silphium; my sister Alex, brother Peter and father, Brian; and my in-laws, David and Julia Newman, chemists with a keen interest in botany who answered my dumb questions with impeccable clarity and did huge amounts of childcare into the bargain.

Anyone seeking more detailed botanical knowledge should google Gernot Katzer's Spice Pages – truly a feast of riches. Anyone interested in the use of spices in antiquity should read Andrew Dalby's *Dangerous Tastes: The Story of Spices* (2000) and *Food in the Ancient World from A–Z* (2003). And for a learned, stimulating overview, Jack Turner's *Spice: The History of a Temptation* (2004) can't be bettered. I enjoyed and made use of John Keay's *The Spice Route* (2005), Giles Milton's *Nathaniel's Nutmeg* (1999) and Bertha S. Dodge's *Quests for Spices and New Worlds* (1988). I'm also indebted to Tom Stobart's *Herbs, Spices and Flavourings* (1970) and Elizabeth David's bracingly belligerent *Spices, Salt and Aromatics in the English Kitchen* (1970).

It has been a pleasure to work with Rebecca Gray, Andrew Franklin, Penny Daniel, Hannah Ross, Anna-Marie Fitzgerald and everyone else at Profile Books; also my agent, Antony Topping at Greene & Heaton. Matthew Taylor copy-edited the text with care and rigour. But I couldn't have done any of this without the support and infinite patience of my wife, Cathy, and our daughters, Scarlett and Molly, to whom this is dedicated with love. Yes, yes – I'm going to tidy the study tomorrow.